AF702299

Theodoret of Cyrus
Commentaries on the Prophets

Theodoret of Cyrus

Commentaries on the Prophets

Volume One

Commentary on the Prophet Jeremiah
Commentary on the Prophet Baruch
Commentary on the Book of Lamentations

Translated with
an Introduction
by
Robert Charles Hill

HOLY CROSS ORTHODOX PRESS
Brookline, Massachusetts

Published by Holy Cross Orthodox Press
50 Goddard Avenue
Brookline, Massachusetts 02445

On the cover: Michelangelo Buonarroti, *The prophet Jeremiah* (detail), fresco, 1508-1512, Cappella Sistine Chapel, Vatican, VC.

LIBRARY OF CONGRESS CATALOGING–IN–PUBLICATION DATA

Theodoret, Bishop of Cyrrhus.
[Commentary on the Prophet Jeremiah. English]
Commentary on the Prophet Jeremiah / Theodoret of Cyrus; translated with an introduction by Robert Charles Hill.
p. cm. -- (Commentaries on the prophets ; v. 1)
Includes bibliographical references and index.
ISBN 1-885652-74-7 (pbk. : alk. paper)
1. Bible. O.T. Jeremiah--Commentaries. I. Hill, Robert C. (Robert Charles), 1931- II. Title. III. Series.
BR65.T753C6813 2006
224′.207--dc22 2005036623

To His Eminence Archbishop Demetrios,
Primate of the Greek Orthodox Church in America,
Theodoret scholar

"Your word is a lamp to my feet and a light to my path"
Ps 119:105

CONTENTS

Abbreviations

Aug	*Augustinianum*
Bib	*Biblica*
CCG	Corpus Christianorum Graecorum, Turnhout: Brepols
CCL	Corpus Christianorum Latinorum, Turnhout: Brepols
DBS	*Dictionnaire de la Bible. Supplément*, IV, Paris: Librairie Letouzey et Ané, 1949
DS	*Enchiridion Symbolorum, Definitionum et Declarationum*, 34th ed., edd. H. Denzinger, A. Schönmetzer, Freiburg: Herder, 1967
DTC	*Dictionnaire de théologie catholique* 15, Paris: Librairie Letouzey et Ané, 1946
EstBib	*Estudios Bíblicos*
ETL	*Ephemerides Theologicae Lovanienses*
FOTC	Fathers of the Church, Washington, DC: Catholic University of America Press
GO	Göttingen Orientforschungen
ITQ	*Irish Theological Quarterly*
JECS	*Journal of Early Christian Studies*
LXX	Septuagint
NJBC	*New Jerome Biblical Commentary*, edd. R. E. Brown et al, Englewood Cliffs, NJ: Prentice Hall, 1990

PG	Patrologia Graeca, ed. J.-P. Migne, Paris, 1857-66
PL	Patrologia Latina, ed. J.-P. Migne, Paris, 1878-90
RSPT	*Revue des Sciences Philosophiques et Théologiques*
SC	Sources Chrétiennes, Paris: Du Cerf
StudP	*Studia Patristica*
TRE	*Theologische Realenzyklopädie*, Berlin: Walter de Gruyter
VC	*Vigiliae Christianae*
VTS	*Vetus Testamentum*, Supplement

Introduction

1. Theodoret, his life and works

Born about 393 in Antioch, Theodoret owed his name to grateful parents, who also were responsible for his entering monastic life at an early age. Since his famous predecessors in that school, if we may use the term,[1] John Chrysostom and Theodore of Mopsuestia – both pupils of Diodore of Tarsus – had been appointed to episcopal responsibilities in Constantinople in 397 and in Mopsuestia in Cilicia in 392, respectively, they cannot have exercised much direct influence on Theodoret's formation. In 423 he was elected bishop of Cyrus, a city about a hundred kilometers northeast of Antioch, perhaps "a little backwater"[2] yet a see with responsibility for eight hundred parishes, Theodoret tells us in his letters. Caught up in the theological turmoil in the wake of the council of Constantinople of 381, he represented the christological positions of the oriental bishops against those supporting Cyril of Alexandria. His episcopal and civic duties, not to mention these theological concerns, did not prevent him from writing numerous dogmatic, apologetic and historical works. In addition, he composed commentaries on Paul's letters and most of the Old Testament. The Commentary on the Song of Songs began the series about the time of the council of Ephesus in 431; and in a letter written in 448[3] shortly before being deposed at the "Robber Council" of Ephesus, he could make the claim to have produced works on "all the prophets, the psalter and the apostle." Theodoret's rapid reinstatement as bishop by Pope Leo followed, and he played a leading role in having the council of Chalcedon convened in 451. He died about 460.[4]

It is rather intriguing that, despite their ranking in the Jewish and Christian Scriptures, both the Book of Isaiah ("the most articulate of all the prophets" in popular estimation, if John Chrysostom is to be believed)[5] and the Book of Jeremiah did not rate alongside Daniel, Ezekiel and The Twelve as those prophetic books whose early commentary prevented Theodoret from beginning his exegetical career with the Psalms.[6] It was only later in a very busy decade (in terms of output) and doubtless a tumultuous one (from the viewpoint of theological currents) before the convening of the council of Chalcedon that he took on and completed the lengthy Commentary on Isaiah and the still imposing, if less lengthy, Commentary on Jeremiah that includes also Baruch and Lamentations – not to mention the Commentary on the Fourteen Letters of St. Paul as well. What an extraordinarily fertile period of biblical commentary!

Whatever the reason for this order of composition, some time around the middle of that decade (the Psalms Commentary composed later than 441) Theodoret sat down with the works of Eusebius of Caesarea and Cyril of Alexandria at his elbow to begin his Commentary on Isaiah with the modest claim, "With the exception of the remarkable Jeremiah, the other prophets' thought we have with God's help explicated as far as is possible." Predictably, this work on Isaiah is still fresh in his mind when he moves promptly to Jeremiah, so that when he comes to 22.7, which in his local text reads, "I shall consecrate destroyers against them," he suggests a meaning "assign" for "consecrate" on the basis that "we cited this explanation in many places in the Commentary on Isaiah." He had not originally intended to include Jeremiah in his compass; he says at the opening, "I had been of the view that there was no need for a commentary on the inspired composition of the divine Jeremiah." What induced him to devote time to it was (if we can take this as more than a conventional remark by an author) that "many studious people kept pressing me to do a commentary on this book as well by claiming that most people do not grasp the sense of the work" – a motive that resembles the didactic purpose of the Commentary on the Psalter, helping people "sing its melodies and at the same time recognize the sense of the words they sing."[7] And there is a sense of perfunctory performance of duty in the Jeremiah work, commentary (at least in the text as we have it) being kept to a minimum – though it is not without a note of self-satisfaction that he brings it to a close in the words, "We added this commentary as well to the other prophetic books, thus leaving not even a single piece of prophecy without comment." And towards the close of his final exegetical work, the *Questions* on Kingdoms and Chronicles, he excuses himself for not restating what he had already covered in the Jeremiah Commentary: "The story of the remaining kings the Prophet Jeremiah reported in many places. For our part, since we commented on that book as well thanks to divine grace, we have presumed it superfluous to comment on it again."[8] Theodoret is surely entitled to congratulate himself modestly thus, informing also Eusebius of Ancyra in a letter dated December 448 that he has commented on "all the prophets, the psalter and the apostle."[9] What a pity that his reward for all the composition in the 440s in response to pastoral needs was his deposition at the Robber Synod of 449, if only for a brief period.

2. *Text of the Commentary; Theodoret's text of Jeremiah*

For the modern reader of Theodoret's Jeremiah Commentary, including Baruch and Lamentations, the text to hand is that of J. P. Migne's *Patrologia Graeca* vol. 81 deriving from the seventeenth- and eighteenth-century editions of available manuscripts. The eighteenth-century editor J. L. Schulze details the characteristics of manuscripts from Augsburg and

Bavaria,[10] the former recommending itself to him whereas the latter departs from Theodoret's typical conciseness through inclusion of excerpts from earlier commentators (as emerges in codex B, for instance, in unlikely expansiveness of commentary on 2.23,30). The casual reader of Schulze's text of Theodoret in PG 81 who does not boast paleographical skills, though finding the Commentary (as has been mentioned) rather perfunctory in the manner of someone bringing a long task to an eventual conclusion, recognizes in it the bishop's typical *syntomia* and all the other marks of his style of commentary. The work is divided into twelve *tomoi* or volumes, each closing with its brief peroration – the bishop's only lapse into parenesis; the first *tomos* opens with a preface and the last closes with a (slightly complacent) conclusion. He does not concede himself the luxury of consulting a Hexapla to find therein the usual added textual resources; Syriac is the only further textual reference of a commentator unable to consult the Hebrew. In short, our available text gives all the signs of a (justifiably weary) Theodoret in a hurry, as distinct from the eclectic, piecemeal impression of a text assembled from the catenae that one gains from the PG 81 Isaiah text deriving from Jacob Sirmond's seventeenth-century edition (by comparison with the SC critical edition).

And yet there have been doubts that the Sirmond-Schulze text in PG 81 comes to us in direct manuscript tradition and is not rather from the catenae.[11] This doubt was reinforced with the discovery in 1899 of a manuscript in the Convent of the Holy Sepulcher in Constantinople containing a text of Theodoret's Isaiah Commentary that differed from Sirmond's, as well as a text of the Jeremiah Commentary on pages 186-314 of this ms. 17 that begins with words that differ from the opening of the PG 81 text. Jean-Noël Guinot, the eminent Theodoret scholar responsible for the *Sources Chrétiennes* edition of the "Constantinople" Isaiah ms. (now in Athens) first photographed and edited by August Möhle, called for a comparison of the two Jeremiah texts to check authenticity, while also lamenting that the precious ms. 17 is in such a condition of decay as to be beyond access.[12] In short, we are left to internal evidence from the Sirmond-Schulze text of the Jeremiah Commentary to decide on its authenticity; I have suggested above, with encouragement from Guinot, that there are compelling grounds for reaching a positive verdict.

It is ironic that of all the Latter Prophets it is Jeremiah which has particularly intrigued biblical scholars on account of the differences between the Greek version and our present Masoretic Hebrew text, which is considerably more lengthy, making a decision on authenticity of patristic commentaries on it all the more urgent. The biblical scholars lament that long sections of the book are to their knowledge "missing from the LXX," on the basis of which they arrive at an estimate of some now irretrievable *Vorlage*, often conceding that the Greek could be closer to it than our Hebrew text.[13] What they generally fail to do is, firstly, to concede that "Septuagint" is not a univocal term but indicative rather of a "collection of translations,"[14] and, secondly, to turn to patristic commentaries like Theodoret's to discover the form of the LXX in use in Antioch, which very often incorporates the "missing" elements of the text.

The precise character of this overall Antioch text is unclear, even if "the ancient sources agree in their affirmation of a recension of the Greek Bible located in the regions of Syria and Asia Minor."[15]. Jerome, for instance, who died about the time Theodoret became bishop, tells us in his preface to the Chronicles of three forms of the LXX current in his time in Alexandria, in Constantinople-Antioch, and in "the provinces in between," respectively;[16] that form in use in Antioch he describes elsewhere as "another version which Origen and Eusebius of Caesarea and all the Greek commentators call the popular text, and which by most is now called the Lucianic text,"[17] thus attributing the Antioch recension to the scholar-priest of Antioch, Lucian, a century earlier – an attribution some modern scholars accept,[18] others reject, preferring to speak of a "*texte antiochien*"[19] or even Palestinian.[20] Antiochene commentators on this text, of course, supply us with clues as to its nature; but, as in the case of Theodoret's other commentaries, modern critical editions tend to steer clear of such exegetical works of the Antiochenes on account of their length and the abundance of their manuscript tradition.[21] We are grateful to Theodoret in particular for our knowledge of the local text, Chrysostom having left nothing substantial on Jeremiah[22] and Theodore's commentary having suffered the harsh fate of most of his works; modern biblical commentators ignore it to their peril, the Antiochene text preserving many readings otherwise classed as "missing" from the LXX and throwing light on that *Vorlage*.[23]

Septuagint scholars, while grateful that Theodoret comments on the whole book, would regret that he seems (in the text as we have it) in a hurry to bring the prophetic corpus to a close; there is not the same (atypical) expansiveness that distinguishes the Isaiah Commentary, in the composition of which he drew heavily on Eusebius and Cyril and at times argued the toss with them. Here Theodoret is often content to paraphrase the prophet's thought, even reducing it to a precis, so that there are sections (in chs. 27 and 32, e.g.) where the text is not cited verbatim. Also, as mentioned above, he forgoes the luxury of consulting textual resources that may have thrown light on obscure readings such as those available in a copy of the Hexapla: another form of the LXX, the three alternative versions associated with the names of Aquila, Symmachus and Theodotion, a Hebrew text and its transliteration. Once only does he refer to other manuscripts, ἀντίγραφα that preserve a different form of the LXX, namely, on the text of 15.15.

The conspicuous exception to this relative neglect of a critical approach to the text is Theodoret's reference to the Syriac version, available by that time in the Peshitta Bible;[24] over and over again he cites the Syriac (his native tongue, after all) to shed light on an obscure reading – a rare practice in the Isaiah Commentary, where, however, the Hexapla was constantly open before him. For instance, an obscure phrase, "shorn in squalor," is applied to Moab both in Isa 16.7 and Jer 48.31: at the former occurrence Theodoret finds an alternative version in Symmachus, at the latter he turns instead to Syriac and finds a different one. Syriac is invaluable to him when his LXX text leaves a Hebrew phrase untranslated, as at 46.17, "'Give Pharaoh Neco, king of Egypt, the name *Saon eebeir emod*,'" on which Theodoret can only comment, "The Syriac rendered it this way, 'Give him the name 'Disturber who missed his opportunity.'" At 25.25 within a Judgment on the Nations, where modern commentators are inclined to say the LXX does not mention place names like Zimri, Theodoret's text reads, "All the kings of Zimri," and he comments, "We found Zimri in the Hebrew and the Syriac," possibly suggesting to an unwary reader a picture of the bishop poring over the Hebrew text were it not for his many solecisms where this language is concerned (adverted to in footnotes below), and his reliance on his native Syriac (a dialect of Aramaic) to access it beyond the transliterated column in the Hexapla. He does not even advert to the acrostic pattern in the Hebrews of the four Lamentations his text preserves, as that feature had likewise escaped him in commentary even on Ps 119.

3. *Nature, purpose, characteristics of the Commentary*

Allowing for these differences and these similarities, arising from circumstances, it is the same approach to the task we recognize in this Antiochene commentator on Jeremiah as in his work on other biblical authors. For him and other ancients this inspired work, *propheteia*, includes also as the work of Jeremiah the four Lamentations (no fifth in his text) and as the work of his secretary the five chapters of Baruch (no Letter of Jeremiah appearing as a sixth). Ever solicitous for his readers' understanding of the material, he wants them to grasp its drift (*dianoia*) and so begins with a statement of the book's theme (*hypothesis*) in a brief foreword or synopsis of content (*protheôria*), succinctly listing the history and the kings of Judah in the period of Jeremiah's ministry, and some topics the book touches on. Theodoret predictably differs from modern commentators in the degree of critical questioning he is prepared to put to the text of "the divine Jeremiah." He does not raise questions of the authenticity of oracles included in the text: when ch. 24 recounts the vision of two baskets of figs, which a modern like William McKane regards as a mere "compilation in which other parts of the Hebrew Bible are used... a historical riddle which cannot be completely solved,"[25] Theodoret engages in no such deconstructive criticism, simply abstracting from the way the vision should be taken and concentrating on its theological import. He is not interested in identifying with form critics the genres exemplified in the oracles, like the *rib* or lawsuit in 2.5ff, and the communal lament in 14.1-10. While he is not prepared like the moderns to debate redactional processes in locating a Jeremianic or Deuteronomic core in passages like 16.1-9, he does show his characteristic flexibility (illustrated also in his debate on authorship of psalms and psalm titles in the preface to that Commentary) in reminding his readers of stages of composition, saying at the opening of chs. 21, 25, 32, "It is necessary to realize that the prophecies do not now occur in order."

As becomes a man in a hurry, and consistent with his professed principle of *syntomia* in his other commentaries, Theodoret promises in his preface, "I shall give particular attention to conciseness as far as possible: of the more obvious matters, on the one hand, I shall give a summary in point form, while taking care to explicate what requires in-depth treatment." His commentary is therefore never expansive, often consisting of paraphrase, though always sensitive to theological import. He sees no point in representing the text of mere narrative, and when ch. 19 gives the account of Jeremiah's buying the earthenware jug and smashing it in the sight of the people, Theodoret reduces it to a brief precis that highlights significance, having already followed the prophet though a prophetic action with the *eikôn* of the loincloth a few chapters earlier.

An incidental advantage of the brisk pace of commentary on Jeremiah is a reduction in the amount of rationalizing to which Theodoret has recourse as a normal ploy, as for instance in the Isaiah Commentary, where often a plethora of alternative readings all had to be justified (without appeal to any Hebrew substrate, of course). Even without conflicting alternative versions in the Jeremiah Commentary, however, Theodoret can get himself into a spot of bother from which escape is possible only by this procedure, as in commentary on the opening verses of ch. 50, an oracle against Babylon: he confuses the principal god of the Babylonian pantheon, Marduk/Merodach (to which the text refers, and with which the god Bel from Nippur had become identified), with the king Merodach-baladan who appears in Isa 39.1 and whom in his final comments on Isa 37 he had credited with the transfer of power from Nineveh to Babylon that had in fact occurred under Nabopalassar. But to such a rationalizer nothing is a problem: a meaning, or meanings, can be found.

> *Bel is disgraced.* It was an idol much honored by the Babylonians; some call it Jupiter, others Kronos. He says it has been disgraced, firstly for being unable to help the worshipers, then for being completely deprived of people to honor it. *The undaunted, the effeminate.* He implied both their power and their luxurious way of life. *Merodach has been betrayed.* They called the first ruler of the Babylonians Merodach. So here he is either mentioning the last ruler, under whom the overthrow of the kingdom occurred, or the first one, who shifted the kingship

from Nineveh to Babylon. You could apply the term *has been betrayed* to the second or to the first, referring to the kingdom in the case of the second; he means all the idols have been disgraced and their weakness made plain.

Relative rarity of this hermeneutical procedure in the commentary is a mercy.

4. *Theodoret as interpreter of Jeremiah*

To Theodoret as an Antiochene, meaning is in the detail; the virtue of precision, *akribeia*, urges recognition of it, even with haste pressing. Three times in the course of the commentary he reminds his readers to distinguish middle voice from active in the verb *krinomai* if the correct interpretation of divine retribution is to be taken. When 25.31 (cf. 2.9,35) reads, "He is entering into judgment with all flesh," Theodoret stresses again the true significance of the morphological detail: "Once again he reveals his ineffable goodness: he did not say, He will judge all flesh, but *He is entering into judgment*, bringing out his characteristic kindness and reproving the ingratitude of the recipients." Perhaps it is only the brisk pace of this work that excludes it from specific mention by Photius in Constantinople in the ninth century in saying of him, "On the whole, he reached the top level of exegetes, and it would not be easy to find anyone better at elucidating obscure points."[26] What is not allowed to pass without comment, even in haste, is the author's figurative language: as ever, whether the author be psalmist, apostle or prophet, Theodoret insists on unpacking every image. When vv.15-16 of the first Lamentation present the wretched fate of Judah under various images (a wine vat, wringing hands, a menstruating woman), he ensures that none escapes without comment, beginning with the wine vat. "*The Lord trampled the wine vat with the virgin daughter Judah. For these things I weep*. Frequently the divine Scripture likens the worst punishment to a wine vat on account of all the bunches of grapes being crushed in the wine vats so that not a single grape escapes."

Also as an Antiochene, to Theodoret figures that involve anthropomorphisms constitute a possible problem for the reader and call for an admonition. Bar 2.16-17 includes the commonest of all figurative expressions in prayer to God, but the commentator feels nothing should be taken for granted. "*Incline your ear, Lord, and listen. Open your eyes and see*. People suffering abuse normally close their eyes when the wrong-doers are seen, and avert the pupils when the abusers call to them; so he expressed this in human fashion: the divinity is not composite but simple and uncircumscribed." The divine considerateness involved in sacred history, as also in scriptural communication, that takes account of human limitations, *astheneia*, and that Chrysostom spoke freely of as *synkatabasis*,[27] Theodoret also if less frequently brings to his readers' notice, even on a rare occasion employing those terms. When the oracle in 7.21 reads, "Thus says the Lord of Hosts, the God of Israel, Add your burned offerings to your sacrifices, and eat the flesh," he suggests the directive should be taken as a concession to human weakness.

> It is made clear also from this that the obsolete prescriptions of the Law had been imposed on account of the Jews' limitations: since they had learned in Egypt how to sacrifice to idols, he wanted to separate them from those practices (in all the prophets he rejects them, remember), yet out of considerateness for their limitations he utters that remark, *Eat flesh*.

Elsewhere (on 9.9) he rephrases the hermeneutical principle in a way that Chrysostom would endorse, "His words are adjusted to our capacity to receive."

The most striking feature of Theodoret's hermeneutics in this work, especially in the wake of the Isaiah Commentary so influenced by Alexandrian interpretation represented by Eusebius and Cyril with their consistently eschatological accent (one of the atypical features of that work), is its consistently historical interpretation – hence the opening summary of events and kings in the *protheôria*. Perhaps the Theodoret who in the preface to the Psalms Commentary pledged to avoid both the excessive historical accent (of Theodore) and "undue relish in allegory" (of Alexandria)[28] could have felt that balance imperiled here – as it was strangely abandoned altogether in commentary on Isaiah. But again haste is to blame: a literal interpretation is more expeditious. There is only a rare essay into typology, and then (as Antioch required) with New Testament support. When the Lord says in 4.4, "Cut away the uncircumcision of your heart" (other forms of the LXX reading "hardness of heart"), Theodoret claims the support of Rom 9.28-29 to comment, "He clearly brought out that the visible circumcision is a type of the invisible, and that if there is circumcision within, bodily circumcision is unnecessary." The accent falls more consistently on the historical realization of prophecy, not the typological, or on what is called "narrative coherence" by Francis Young (we might rephrase it as prophetic coherence, or Young's own "textual coherence"), who goes on to say of Antiochene exegesis, "What we do have is an important stress on the 'reality' of the overarching narrative from creation through fall to incarnation and redemption."[29] Not only will Theodoret frequently go to some trouble to show from history that "the prophecy proved to be reliable"; but as in the case of the description of Jerusalem as a fruitful vine that became wild in Jer 2.21, he looks back to see this paralleled in the Song of Moses and forward to Jesus describing himself as the true vine in the Johannine Supper discourse. His unremitting attention to textual details of history, geography, topography and the natural sciences – typical of Theodoret – also exemplifies this interest in coherence.

5. Theological accents in the Commentary

If the commentator's haste (or the history of our text) keeps to a minimum the rationalizing necessary to harmonize a range of versions, and sharpens the hermeneutical focus on the history of Judah vainly resisting the conqueror, so the repression of a messianic interpretation of oracles lessens the need to engage in polemic a range of christological adversaries. As with any Old Testament text commented on by the Fathers, of course, the Jews, their prerogatives, their fate and its well-worn justification come in for mention, and this work is no exception. Theodoret can come through as one who has no quarrel with (Old Testament) Judaism, on the one hand, and on the other as a keen critic of the Jews, who deserved what they got. He is happy enough for a while to second Baruch's interpretation of "the fountain of wisdom" (3.12) as the Law; but when wisdom in 4.1 is defined as "the book of the commandments of God, the Law that will last forever," he is quick to interpose against the author, "the old covenant came to an end." He can piously close ch. 23 and tome 5 with the exhortation, "May we follow both the Old Testament and the New Testament words," seeing both inspired, as he says elsewhere in his works, but then uncharacteristically blurt out in protest on the messianic prophecy in vv.5-6 of that chapter, "The stupid Jews shamelessly endeavor to apply this to Zerubbabel," a figure who never ceases to get under his skin as a rival to Jesus.

Otherwise the rogues' gallery of heresiarchs found in other works do not figure here. Mention of creation of all things by the Lord, as at 10.11-12, can prompt a rebuttal of subordinationism (Arius going unnamed). And when Baruch 3.37 speaks of Wisdom coming to live on earth, Theodoret envisages another possible misunderstanding of Jesus in the scheme of things, rejecting any possible identification of him with such a created Wisdom-figure (his Hebrew not being at a level to suggest to him that the verb in Prov 8.22 may mean "acquire" rather than "create").

> The verse gives a clear reference to the incarnation of the only-begotten and to the fact that he is creator of all and fountain of wisdom. He is therefore also its creator and lord; of him it says in Proverbs, "The Lord created me as the beginning of

ways in his work": it is not God the Word who says this, but the wisdom of God the Word developed by him.

Without any provocation Theodoret in the course of the Commentary comes out with one of those expressions of the hypostatic union in Jesus, arising from an ill-considered comparison of his own, that leave something to be desired. It occurs in connection with the burning of Baruch's text of Jeremiah's oracles by Jehoiakim recorded in ch. 36, the sequel to which Theodoret expresses thus, "The God of all bade Jeremiah write the former oracles in a different book: whereas the writing matter was consumed by fire, the divine Law remained intact; likewise also the Word, when the body that was assumed suffered, remained immune to suffering." The Christology could be paralleled from his other works.

Otherwise, the Commentary provides little exposure of Theodoret's theological positions. He is always short on moralizing, studiously avoiding any trespassing on the role of a preacher; parenesis occurs only, and very briefly, as a peroration to close each volume, and when the last chapter of Jer concludes with Judah's deportation and a final act of kindness to King Jehoiakim, at a point where a commentator might be allowed his own reflection on this proverbially moral book, all Theodoret thinks proper is this: "Now, this proclaims the Lord's lovingkindness: in punishing he is merciful, in applying correction he consoles, and the justice of his verdict he tempers with lovingkindness." Haste it is, on the other hand, that is responsible for the paucity of sacramental reference in the text, which the bishop can normally not resist; he sees in 31.34, "I shall no longer remember their sin," a reference to baptism as a sacrament of reconciliation, but otherwise does not pause to comment in this vein.

It would not be an Antiochene work, especially by a pastor, despite all his parenetic restraint, if some clue did not emerge as to the balance in the process of virtuous living and the whole process of salvation between divine grace and human effort. In preface and conclusion he sees both influences at work, as he also admits to be writing for the benefit of those "fond of God and of hard work." Pelagians, whose cause Theodoret has been thought to support,[30] could find no encouragement in this work. The topic of sin, which predictably in comment on a prophet with a reputation like Jeremiah's arises frequently, leads Theodoret more than once to attribute responsibility not to any flawed human nature but to free will, *gnômê*, or indifference, *rhathymia*. Such is his response when in v.39 of the third Lamentation the question is posed, "*Why will any living mortal complain, a man about his sin?* In other words, it is indifference, not nature, that is responsible for sin, as a result of which the judge also imposes punishment on the sinners."

6. Theodoret's achievement in the Commentary on Jeremiah

In short, by whichever way this work of commentary has reached us – whether by direct manuscript transmission or through the catenae – the marks are there of a style we associate closely with Theodoret, even if his preference originally had been not to undertake it. We are pleased that he did. Not only does he assist us (if, unlike many modern biblical commentators, we are prepared to read the work) to retrieve a biblical text notoriously under question. But as well the Jeremiah Commentary seems to represent the kind of immediate response to his local LXX text the busy bishop is inclined to and capable of when time does not afford him the luxury of consulting a range of textual resources (the Peshitta aside) and hermeneutical opinions to which in a situation of greater leisure (for instance, in composing the Isaiah Commentary represented in the "Constantinople" ms. 17) he might turn. From an "exegetical"[31] point of view, at any rate, may we class this work as vintage Theodoret? While not prepared to join modern authors in deconstructing the text or acknowledging a composite text, he does allow for the fact that Jeremiah's oracles being read by his readers have been assembled at a later period. He is as interested in having those readers grasp the drift of obscure passages as he was earlier in his career with the Psalms. He unpacks every image, even supplying some of his own, in this process of clarifying obscurity. Unlike the Isaiah Commentary, where he was tapping into the hermeneutic of another school, here Theodoret adopts a more typically Antiochene accent on the historical background to Jeremiah's ministry, the *alêtheia*. In the text as we have it, the Commentary reveals little by way of distinctive christological or other theological positions, and little theological jousting. Yet the work provides us with a unique piece of Antiochene commentary on three books of the Old Testament – Jeremiah, Lamentations and Baruch – as he will later leave a unique patristic commentary on Ruth and Chronicles. In short, we can concede that in later life, when revisiting the period of Jeremiah's ministry in his *Quaestiones* on Chronicles, Theodoret could justifiably observe with some pride of his work on Jeremiah, "That book in its entirety we commented on as well, thanks to divine grace."[32]

Select Bibliography

Azéma, Y., *Théodoret de Cyr. Correspondance* I,II (SC 98,111, 1964,1965)

Bardy, G., "Théodoret," DTC 15, 1946, 299-325

____, "Interprétation chez les pères," DBS IV, 1949, 569-91

Barthélemy, D., *Les Devanciers d'Aquila*, VTS X; Leiden: Brill, 1963

Canivet, P., *Histoire d'une entreprise apologétique au Ve siècle*, Paris: Bloud & Gay, 1957

Drewery, B., "Antiochien," TRE 3, 103-113

Fernández Marcos, N., "Some reflections on the Antiochian text of the Septuagint," in *Studien zur Septuaginta – Robert Hanhart zu Ehren*, ed. D. Fraenkel, U. Quast, J. W. Wevers; MSU XX; Göttingen: Vandenhoeck & Ruprecht, 1990, 219-29

____, *The Septuagint in Context. Introduction to the Greek Versions of the Bible*, Eng. trans. Leiden-Boston: Brill, 2000

____ and J. R. Busto Saiz, *Theodoreti Cyrensis Quaestiones in Reges et Paralipomena*, Textos y Estudios "Cardenal Cisneros" 32, Madrid: CSIC, 1984

Guinot, J.-N., *Théodoret de Cyr. Commentaire sur Isaïe* I,II,III SC 276,295,315, 1980,1982,1984

____, "Théoderet a-t-il lu les homélies d'Origène sur l'Ancient Testament?" *Vetera Christianorum* 21 (1984) 285-312

____, "Qui est 'le Syrien' dans les commentaires de Théodoret de Cyr?" *StudP* 25 (1993) 60-71

____, *L'Exégèse de Théodoret de Cyr*, Théologie Historique 100; Paris: Beauchesne, 1995

Hill, R. C., "On looking again at *synkatabasis*," *Prudentia* 13 (1981) 3-11

____ , *Theodoret of Cyrus. Commentary on the Psalms*, FOTC 101,102; 2000, 2001

____ , *Theodoret of Cyrus. Commentary on the Song of Songs*, Early Christian Studies 2; Brisbane: Australian Catholic University, 2001

____ , "Two Antiochenes on the Psalms," *StudP* 34 (2001) 353-69

____ , "Theodoret wrestling with Romans," *StudP* 34 (2001) 347-52

____ , "*Orientale lumen*: western biblical scholarship's unacknowledged debt," in L. Cross, ed., *Orientale Lumen Australasia-Oceania 2000*, Melbourne: Australian Catholic University, 2001, 157-72

____ , *Theodoret of Cyrus. Commentary on the Letters of St Paul*, 2 vols; Brookline MA: Holy Cross Orthodox Press, 2001

Jellicoe, S., *The Septuagint and Modern Study*, Oxford: Clarendon, 1968

Jones, D. R., *Jeremiah*, New Century Bible Commentary, Grand Rapids: Eerdmans, 1992

Kelly, J. N. D., *Early Christian Doctrines*, 5th ed.; New York: Harper & Row, 1978

McKane, W., *Jeremiah 1-25, 26-52*, International Critical Commentary, Edinburgh: T&T Clark, 1986, 1996

Provan, I. W., *Lamentations*, New Century Bible Commentary, Grand Rapids: Eerdmans, 1991

Quasten, J., *Patrology* III, Westminster MD: Newman, 1960

Schäublin, C., "Diodor von Tarsus," *TRE* 8,763-67

____ , *Untersuchungen zu Methode und Herkunft der Antiochenischen Exegese*, Theophaneia: Beitrage zur Religions- und Kirchengeschihte des Altertums 23; Köln-Bonn: Peter Hanstein Verlag, 1974

Wallace-Hadrill, D. S., *Christian Antioch. A Study of Early Christian Thought in the East*, Cambridge: CUP, 1982

Weitzman, M. P., *The Syriac Version of the Old Testament*, Cambridge: CUP, 1999

Young, F., *From Nicaea to Chalcedon. A Guide to the Literature and its Background*, Philadelphia: Fortress, 1983

____ , *Biblical Exegesis and the Formation of Christian Culture*, Cambridge: CUP, 1997

Ziegler, J. (ed.), *Jeremias, Baruch, Threni, Epistula Jeremiae*, Septuaginta XV, 3rd ed.; Göttingen: Vandenhoeck & Ruprecht, 1976

The Blessed Theodoret
Bishop of Cyrus

Commentary on the Book of the Prophet Jeremiah

Preface

I had been of the view that there was no need for a commentary on the inspired composition of the divine Jeremiah.[1] Since, however, many studious people kept pressing me to do a commentary on this book as well by claiming that most people do not grasp the sense of the work, I shall attempt, after praying for divine grace to cooperate,[2] to meet the demand. Now, I shall give particular attention to conciseness as far as possible:[3] of the more obvious matters, on the one hand, I shall give a summary in point form, while taking care to explicate what requires in-depth treatment, on the other. Firstly, however, I shall enunciate the theme of the work.[4]

Foreword[5]

King Josiah had for his father Amon, an impious man, and for his grandfather Manasseh, who had been the father's instructor in impiety. He himself, on the contrary, took the opposite path to them, and sided with the party of the godly. For children, however, he had those who, on the one hand, showed no interest in their father's virtue and, on the other, imitated their forebears' godlessness. Knowing this in advance, therefore, the God of all elected the prophet in the thirteenth year of Josiah's reign and bade him foretell the calamities that would befall both city and people. He persevered in prophesying this, not only for the remaining years of Josiah but also in the time of Jehoahaz, who was Josiah's son and succeeded to the throne, and in the time of Jehoiakim, the latter's brother and son of Josiah, and actually in the time of Jeconiah,[6] who was Jehoiakim's son and Josiah's grandson, and likewise also in the time of Zedekiah, (497) who was also son of Josiah. The result was that the whole period of his prophesying was forty-two years minus a few months. He foretold the siege conducted by the Babylonians, the ensuing famine, the razing of Jerusalem, the burning of the divine Temple, and the deportation of the people. He forecast also the captives' return, the overthrow of the Babylonians and in fact the various punishments of a great number of other nations. He also predicted the granting of the New Covenant, the end of the Old one, the calling of the nations and the future salvation of the world.[7]

Chapter One

The word of the Lord, which came to Jeremiah, son of Hilkiah, from a family of priests, who dwelt in Anathoth (v. 1).[8] The prophet was accorded a double grace, the priestly and the prophetic: he took one from his lineage, and received the other from the gift from on high. He also mentions the period of his prophesying: *In the days of Josiah,* the text goes on, *son of Amon, king of Judah, in the thirteenth year of his reign* (v. 2). He makes mention also of those who reigned next up till the end of the siege.[9]

The word of the Lord came to me, saying, Before I formed you in the womb I knew you, and before you left the womb I consecrated you (vv. 4-5). The election was not without basis: knowledge preceded it. He had knowledge, note, and then he consecrated; for he knows everything before its coming to be. Now, the word *consecrated* he employed to mean "appointed." Then he mentions also the task for which he selected him, *I appointed you as prophet to the nations*: he prophesies not only Jews' fortunes but also the other nations'. *I replied, O Lord and Master that you are, see, I do not know how to speak, because I am a child* (v. 6). The (500) prophet recognized the one addressing him – hence his giving him a title to do with lordship. When the mighty Moses was once speaking, remember, and wanted to learn the divine name, the Lord said, "I am the one who is."[10] He imitates Moses' piety by saying youth is not up to prophesying.

The Lord, however, urges him not to put forward the excuse of youthfulness, but to do as he is told. He also dispels his apprehension: *Have no fear in their presence*, he goes on, note, *nor be frightened of them* (v. 8). Then he brings out also the reason for confidence: *Because I am with you to deliver you, says the Lord*. The Lord God said this also to the divinely-inspired Moses: when he dreaded the role of service and said, "Who am I to go to make my way to Pharaoh?" the Lord said, "I shall be with you."[11] He gave this firm promise to the sacred apostles as well: after bidding them make disciples of all the nations, and as God knowing in advance that doubts rose up in their hearts about the possibility of eleven mere men bereft of eloquence converting the whole world, he resolved their uncertainty and dispelled their fear by saying, "And behold I am with you all days to the end of the age."[12] He said this here as well to the prophet, *I am with you to deliver you, says the Lord*.

His action confirms his word: *He stretched out his hand*, the text goes on, *and touched my mouth, and the Lord said to me, I have put my words in your mouth* (v. 9). He explains also what the words are: *See, today I have set you over nations and kingdoms to root up and to pull down, to destroy and to overthrow, to build up and to plant* (v. 10). He prophesied, notice, not only the captivity of the Jews but also the release provided by Cyrus; he also prophesied for many other nations not only a range of calamities but also the salvation provided by the incarnation of Christ the Lord. Hence he cited the uprooting and destroying in connection with the disasters, and the building up and planting in connection with the opposite.

After that he shows him a nut-bearing twig or, according to the Syriac and the Hebrew, a twig bearing almonds; all texts in fact referred to it as a twig.[13] The prophet was asked what was seen and made his reply. The Lord said to him, (501) *Your vision was good, for I am watching my words so as to enact them* (v. 12). By *watching* he refers to his anxiety to inflict punishment, and by sleeping his longsuffering; blessed David, remember, said, "Wake up! Why do you sleep, Lord?" and again, "The Lord awoke as though from sleep."[14] Now, the almond-bearing twig suggests the rapidity of the punishment: this tree flowers before the other trees. According to the Septuagint, on the other hand, this is the meaning to be taken: the nut itself has a bitter and rough covering, but hidden under it is the edible part; likewise discipline has painful aspects, but what follows that is advantageous.

Then he gives him a glimpse also of *a boiling kettle facing away from the north* (v. 13). By kettle he refers to Jerusalem, with Babylon the fire, calling it north: Babylon is north of Jerusalem. The divinely-inspired Ezekiel also calls Jerusalem a kettle and its inhabitants meat.[15] Then he explains more clearly what was said in figurative fashion: *See, I am in fact summoning all the kingdoms of the kingdoms*[16] *from the north, says the Lord; they will come, and each of them shall set their throne at the entrance of the gates of Jerusalem, upon all its walls, and upon all the cities of Judah* (v. 15). To bring out the justice of what is done he adds, *I shall speak with my judgment against them in regard to all their wickedness in forsaking me, sacrificing to foreign gods, and worshiping the works of their hands* (v. 16). What could be more foolish than this impiety? What more righteous than the retribution? I mean, they for their part forsook their own maker, and turned things of their own making into gods, whereas he after showing longsuffering at great length deprived them of his characteristic grace; once deprived of it they became enslaved to unholy men.

He bids him gird his loins – that is, attire himself in neat and manly fashion – and by reminding him of the promises already made he dispels his fear. He says he has the appearance of an iron pillar, a bronze wall and a strongly fortified city, in the sight not only of the priests of the Jews and their rulers but also of the very kings and the whole body of their subjects. He promises him not peace and tranquility but contests and victory. (504) *They will make war against you*, the text goes on, *and will not prevail against you, because I am with you to deliver you, says the Lord* (v. 19). He made this promise also in respect of the Church, saying in regard to the most divine Peter, "On this rock I shall build my Church, and hell's gates will not prevail against it."[17] He did not say, they will not make war, but though warring they will not prevail; after all, contestants are required for victory to be won.

Chapter Two

After this he bids him speak to the inhabitants of Jerusalem. *The Lord says this: I remember the grace of your youth and the love of your maturity, when you followed the holy one of Israel in the desert, in a land not sown, says the Lord* (v. 2). He called the beginning of Israel's vocation *youth*: when they suffered hardship in Egypt they murmured, whereas he had pity, and by employing Moses as his minister he delivered them. He adopted the phrase *the love of your maturity* ironically: Jews never had perfect love for their benefactor. The hymn-maker David also teaches us this: "They loved him with their mouths, and they lied to him with their tongue; their heart was not steadfast with him, nor were they faithful to his covenant."[1]

Israel holy to the Lord (v. 3), meaning, From the beginning I esteemed you ahead of the other nations, and you were styled my people. Likewise blessed Moses also said, "The Lord's portion was his people Jacob, Israel the division of his inheritance."[2] *First-fruits of his offspring*: he chose him before all the others – hence his words to Pharaoh as well, "Israel is my firstborn son,"[3] and his similar words through another prophet, "Like grapes in the wilderness I found Israel, and like the early fruit of the fig I found your fathers."[4] *All who eat it will go astray, evil will befall them, says the Lord*: those who fought against Israel were not fighting as though they ministered to the Lord; instead, it was as though they were able to prevail over God himself. Likewise Sennacherib also said, "Do not let your God in whom you rely deceive you with the promise that the Lord will deliver Jerusalem from my hand."[5] For this reason he threatened them as well with retribution.

Then he says to the whole people, (505) *What fault did your ancestors find in me that they separated themselves at a distance from me, went after worthless things and became worthless?* (v. 5) Who can adequately measure up to extolling the Lord's lovingkindness? I mean, instead of judging as a judge, he offers a defense as a guilty party and is prepared to have proof given that he has not done what had to be done; and though all-holy God he says to lawless human beings, What sin have I committed? What wrong have I done? Speak, prove your case. On the basis of what accusation did your ancestors abandon me, their benefactor, on the one hand, and on the other become enslaved to idols made by hand? It was I in fact who freed them from the slavery of the Egyptians, led them through a trackless land, regaled them in the waterless desert with a stream of abundant water, and brought them into the promised land, which is mother of multifarious crops. By mention of Carmel he signified the whole land of promise;[6] yet despite enjoying these things, far from acknowledging their benefactor they imitated the shameless behavior of their ancestors.

Then he launches into an accusation of each class individually. *The priests did not say, Where is the Lord?* (v. 8). This was the most unholy action of all, the guides proving to be leaders in error. *Those who handle the Law did not know me.* Here he accuses scribes and teachers, who though interpreters of the Law were the first to transgress it. *The shepherds acted impiously towards me*, a name he gave the kings. *The prophets prophesied by Baal.* By *prophets* he refers to the false prophets,[7] just as he likewise refers to those not really gods as gods. *And went after things of no value.* He brought out the extremity of their folly: forsaking the source of the manifold good things, they worshiped the useless idols.

For this reason I shall come to judgment on you, says the Lord, and I shall come to judgment on the children's children (v. 9). He persists in his moderation: he did not say, I shall pass judgment on you and your offspring, but *I shall come to judgment* on you and on them, that is to say, I shall hold a trial and I shall cross-examine offenders.[8] Now, to bring out the extremity of the offense he bids them examine the nations' way of living, both west and east, and learn whether some of them changed their ancestral gods. By Kittim he refers to Cyprus, to the islands adjacent to it, and by mention of them to the western regions, and by Kedar to the inhabitants of the desert in the direction of the rising sun, and by mention of them (508) he hints at the eastern regions.[9] His point is that these people followed their ancestral customs and the gods they were taught to worship, whereas the Jews denied the true God. This was the reason he said heaven was appalled and earth horror-struck – not that the elements enjoy the faculty of reason, but because blessed Moses summoned them to witness as encompassing all created things: "Hearken, O heaven, and I shall speak; let earth listen to the words of my mouth."[10]

Because my people have also committed two evils: they have forsaken me, a spring of living water, and dug for themselves broken cisterns that are not capable of holding water (v. 13). He called the idols *broken cisterns*: the cistern is made by hand, and does not have a spring of water; instead, it receives the water that comes from the clouds and is collected from hither and yon, and if it is cracked and broken, it immediately loses the water gathered from heaven.[11] Such is the nature of idols: they depend for their substance on matter and artifice, and the beauty they acquire from these sources time wipes out. The true God, on the other hand, is a spring of everlasting life.

Surely Jacob is no slave, or Israel a home-born servant? Why did he become booty? Lions kept roaring at him (vv. 14-15). Everyone knew, he is saying, that I freed them from the slavery of the

Egyptians; it was clear to everyone that it was in reliance on my providence that they were sufficient even of themselves. This was in fact conspicuous and remarkable. What, then, was the cause of their captivity? Why did they ever fall victim to the kings assailing them (calling the kings lions)? He says they both divided their land and burned the cities. You suffered this at the hands not only of Assyrians but also of Egyptians. He continues, in fact: *People of Memphis and Tahpanhes knew you and mocked you* (v. 16): the people who endured those notorious misfortunes on your account I finally consigned to the depths of the sea.

Then he explains the reason for the weakness. (509) *Was it not your forsaking me that brought this upon you? says the Lord your God* (v. 17). Then he indicates also the beginning of the revolt. *At the time I was guiding you through the desert*: as soon as you were freed from Egypt you abandoned me and made a god of a calf. *What good to you now is the way to Egypt, to drink water of Gihon? What good to you is the way of Assyrians, to drink water of the rivers?* (v. 18) When they were attacked by Syrians, they called on the Assyrians for assistance; and when Assyrians assailed them, they had recourse to Egyptians (referring to the Nile as *Gihon*). *Your revolt will chastise you, and your wickedness censure you. Know and see that your forsaking me is harsh and bad for you, says the Lord your God; I was not pleased with you, says the Lord your God* (v. 19):[12] you did not call on me for assistance, but on them – hence I handed you over to them. Those who crucified the Savior also suffered something like this: denying him they said they had no king but Caesar – hence he handed them over to Caesar.[13]

Because ages ago you broke your yoke, snapped your bonds and said, I will not serve you (v. 20): your habits go back a long way; in olden times you broke the yoke of the Law and adopted the ways of the lawless nations, and you preferred the altars and groves to the ritual of the Law. *I, on the contrary, planted you as a fruitful vine, completely true* (v. 21). It was not without purpose that he included *completely*: there were pious men among them, both the divine prophets and those following them; so his meaning is, I wanted you all to be like that, having cared for all equally. *How did you turn from me to bitterness and become a wild vine?* If it had remained true, it would not be wild; but since it turned to bitterness, it is called no longer true but wild. The mighty Moses also spoke in similar terms: "Their vine comes from the vine of the Sodomites, and their brushwood from Gomorrah; their grapes the grapes of gall, their clusters bitter."[14] Hence they also offered gall to the Lord. But since they inflicted abuse on the divine planting, turned to bitterness and produced thorns instead of grapes, (512) Christ, who comes from them according to the flesh, calls himself true vine, saying, "I am the true vine," and gave the term "branches" to those believing in him.[15]

Even if you wash in soap and cover yourself in grass, in my sight you are stained with your iniquities, says the Lord (v. 22). By *grass* he refers to the soaps derived from the soil, and by these words he brings out in figurative fashion that it is not the aspersions prescribed by the Law that bring about release from sins but sincere repentance and renouncing vice. After this he reproves their shamelessness. *How will you say, I am not defiled and have not gone after the Baal?* (v. 23) Then he brings out the notoriety of their godlessness: *Look at your ways in the graveyard, and know what you have done.* By *graveyard* he refers to the place of the tombs; in that place they made a holocaust of their sons and daughters to the idols.[16] *Late did they lament in their own voice.* He used *late* to mean tardily: after the experience of sufferings, he is saying, they had a sense of lawlessness. The prophet says as much afterwards, also, giving a glimpse of the ten tribes grieving and saying, "Later I repented of captivity."[17]

They expanded their ways at waters of the wilderness (v. 24).[18] By *expanded* he indicated the insatiable desire for impiety. He called the idols *waters of the wilderness* insofar as they create devastation and are the source of ruin. *They were carried away with the lusts of their soul*: what they wanted to hear the false prophets made it their business to prophesy; he used *carried away* of the false prophets. *They have been surrendered; who can make them repent?* With God surrendering them, who will be able to help? He speaks in similar terms through the mighty Moses.[19] *Everyone seeking them will have no problem; they will discover them in their lowliness*: they became vulnerable by embracing impiety.

After this he teaches that, though often (513) advised to desist from their harmful ways, they were bold and blatant in professing their revolt. For that reason, however, he says, I shall envelop all equally in shame – kings, rulers, priests, and the prophets of falsehood; they will be like a thief caught in the act of theft, utterly crestfallen. After all, while calling the gods made from wood and stone fathers and parents, they turned their back on me and avoided me like an enemy. *In the time of their troubles they will say, Arise and save us* (v. 27). This is a particular mark of extreme shamelessness, suffering from ingratitude while enjoying the good things, on the one hand, whereas on the other begging for assistance when in need of them. *Where are your gods which you have made for yourselves? Will they not rise up and save you in your time of trouble?* (v. 28) He brings out also their vast number: *Because your gods are as numerous as your cities, Judah, and to the number of Jerusalem's thoroughfares they sacrificed to the Baal.*[20]

Having thus demonstrated the honor given to the false gods, their number and their impotence, he mildly upbraids the ingrates. *Why do you speak against me? You have all profaned me and you have all wronged me, says the Lord* (v. 29). He recalls also the chastisements inflicted on them. *In vain did I strike your children, you did not accept correction* (v. 30): you neither acknowledged the benefactor when receiving benefit, nor desisted from impiety when chastised. I for my part, however, handed over to slaughter also those responsible for the error.[21]

You heard the word of the Lord. The Lord says this: Surely I have not been a wilderness to the house of Jacob, the land made barren, since my people said, We shall not be subject, and we shall not come to you? (v. 31). He says this ironically, meaning, Surely I am not like the idols? Surely I did not, like them, provide them with no good fruit, and for that reason they shunned my service? He shifts to a different figure as well, saying, Every bride is concerned for her adornment and every maiden is careful of her bodice, whereas my so-called (516) people spurn the one who cares for them. He repeats the irony: *Why do you still take pains with your ways to seek the object of your affections?* (v. 33) What else are you prepared to add to the aforementioned, he is saying, so as to bring about my love for you? *That is not the way*: none of those things prompts love – quite the contrary: it leads to hate; you have not only run headlong into impiety but have also perpetrated murder.

On your hands, in fact, he goes on, *is found the blood of innocent people* (v. 34). Blessed David also said this, "They sacrificed their children to the demons, and poured out innocent blood, blood of their sons and daughters, whom they sacrificed to Canaan's graven images, and the land was stained with their blood."[22] To emphasise that, far from doing this furtively, they committed it openly, he went on, *I did not find them in holes in the wall, but under every tree*: it is not as though they do this secretly like burglars, not as though they tried to escape detection when in their case they were committing this lawlessness; rather, every hill and every grove was the scene of their impiety, and shameless and loathsome as they were, they even denied what was brazenly done.

You said, I am innocent; let his anger be directed away from me (v. 35). Hence he went on, *Hence I have a case against you for saying, I have not sinned.* He does not say, I shall pass judgment on you, but I have a case against you, that is, I sit as judge and accuse you of lying and shamelessly denying the charge.[23] *Because you have not the slightest worry about adopting other ways for yourself* (v. 36): shamelessness befits iniquity. In this he suggests something else as well: Just as by your appeal to the Assyrians you gained nothing by way of assistance, so too now by having recourse to the Egyptians you will thereby gain no benefit. He implies as much, in fact, by what follows. *You will be put to shame by Egypt, just as* (517) *you were put to shame by Assyria. For from there as well you will come away, and your hands will be on your head* (vv. 36-37). It is typical of the grieving to put their hands folded on their heads. The cause of the troubles, *Because the Lord had frustrated your hope, and you will not prosper in it*: if you had placed your hope in God, you would have reaped timely fruit from your hope; but since you had confidence in human beings, you are disappointed in your hope.

Chapter Three

After this he observes that, whereas any woman who leaves her husband for a relationship with another man cannot return to her former husband, the Law forbidding it, you forsook me who was related to you by Law, and related yourself to unholy demons. Then, when you felt the harm, you returned to me, and I did not refuse to take you back. If, however, you think I said this idly, *Direct your eyes straight ahead and see how could it be you were not sullied* (v. 2), that is, polluted; he says as much to her, remember, through Ezekiel, "I found you stained in your blood."[1] This is also the version of the Syriac.[2]

He says in what follows, You not only welcomed all-comers, but even went out looking for them; you waited around in the streets like carrion-crows, awaiting their arrival, and you filled the land with your defilements, having recourse to many shepherds in place of one. By many shepherds, note, he referred to the idols: just as the fathers of falsehood were called gods by arrogating to themselves the divine name, so too they were given this name by stealing the name of the true shepherd.[3] *You had the face of a whore, being shameless before everyone* (v. 3): just as those who sell their charms wash the shame from their foreheads and make themselves available to everyone, likewise in your case, instead of keeping your favor for someone, you gathered the crop of good things from me and took up service with idols; but falling foul of calamities and experiencing their weakness, you went looking for my help.

Did you not address me as house and father, responsible for your maidenhood? (v. 4) Did you not in former times apply to me terms of belonging, calling me at one time father, at another first husband, and at another house of refuge? This is in fact the way blessed (520) David also puts it, "Be God protector for me, and a house of refuge to save me."[4] *Surely it will not continue forever* – that is, your falsehood and the mockery of your words – *or be preserved to the point of victory?* (v. 5) Surely you do not think that by this you will prevail and be victorious? Then with irony, *Lo, you have said and done these wicked things and have succeeded*, that is, Consider that you have done your mocking and got away with committing these acts of lawlessness.

After this he says God spoke to him in the days of King Josiah. *Did you see what the house of Israel did to me?* (v. 6) Since they were absent, being enslaved in Babylon, he teaches the prophet the justice of the retribution. *They betook themselves to every high hill and under every green tree, and they played the whore there*. Then he brings out his own goodness and longsuffering: *I said, After her playing the whore like this she will return to me; but she did not return* (v. 7). It was thus willingly she brought on ruin, not embracing life according to the Law from the outset, nor prepared to be converted after her impiety.

Then he increases the accusation against the tribe of Judah.

Judah, her faithless sister, saw her infidelity, and saw that for all the adulteries in which the house of Israel had been apprehended I had sent her away and given a bill of divorce in her hands. Judah, her faithless sister, was not afraid; she went off and herself likewise played the whore (v. 8). Though perceiving both her sister's wickedness and the penalty inflicted on her for it, she did not avoid repeating the wickedness; instead, she followed in her footsteps. *Her whoredom was as nothing to her* (v. 9): she thought nothing of committing lawlessness. By *whoredom* he refers to idolatry: forsaking God, who was called their bridegroom, they worshiped the idols. *She polluted the earth, sacrificing her children to the demons;*[5] *she committed adultery with stone and tree.* He leveled the charge of whoredom with clarity.

Then he brings out in many ways that she did not abhor her sister's impiety, though perceiving her ruination, and that the ten tribes had more excuse than the tribe of Judah since, though seeing their calamities, it continued doing what brought them on. Hence the prophet is bidden prophesy this to them. (521) *Go, proclaim these words to the north, and say, Turn back to me, house of Israel, says the Lord. I shall not harden my face against you, because I am merciful, says the Lord, and I shall not be angry with you forever* (vv. 11-12). Immeasurable the Lord's lovingkindness: despite the great lawlessness he looks only for repentance. He also brings out the form it takes: *Only acknowledge your iniquity, that you have profaned the Lord your God* (v. 13) – the beginning of recovery is the experience of ill-health. And *you poured out your ways on foreigners*: forsaking your God, Lord, maker and benefactor, you related yourself to foreigners. Who were they? *Under every green tree.* He brought out the uselessness of the error, plants made into gods being fruitless. *You did not obey my voice, says the Lord.* When he gave the Law, remember, he said, "You shall have no other gods but me."[6]

Turn back, rebellious children, says the Lord (v. 14). He calls them recalcitrant children on account of his ineffable goodness. *Because I shall be your master*: once more I shall look after you and accord you every care. *I shall take you, one from a city and two from a family, and I shall bring you into Zion. I shall give you shepherds after my own heart, and they will shepherd you as shepherds of understanding* (vv. 14-15). This happened in the manner of a type in the time of Zerubbabel: they returned under Cyrus the Persian, with Zerubbabel son of Shealtiel and the high priest Jeshua son of Jozadak as shepherds;[7] piety and good order distinguished them both. In reality, however, the prophecy reached fulfillment after the incarnation of our God and Savior: from Jews the Lord chose *one from a city and two from a family*, and appointed them *shepherds after his own heart*, namely, the sacred apostles. This was the very reason he also said to the most divine Peter, "Simon Jonah, do you love me? Shepherd my sheep."[8]

To the fact that the prophecy has this sense, what follows testifies. *In those days and at that time they will call Jerusalem the Lord's throne, and all the nations will be gathered to it in the name of the Lord in Jerusalem. They will no longer follow in the wake of the reasonings* (524) *of their evil heart* (v. 17). Now, this did not happen after the return from Babylon: the nations did not then forsake their impiety. After the incarnation of our God and Savior, the divine apostles carried the saving message to the whole world, while those in thrall to the previous error abandoned it; they worship the God of all, and they all make their way to Jerusalem as though to the divine throne. He then brings out that after the return from Babylon the tribes would no longer be separated but would come together and occupy the ancestral land.

Then the prophet, pleased with the glowing promises, says, *I said, May it happen, Lord* (v. 19). After this interjection, the prophet concludes the divine promise: *I shall rate you as children*: once more you will be styled my children. *And I shall give you a chosen land, a celebrated inheritance, belonging to God the master of nations.* This was the way he referred to the promised land. He called him *God the master of nations* to bring out that he is God of all and creator of all, and that the nations will attain knowledge of God and the grace of the Spirit will transfer to them. After this he advises them to acquire the affection children have for their father, and enjoy divine providence. Then he accuses them of imitating an adulterous woman sinning against her husband, not only the ten tribes but also the tribe of Judah, and of breaking the covenant with their bridegroom.

He also foretells the repentance of the ten tribes: the disaster of the captivity instilled in them a sense of their transgression. *A sound of weeping and begging was heard from the lips of the children of Israel, because they committed wrong in their ways and forgot the holy God* (v. 21). Perceiving their repentance, he urges them to persevere in it, saying, *Return, returning children, and I shall heal your bruises* (v. 22). He not only promises healing, but also explains what words must be used, as if to say, Put it this way, *Lo, we shall be your slaves, because you are the Lord our God*: we renounce the error, we abhor the service of the demons, we know you alone are Lord and God. *Truly the hills and the power of the mountains are a delusion.* (525) *Instead, salvation for the house of Israel is through the Lord God* (v. 23): we learned through experience that you alone are the source of good things, whereas the groves and the hills are loss and ruin.

From their youth, however, shame consumed the labors of our fathers, who incinerate their sheep, their sons and their daughters (v. 24).[9] He brought out both the extraordinary degree of honor they offered to the idols, burning alive the sons and daughters as well as the sheep, and also the fact that they not only gained no advantage from this but incurred shame as well in addition to the loss of their lives. In what follows, in fact, he admits as much: *We lay down in our shame, and our dishonor enveloped us, because we and our fathers have sinned in the sight of our God from our youth to this very day, and we have not listened to the voice of the Lord our God* (v. 25). The divine apostle also says shame is the fruit of sin, putting it this way, "So what fruit did you then receive from what is now to your shame?"[10]

Chapter Four

Having thus taught them to pray, he promises them also enjoyment of good things, provided they forget about the idols (referring to them as abominations) and transfer their adoration to the true God so as to make their oaths no longer by the idols but by him, keeping to the truth and not falsehood. He says as much, in fact: *If you swear, The Lord lives, in truth, in justice and in righteousness* (v. 2). In the sacred Gospels, by contrast, he made more perfect prescriptions than these: "It was said to the ancients, You shall not swear falsely: you shall discharge your oaths to the Lord. But I tell you, do not swear at all."[1] He bids Jews, being weak as they are, to swear by him so that through the habit of swearing they may learn to adore him alone; and he promises that, if this is done, *nations will give blessing through him, and through him will praise God in Jerusalem* – in other words, when they became religious, many of the neighboring peoples learned about religion.

Then he shifts his attention from Israel to Judah, saying, *Break up your fallow ground, and do not sow on top of thorns* (v. 3). Tend your souls, he is saying; root up the memory of the idols (referring to them as *thorns*). *Circumcise yourselves to your God* (v. 4). Then he brings out what God's circumcision is like. *Cut away* (528) *the uncircumcision of your heart, men of Judah and the inhabitants of Jerusalem.* He clearly brought out that the visible circumcision is a type of the invisible, and that if there is circumcision within, bodily circumcision is unnecessary. Taking a lead from this text the divine apostle wrote to the Romans, "A person is not a Jew, you see, who is one outwardly, nor is circumcision what is outward, in the flesh; rather, a person is a Jew who is one inwardly, and circumcision is of the heart, in spirit and not in letter. That person's commendation comes not from people but from God."[2] He had heard, note, what God said through the prophet, *Circumcise yourselves to your God, cut away the uncircumcision of your heart, men of Judah and the inhabitants of Jerusalem, lest at some time my wrath issue forth like fire and be set alight, and there be no one to extinguish it in the face of the wickedness of your exploits*: you alone are able to extinguish it by repenting; but since you do not fall to repentance, no one is capable of ridding you of the penalty.

To scare them he bids him tell Jerusalem and all the tribe of Judah to sound the trumpet and to signal to everyone the enemies' attack so that they may take refuge in the fortified cities, especially in Zion as the most secure. He urges them in the words, *Hasten, do not dally, don sackcloth, because I am bringing troubles from the north and great tribulation* (v. 6). He speaks of it in a figurative manner, referring to Nebuchadnezzar as a lion, and Babylon as his lair, from which he launches his attack to burn down cities and tear places to pieces. *For this very reason weep and wail because the fury of the Lord's wrath has not been averted from you* (v. 8). He prophesies also the dread felt by the king, both Jehoiakim and after him Jeconiah, and finally Zedekiah; he prophesies also the fear felt by the rulers and priests.

After this the prophet says to the Lord, *Surely you would not use deceit to deceive God's people and Jerusalem, saying, There will be peace, and lo, the sword has touched their very lives?* (v. 10). The prophet was not speaking factually in saying this: since the false prophets promised peace, claiming God guaranteed it, to accuse them of falsehood he used those words. *At that time they will say to this people and Jerusalem that there is a breath of error in the wilderness, a way of the daughter of my people not pure or holy.* (529) *A breath of fulfillment will come to me from them* (vv. 11-12). From experience itself, he is saying, they will learn in the time of the calamities that a breath of deceit was uttered by the false prophets, not pure or holy or a breath of fufilment – that is, not completing the Trinity;[3] from them the present troubles came to me. *Rather, now it is I who shall speak judgments against them*, that is, these calamities I shall justly inflict on them. And he lists them, comparing the chariots to cloud and tempest, and the speed of the horses to eagles.[4] He also prophesies the future lament, *Woe to us, we are suffering hardship.*

After this he advises them to secure the fruit of salvation by repentance. *Wash your heart of evil, Jerusalem, so as to be saved. How long will your wicked plans remain in you?* (v. 14) In other words, the wickedness of your thoughts has proved to be the source of your troubles. *Hence a voice of one announcing will come from Dan, and hardship will be reported from Mount Ephraim* (v. 15). Dan was the name give to the present Paneion; it was part of Israelite territory, and the story of the Kings mentions it, "from Dan to Beersheba."[5] It was situated, like Mount Ephraim, to the north of Jerusalem, and from there the Babylonian made his advance. Both the prophet and the fourth book of Kings mention it,[6] saying that Nebuchadnezzar's men brought the captives to Riblah in Hamat. Riblah is a town now called Emesa, so it is clear that it calls the great Hamath Emesa, whereas the other Hamath is called Epiphaneia,[7] the name it has to this day in the local language.

Since, then, they came in haste from that quarter and were looking forward to disasters: *Lo, hordes are coming from a distant land, and have communicated their voice to the cities of Judah. They were in a circle around her as though guarding a field* (vv. 16-17): just as people guarding seeds or vines (532) guard them carefully and forbid travelers to pass through them, so those besieging Jerusalem will allow not a single person to escape. Both the prophet and the fourth book of Kings[8] report that they also built a wall of squared stones around it so that none of the inhabitants might get away. You are to suffer this, he says, *because you neglected me, says the Lord. Your ways and your habits brought this on you, your very wickedness in its harshness, in its reaching to your heart* (vv. 17-18): you are enduring fitting punishment for your exploits, and reaping what you sowed.

After prophesying this the prophet feels sorry and grieves deeply for them, and he says his entrails are in turmoil and his heart strings plucked; he resembles a mother tearing her hair at the loss of her children. *My soul is on edge, my heart has gone to pieces, I shall not keep silence; because my soul heard the sound of a trumpet, the cry of war, it signals distress and tribulation* (vv. 19-20): this is what the trumpet signifies, these the evils it portends; it means the land has suffered distress, the tent has been dismantled and the coverings scattered. By this he hinted at the destruction of the city. He narrates also the multitude of the fugitives, and speaks in God's person: *Because those leading my people did not know me, their children are foolish and lack understanding* (v. 22). And in case they be thought deserving of pardon for being foolish, he immediately added, *They are smart at evildoing, but of doing good they have no knowledge*: this is the worst of it, that they used their brains for nothing, like people drunk on wine and murderers with a knife.

I gazed on the earth, and lo, nothing; and on the sky, and its lights were not there. I looked at the mountains, and lo, they were trembling, and all the hills were in disorder. I gazed, and lo, there was no human being alive, and all the birds of heaven were terrified (vv. 23-25). People caught up in disasters normally have this experience: they think light is not light, day is not day, and pleasant things are not pleasant; for them everything is changed into its opposite. *I looked, and lo, Carmel was desolate, and* (533) *all the cities were consumed with fire in face of the Lord and were wiped out in face of his wrath* (v. 26). While it is plausible that Carmel itself was ravaged by the enemies' advance, my own view is that in this case Jerusalem is referred to as Carmel by metonymy in view of the great number of its inhabitants.[9]

The Lord says this, All the land shall be desolate, but I shall not bring about the end (v. 27). By *all the land* he means Palestine; and he promises the recall. Then he gives this exhortation, *Let the earth grieve for this, let heaven above be darkened, because I have spoken* (v. 28): creation is in harmony with its maker. *I am ready for battle,*[10] *and I shall not relent.* The phrase *I shall not relent* is anthropomorphic, the divinity being immune to passion, and it has the meaning, I thought fit to exact retribution.[11] *I launched the attack and shall not be diverted from it,* that is, from the attack. He explains what it is like: through fear of the horses and the archers all were put to flight, and some endeavored to put their trust in the mountains and others in the groves; many also abandoned the cities and occupied the crests of the mountains.

Then to Jerusalem: *And you, poor wretch, what will you do?* – that is, where will you flee? what place will you escape to? *If you donned scarlet and prettied yourself with gold ornaments, and if you painted your eyes, your makeup was in vain: it is your life they are after* (v. 30). They were in the habit of beautifying themselves on the festivals of the demons; he reminds them of this ornamentation, and points out that it is all useless and futile. In fact, they gained no assistance from the demons, who proved rather a source of these troubles for them. *For I heard a sound as though of a woman in labor, your groans as though of someone giving birth to her first child* (v. 31). By this figure he expressed the extent of the pangs.[12] *Woe is me, that my soul fails me at the sight of the victims.* He fulfills the divine law, "Weep with those who weep,"[13] also suffering with those who are punished.

Now, as we take a pause at this point,[14] we urge those who light upon the book to shun the deceit of the demons while in every way serving God. This, after all, is the way we shall succeed both in enjoying his providence in this life and in attaining the future goods, thanks to the grace and lovingkindness of our Lord Jesus Christ, to whom with the Father together with the all-holy Spirit be glory, honor and power, now and forever, for ages of ages. Amen. (536)

Chapter Five

Run around the streets of Jerusalem, see and discover, look in its alleys to find a man in it, anyone to be found doing justice and seeking faith, and I shall be merciful to them, says the Lord (v. 1). Not to be surpassed their impiety and the Lord's lovingkindness: whereas they proceed in concert to lawlessness, he promises pardon to everybody on the basis of one single person living according to the Law. *See and discover, look* means, Search with all diligence. *They say, The Lord lives, yet they take false oaths* (v. 2). In what was said before he urged them not simply to direct their oaths to him but to swear truthfully.[1] *Your eyes are on truth* (v. 3), that is, you testify to what I say, observing everything.[2] *You flayed them all, and they were not distressed, you reduced them to extremes, and they were unwilling to accept correction.* While the former statement suggests moderate correction, the phrase *reduced them to extremes* suggests aggravated correction – yet on account of their stubborn attitude it did them no good. He says as much, in fact, in what follows, *They made their face harder than rock, and refused to turn back.* He suggests in these words their shamelessness and disobedience.

And I said, Perhaps they are poor – hence their inability and their ignorance of the way of the Lord and their God's judgment. I shall betake myself to the well-off, and speak to them, because they know the way of the Lord and God's judgment (vv. 4-5). By *well-off* he referred to the priests and the teachers of the Law, and by *poor* to the rest insofar as they did not possess the wealth of divine knowledge. Yet he accuses both of lawlessness, proceeding in this way: *Lo, in concert they broke the yoke, they snapped the bonds.* It was not without purpose the prophet said this; instead, since the Lord promised lovingkindness provided he found someone *doing judgment and seeking faith,* he explains that, though he went looking as he was bidden, he found they had all broken the yoke of the Law.

Hence a lion from the forest struck them, a wolf destroyed them at their very houses, (537) *and a leopard kept watch against the cities* (v. 6). By *lion* he refers to Nebuchadnezzar, and by *wolf* (in my view) to the captain of the guard Nebuzaradan, who was later given the commission to burn down the city and the divine Temple and to reduce the survivors to slavery;[3] and I think Antiochus Epiphanes is referred to by *leopard*, the divine Daniel seeing the kingdom of Macedonia likened to a leopard.[4] You will be hunted down by all these, he is saying, on account of the error of the idols.

Then in teaching mode, *For which of these am I to show mercy to you?*[5] (v. 7) He mentions also the kinds of lawlessness: Not only do you and your children swear by things that are not gods, but as well you make others swear by them, whereas I for my part regaled you with an abundance of good things (the meaning of *I gave them their fill*). In addition to this you violated other people's marriages to the point of your lasciviousness resembling lusty stallions. Then in argumentative fashion, *Am I not to take account of such things, and is my soul not to be avenged on such a nation?* (v. 9) Is it possible, he is saying, for me to overlook this? How could the due verdict be set aside? For this reason he delivers it, and orders the walls to be destroyed and the ramparts to be overturned;[6] but he tempers justice with kindness. *Do not bring on the end: leave its foundations, because they belong to the Lord.* In this he hints at the recall and the rebuilding.

He also foretells the responsibility for the troubles in their being lawless and ungrateful to their benefactor, their turning insolent and presuming they would prove superior to the troubles. *Evils will not come upon us, nor shall we see sword and famine* (v. 12). The false prophets were responsible for this; in what follows he charges them with it. *Your prophets were all wind, and the word of the Lord was not with them* (v. 13). The phrase *all wind* indicates the futility and falsity of what was said: they had no share in the divine Spirit. This is the reason he says to the prophet, The word which I utter through your tongue will consume them like fire; and he gives a glimpse also of the manner of retribution. *Lo, I shall bring upon you, house of Israel, a nation from afar, says the Lord; it is an ancient nation* (v. 15). He means the Assyrians: he calls them *an ancient nation* since their kingdom is older than all others, Nimrod being the first to rule over them after the flood.[7] Then he mentions the foreign character of their language. He also compares their quiver to an open tomb on account of the deathly blows of (540) their arrows and the accuracy of their archery.[8] He mentions also the devastation of the land, the sacking of the homes and the slaughter of the people.

He forecasts, nonetheless, both the destruction of the enemies and the people's recall. *I shall not bring you to an end* (v. 18). Since they suffered from insensibility and did not see their own lawlessness, and instead said, *Why did the Lord our God do all these things to us?* (v. 19), he bids the prophet say to them, *In return for your forsaking me and serving other gods in your land, just so you will serve other people in a land that is not yours.* The sentence of retribution is just: Since you denied my kingship (he is saying), I shall hand you over to other masters. He bids them listen carefully to this, and calls them stupid and uncomprehending, since they did not use their bodily senses as they should: *They have eyes but do not see, they have ears but do not hear* (v. 21). He also shows them to be less rational than inanimate things: the sea respects its boundaries (he says), I put boundaries on it, not a wall of steel but the simplest sand – yet though tossed and disturbed it does not exceed its boundaries, instead reversing when it approaches them.[9] They, by contrast, though endowed with reason, preferred irrationality.

This people's heart has become disobedient and unbelieving (v. 23): they do not appreciate the good things provided by me; I unceasingly provide them with rain in the morning and in the evening. Furthermore they also enjoy the fruits of the earth; he said as much, in fact, *ordering a harvest at the time of abundance* (v. 24): he employs his will like an order, and grants abundant crops from the earth. Nevertheless, on seeing you acting lawlessly, he deprived you even of the good things. *Impious people, in fact, have been found among my people, and they have set traps to destroy men, and they have ensnared them. Like a trap that is set and is full of birds, so their houses are full of guile* (vv. 26-27). By this he indicated their underhand schemes.[10] He mentions also the wealth accruing from iniquity, the arrogance and lawless living stemming from wealth, and the iniquity done to orphans and widows.

After this he proceeds, *Shall I not take account of these things, and shall my soul not be avenged on such a nation?* (v. 29) Foreign to my righteousness, he is saying, is neglect of such things. (541) *Stupor and dread fell upon the earth* (v. 30). Whenever we see something being done lawlessly despite all expectation, we are accustomed to say, I was appalled by this, staggered to hear it. Then he cites the causes of it. *Your prophets prophesied iniquitous things*, that is, false things, *and the priests clapped their hands* (v. 31) – a sign of conspiracy. *My people preferred it like that.* He suggested the wicked concert of all parties. *What will you do in the wake of it?* – that is, when punishment is imposed (which he portrays in what follows).

Chapter Six

He bids the people of the tribe of Benjamin, which was linked to the tribe of Judah, sound the trumpet and get ready for battle array, as though the enemy from the north were launching an attack against Jerusalem. He calls her, in fact, beautiful and pampered – beautiful on account of the beauty of the buildings, and pampered on account of the luxurious lifestyle of her inhabitants.[1] *Shepherds and their flocks will come, and fix their tents on her, and each will shepherd his herd with his own hand* (v. 3). By *shepherds* he refers to the kings who shared command with Nebuchadnezzar, and by *flocks* and *herds* to the armies serving under them, suggesting by this the siege of the city. Then he mentions also the movements at midday, the assaults in the evening and the attacks by night, and he gives orders to cut her down like a barren tree, being completely false to the extent of her ability. This is in keeping with what was said before.

As a cistern keeps its water fresh, so she keeps her wickedness fresh (v. 7). The city dedicated to God should have taught good order, even when welcoming those addicted to lawlessness. As it is, however, it is accused of the opposite, having become an actual teacher of impiety; and as the cistern changes the temperature of water, so she changed those arriving in her into vicious ways (by city referring not to the buildings but to the inhabitants). *Godlessness and wretchedness will be heard within her in my sight forever*: instead of revering my dwelling there, they were guilty of godlessness in my sight. *Learn your lesson in hardship and scourging, Jerusalem, lest my soul ever desert you* (544) *and I make you a desolate land, never to be inhabited* (v. 8). This also suggests the Lord's ineffable lovingkindness: though making dire threats against her, he promises her immunity from these if she changed.

Since they did not accept the proposal, however, he invites the enemy as harvesters, bids them garner them all like fruit of the vine, and explains the reason. *To whom shall I speak and solemnly protest, and it will be heard? Lo, their ears are uncircumcised, and they cannot hear. Lo, the word of the Lord came to them as a reproach; may they be unwilling to hear it* (v. 10). He refers to their ears as uncircumcised for accepting everything uncritically. They themselves were like that: though readily accepting what was prophesied by the false prophets for their delectation, they were unwilling to heed the divine words, mocking and jeering at the prophets.

Then he brings out the extraordinary degree of longsuffering. *I filled out my wrath and held it in, and did not put an end to them* (v. 11) – that is, I was bent on punishment, and once more I vouchsafed them pity and pardon. He threatens, however, to inflict a like punishment on both young and old, on both men and women, since all alike loved lawlessness, even those entrusted with priesthood, along with those presuming to make false prophecies.[2] He mentions also what has been perpetrated by them. *They treated the people's wound without due respect, spurning me and saying, Peace, peace*; then as a question, *and where is there peace?* (v. 14) Whereas the ailments should have been tended with very harsh remedies, he is saying, they applied to them the promise of peace – so where is the fulfillment of their words? In fact, instead of peace they see destruction. He brings out also the excess of their brazenness: though confounded in their false prophesying (he is saying), they could not bring themselves to blush. In fact, he says as much, *They did not blush though confounded, and did not acknowledge their own dishonor* (v. 15). Nevertheless, he is saying, in due course they will pay the penalty for what they have committed: *At the time of their being called to account they will be weak, said the Lord.*

At this point he both brings out the Jews' lack of response and proclaims the calling of the nations. *The Lord says this: Stand in the roadways and look; ask eternal paths and see what is the good way, and walk* (545) *in it, and you will find sanctification for your souls* (v. 16). While the holy prophets are many ways, our Lord himself is the truly good way – in fact, listen to his words, "I am the way, the truth and the life."[3] But each of the prophetic ways leads to this way, Moses the lawgiver hinting at this in his words, "The Lord our God will raise up for you from among your brethren a prophet like me"[4] and so on. David, king and prophet, and also Isaiah, Micah, Ezekiel and each of the prophets give a glimpse of this way. And as there is one way leading to the biggest cities which we are accustomed to call kingly and royal, whereas to it some paths conduct people from town and country, so there is one way leading to the Father, the only-begotten Son of God, while like certain paths the blessed prophets lead people choosing to travel by them to this way. The prophetic word, therefore, bids Jews to search out the prophetic ways,[5] and through them to discover the good way and travel in it. In customary manner, however, they resist, and do not carry out what is bidden: *They said, We shall not go*. Nevertheless, he offers them still further exhortation: *I appointed watchmen for you: listen to the sound of the trumpet* (v. 17). Once again he calls the prophets *watchmen*, saying also to Ezekiel, remember, "I gave you as a watchman to the house of Israel."[6] By *trumpet* he refers to the preaching of the apostles; those called to be watchmen prophesied it, too. But still Jews resist again, and openly declare, *We shall not listen*.

Having brought out their opposition, therefore, he foretells the responsiveness of the nations. *For this reason the nations listened, and those shepherding the flocks in them* (v. 18).[7] By *shepherds* he refers to their guides, not simply those accorded spiritual guidance but also kings and rulers, these having accepted the divine message. This is the way the divine apostles Barnabas and Paul also behaved: entering a certain synagogue they principally engaged the Jews in discussion, but when they perceived their unbelief, they said, "It was necessary to speak the word of God to you first, but since you resist it and pass judgment on yourselves as unworthy of eternal life, lo, we turn to the nations, the Lord having given us this direction, I set you as a light of nations to be (548) a light of nations, to be for salvation to the ends of the earth."[8] The prophecy has its fulfillment, therefore.

At this point the inspired word threatens the unbelieving Jews with a retribution befitting their opposition; but it also prohibits worship according to the Law. *Why do you bring me incense from Sheba and cinnamon from a distant land? Your burned offerings are not acceptable, and your sacrifices do not please me* (v. 20). If these things were thought obsolete even when the Law was in force, it was futile and foolish of the Jews after the cessation of the Law to devote themselves to the obsolete prescriptions of the Law as though they were required. He foretells also once more the infirmity to which they were reduced, not only by being forced into slavery but also in appearing to everyone to be accursed.

Then he shifts the prophecy to the Babylonians and the kings serving with him, and he describes their power, their armor, and the savagery and ferocity of their attitude.[9] He mentions also the dread of them. *Their hands hung loose, distress caught hold of them, pangs like a woman in labor* (v. 24). He bids them not to peep out from the cities with the enemy arrayed before them. He bids Jerusalem don sackcloth, scatter dust on their heads, and imitate the grieving for an only child. Then he urges the prophet to see their transgressions. *I have appointed you as a tester amidst my people in their confinement, and you will know how to test their ways* (v. 27) – in other words, Do not tire yourself out going about many cities and fields: they are all gathered in Jerusalem on account of the war.[10]

He gives him evidence of the perversity of their attitude: *All are disobedient, taking twisted paths, like bronze and iron; all are corrupt* (v. 28), that is, base, with nothing of true value in them. *Bellows failed in the fire, lead failed; a silversmith works the silver in vain, their vices are not consumed* (v. 29). By *silversmith* he refers to the word of correction, by *fire* and *lead* to the punishment itself, and by *bellows* to the divine sentence in which the punishment is pronounced. The workers of silver, in their wish to purify the silver, normally add lead so as by means of it to consume impurities. The Lord therefore says, I employed various means in my wish to change them, and applied a range of chastisements, but they remain unaffected. Hence the text goes on, (549) *Call them rejected silver, because the Lord rejected them* (v. 30).[11] He persisted with the comparison: No approach got the better of their wickedness. Now, he says this by way of criticism, not of nature, but of their choice: being himself the maker of nature, he would not criticize what he had made, whereas they were creators of their choice.[12]

Chapter Seven

After this the prophet explains that he was bidden stand in the gates of the divine Temple and propose the inspired word to all those entering.[1] It contained good advice and a promise of good things. *Correct your ways and your doings, and I shall make you dwell in this place* (v. 3). He accuses also false prophecy. *Do not trust in yourselves or in false words, because it will be of no benefit to you at all to say, It is the Temple of the Lord, Temple of the Lord, Temple of the Lord* (v. 4). They were deceiving themselves by saying, How could anyone overcome the divine Temple? He urges them, on the contrary, not to put their trust in those words, but rather to embrace the change in their life for the better, to fear judgments, to accord care to those needing it, to put a stop to their former bloodletting and worship of the idols. By doing this, he says, in fact, you will not be refugees but will remain in your ancestral land, whereas by committing the opposite and taking the course of utter lawlessness you will reap the fruit that is in keeping with your exploits. Far from having regard to false repentance, you see, I cannot bear false words, seeing all that happens as I do. *Lo, I am watching, says the Lord* (v. 11). Neither can I bear the house dedicated to me being a den of brigands.

He next confirms what was said from past events. *Go to my house in Shiloh, where I first gave my name a dwelling place, and see what I did to it in the face of the wickedness of my people Israel* (v. 12). The place Shiloh is located in the ten tribes; it, too, was wiped out when the Assyrians made war on them. The Lord therefore gives orders to trust not in the Temple but in life according to the Law. Hence he adds that that house, too, will suffer the same fate and they in turn will endure the punishment of their brethren. *I shall cast you away from my face, as I cast away your brethren, all the offspring of the children of Israel* (v. 15).

He also forbids (552) the prophet from offering any appeal on their behalf: *I shall not listen to you* (v. 16). And to bring out that it was right that he should turn away from them, he went on, *Do you not see what they are doing in the cities of Judah and the thoroughfares of Jerusalem? Their children are collecting wood, their fathers kindling a fire, and their women grinding suet for making sponges for the heavenly host. They poured libations to other gods to provoke me* (vv. 17-18). Those with raisins, dates and other such things at home would offer them to the idols. About this he says through another prophet as well, "They loved pastry with raisins."[2] So he says to the prophet, Do not take it amiss that you do not persuade me with your intercession: while you are interceding, they en masse provoke me by attending to the worship of the demons. Then he makes clear that whereas he receives no harm from their lawlessness, they are bringing on their own ruin because of it: *Surely it is not I whom they provoke, says the Lord, but themselves, to bring a blush to their own faces?* (v. 19) He mentions also the manner of the shame, threatening the destruction not only of people but also of cattle, and as well ruin of plants and devastation of land.

He also cancels the worship according to the Law. *Thus says the Lord of Hosts, the God of Israel: Gather your burned offerings along with your sacrifices, and eat flesh, because I did not speak to your fathers or command them on the day I brought them up from Egypt in connection with holocausts and sacrifices. Instead, I gave them this command, saying, Listen to my voice, and I shall be God for you, and you will be a people for me and walk in all the ways that I command you so that it may be well with you* (vv. 21-23). It is made clear also from this that the obsolete prescriptions of the Law had been imposed on account of the Jews' limitations: since they had learned in Egypt how to sacrifice to idols, he wanted to separate them from those practices (in all the prophets he rejects them, remember), yet out of considerateness for their limitations he utters that remark,[3] *Eat flesh*, that is, Though I reject the sacrifices, I shall not oppose your partaking of flesh. After all, he declares in the Law (553) that those wishing to partake of flesh in their own cities and towns should "perform sacrifice, pour out the blood on the ground and partake of it," not as though sacrificial but as ordinary flesh, a veto being imposed on performing sacred rites outside the designated place.[4] Hence he says, "Eat it like gazelle and deer," that is, like the animals not offered on the altar.

He next recounts also the limitations of their ancestors: against my advice, *they walked in the way of the desires of their wicked heart* (v. 24). He brings out also the fruit springing from this. *They turned backwards and not forwards. From the day your ancestors came out of the land of Egypt to this day* (vv. 24-25): on account of their own lawlessness they were handed over at one time to the Moabites, at another to the Ammonites, at another to the Midianites, and frequently to Philistines. He gives evidence also of his characteristic care: I did not cease speaking constantly to them through the prophets and urging them to better things; by persisting in their opposition they became worse than their ancestors in resisting the words from those prophets. Still, be quite clear in accusing them, and say, *This is the nation that did not listen to the Lord their God or accept correction* (v. 28). It is the cause of the unbelief, *faith has failed and is removed from their mouth.*

Then he bids them lament, adopt the guise of a mourner and shave their head as though the chosen people has been rejected. And to make clear that his anger is justified, he reveals the awful description of their impiety. *Many arrayed the abominations in the house where my name is invoked, so as to defile it* (v. 30). Manasseh, son of Hezekiah, perpetrated this, and those coming later imitated the impiety perpetrated.[5] The divine Ezekiel is a witness, brought back in a spiritual manner from Babylon to Jerusalem, and he reports on the awful transgressions he witnessed in the Temple.[6] He censures them for making burned offerings of both their sons and their daughters to the demons: *This I did not command them, nor did I imagine it in my heart* (v. 31): after allowing the sacrifices of brute beasts to happen on account of their infirmity, how could I bring myself to legislate for such bloodletting? He mentions the altar of Topheth, called after some idol; the word means imprisonment or devouring.[7] He says that in this place a lot of them were slaughtered and exposed for the eating and feasting of birds and animals; but that the (556) name should be changed, and it should no longer be named Valley of the Son of Hinnom but Valley of the Slaughtered. And he predicts that the city of utter joy will become desolate.

Chapter Eight

He predicts also that Babylonians will attack and not only consign the living to slaughter but also subject to mockery the priests and kings long dead, dig up their graves and leave their bones unburied so as to expose them to sun, moon and stars. They loved worshiping the latter, he is implying, and they will gain no assistance from them. *Because they chose death rather than life* (v. 3). After saying this and similar things at length,[1] he once more extends his hand, urging them to repent. *Does not the one who falls get up, and the one who turns away turn back?* (v. 4) Then he threatens unbelievers, *Why did this people and Jerusalem turn away with a shameless turning, wax mighty in their willfulness and refuse to turn back?* (v. 5) He clearly taught us that wickedness is the result not of nature but of free will.[2]

After this he levels an accusation at the unrepentant attitude: *They say, There is no one who repents of their evil, claiming, What have I done?* (v. 6) This attitude is productive of unremitting wickedness; what follows suggests as much. *The runner was exhausted from his running, like a horse on its haunches in its whinnying*. The Syriac rendered it this way, "All proceed by their own volition, like a horse bent on warfare:" forsaking the divine Law, they follow their own ideas.[3] In the Greek tongue, however, the meaning to be taken is that there is no right time or satisfaction in running: a horse that has recourse to its pace and its whinnying sweats after the effort – and they gained no satisfaction from their vices. What follows is also in harmony with this sense: *The hawk in the sky knows its time; turtledove, cicada and swallow, field sparrows, observe the time of their arrival, whereas my people have no knowledge of the words of the Lord* (v. 7). He heightened his accusation by reference to the irrational creatures: the winged creatures know the difference in seasons, and shift from place to place at different times, discovering by nature what is to their advantage, whereas these people, though sharing in reason, do not reap the advantage of the Law. The hawk, of course, is a bird; some say the kite bears this name. (557)

How will you say, We are sages, and the Law of the Lord is with us? (v. 8) Not having a sense of one's own derangement is the sign of extreme dementia, like transgressors not knowing their sin. *A false reed has become futile for scribes. Reed* and "rope" are names often given to the inheritance;[4] the meaning is that it has not benefited from the letter of the Law on account of their love of falsehood. This is the reason, he is saying, that those calling themselves sages will be confounded. *I shall give their wives to others, and their fields to the heirs* (v. 10). By *heirs* he referred to the enemy as coming into control of their possessions. Now, he says he will do this on account of the common lawlessness of all, priests and false prophets alike, who by promising peace hindered the people's repenting. He threatens them with infertility of land, terror and flight. By *lethal snakes* (v. 17) he refers to the enemy, whom it is impossible to charm, as they do not yield to our appeals.[5]

Then he foretells the captivity. *Lo, sound of a cry of the daughter of my people from afar* (v. 19). Then by way of a question, *Is the Lord not in Zion, her king not there?* The God of all is everywhere (he is saying): so why on earth has he handed them over to the enemy? *Because they provoked me with their tongues, and with their futile practices of foreign origin*: life in violation of the Law and the impious worship of the idols proved for you the cause of these troubles. *Summer has passed, harvest is over, and we are not saved* (v. 20). In this he made clear the long period of the siege and the seventy years of servitude.

Now, it behooves us to make their chastisement an occasion of benefit. "Whatever was written before," remember, according to the divine apostle, "was written for our instruction, so that through endurance and the encouragement of the Scriptures we might have hope."[6] May it be the good fortune of us all to attain this through our Lord Jesus Christ, to whom with the Father and the all-holy Spirit belong glory and power, now and forever, for ages of ages. Amen.

With the bruise of the daughter of my people I am bruised. I am overcome with difficulty; pangs like those of a woman in labor have overwhelmed me (v. 21). The prophet both grieves for the transgressions committed by the people and describes the calamities befalling them on their account. (560) By *daughter of the people* he refers to the city, since they had built it, and by *bruise* he refers to the blow arising from the sin. *Is there no balm in Gilead, are there no physicians there?* (v. 22) By *physicians* he refers to the priests, and by *balm* he refers in figurative manner to spiritual teaching. Gilead was a city of priests;[7] his complaint therefore is that though there were priests and legal prescriptions available, the city in its failings did not even undergo repentance.

Chapter Nine

For this reason the divine prophet asks for a flood of tears to match his suffering so that by night and by day he may bewail the wickedness of his fellows. He asks also for some remote place on the edge of the wilderness, and longs to spend his time there so as not to hear of the evils perpetrated by the people: all have violated other people's marriages (he says), and they form a league bent on all sorts of lawlessness (referring to this as *a band of traitors*).[1] *They bent their tongue like a bow* (v. 3), concocting a plot, weaving a tissue of flattery, scheming against their neighbor. He says as much, in fact: *Falsehood and not trust prevailed in the land, evil emerging from evil.* In this he indicated the unchanging character of wickedness, evils following upon evils, and the responsibility for them the neglect of divine things, as he went on to say, *They did not know me, says the Lord.* To bring out more clearly the wickedness endemic among them, he recommends them not to trust a friend or even a family member, since both employ deceit and trickery and are devoid of truth: *interest piled upon interest, trick upon trick* (v. 6).[2]

Once again he makes mention of the contempt for God: *They refused to know me, says the Lord. Hence the Lord of Hosts says this: Lo, I shall submit them to fire and testing* (vv. 6-7). By *fire and testing* here he referred to war and what springs from it; likewise too the divine David on the part of those in Babylon, "Because you put us to the test, O God, you submitted us to fire as silver is put into the fire"[3] – but this was said by the band of the pious, who were put to the fire and proved upright, whereas here the firing results in proof of baseness. He outlines also the kinds of wickedness, comparing the tongue to a shaft and (561) saying their words are full of deceit: they speak of peace but plot trickery.

Shall I not take account of these things? says the Lord. Shall my soul not be avenged on such a people? (v. 9): it is improper for such a judge to leave unpunished such wickedness (by *taking account* referring to punishment). He used the phrase *my soul* in human fashion: the divine is not composed of body and soul, being simple, lacking composition and form. His words are adjusted to our capacity to receive.[4]

He next urges these same people to grieve for the devastation of both roads and mountains: they are devoid not only of people but also of cattle and birds, birds preferring to dwell in inhabited regions, whereas there is a great lack of them in deserts. He also threatens captivity and devastation of the city, and says it will become an abode of serpents, such wild creatures generally disappearing when people are about, but increasing in numbers and multiplying when they are absent.[5]

What person is wise enough to understand this, and to whom has the word of the mouth of the Lord come? Let them report to you why the land has been ruined and so burned to a desert as to be impassable? (v. 12) He bids those accorded divine grace to level the charge and explain the reason for desolation. He himself does so, telling them they had abandoned the Law given for salvation, while at the same time having recourse to futile words and opting for the worship of the idols. *For this reason I feed them bread of distress and shall give them a draught of bile to drink* (v. 15). By this he indicated the harsh and distressing life. *And I shall scatter them among the nations whom neither they nor their fathers have known, and I shall send the sword against them to the point of consuming them with it* (v. 16). He indicated by this two punishments: slaughter in war and life in captivity – they took off into captivity those who had survived war.

To increase their dread he bids the mourners be summoned and give vent to a flood of tears. He urges the women as well to teach their daughters to mourn, there being no longer room for joy. And he proceeds to give also the reason for the laments: *Because death entered through your windows, it advanced into your land to destroy children from inside and youngsters from the streets* (v. 21). By (564) *windows* he refers to the error of their thinking: through them they gave entrance to the error and the blow inflicted by it.[6] You would not be wide of the mark, on the other hand, to call the body's senses *windows* – sight, taste, smell, hearing and touch: through them both life and death can enter. For example, the person who looks with restraint reaps life, while the one looking immoderately gains death, and the truthful tongue procures salvation for the soul, while the lying one brings about ruin; and likewise with the rest, as you can easily learn.

The Lord says this: People's corpses will be a lesson upon the face of your countryside, and like chaff behind a reaper, with no one to gather it (v. 22): what happens to you will be an occasion of great benefit. He refers to it, note, as *a lesson*: the phrase *like chaff behind a reaper* suggests the untold number of the corpses; and since there were many among them who took pride, some in wealth, some in wisdom, some in health of body, he urges them to glory not in these things but in knowledge of God and in righteous behavior. Since, on the other hand, some were puffed up on the score of circumcision, to suppress their conceit he brings out that most of the other nations were circumcised as well; and he foretells also their future calling and salvation. *Lo, the days are coming, says the*

Lord, and in the case of all the circumcised I shall take account of their circumcision – Egypt, Judah, Edom, the children of Ammon, the children of Moab and all those with shaved faces dwelling in the desert (vv. 25-26). Idumeans, descendants of Esau, were circumcised according to the law given to Abraham, and Ammonites and Moabites as neighbors were jealous of the relationship. The descendants of Ishmael and Keturah were also circumcised according to the ancestral law; he refers to them as *having shaved faces* because they were in the habit of plucking the hairs of their cheeks. The people's sojourn taught the Egyptians circumcision; he associated Judah with them to suppress the latter's conceit. In what follows, at any rate, he levels a heavier accusation at them: *Because all the nations are uncircumcised in the flesh, and the whole house of Israel is uncircumcised in their heart.* The Old Testament thus brings out both the usefulness of spiritual circumcision and the deformity of bodily circumcision: he levels no accusation at the uncircumcised nations – only at Jews, circumcised in body but with their heart uncircumcised.[7] (565)

Chapter Ten

The Lord says this: Do not come to knowledge from the ways of the nations, nor have fear of the signs of heaven (v. 2). By *nations' ways* he refers to the ancient error; he has called astronomy and astrology *signs of heaven*, which he does not allow them to heed – only to trust the Lord of heaven. He mocks also the paraphernalia of the idols, and says that some are made out of wood, others of gold and silver, and require hammer, nails and other tools; that they also require a craftsman and hands skilled in these materials; and that silver is mined in one place, gold in another. By *Tharsis* (v. 9) he refers to Carthage, its silver being greatly prized: even today, of course, those in pursuit of wealth explore Africa. It is not right, therefore, to reverence things of this nature: they have no capacity to help or harm.[1]

Having thus shown the idols to be ridiculous, he composes a hymn to the God of all. *Whence could anyone be like you, O Lord? You are great, and your name is great in its power. Who will not fear you, King of the nations?* (vv. 6-7) With this he demolished the Jews' self-importance: he did not say, The Lord's portion is Jacob, his people; instead, he called the God of all *King of all the nations*, predicting the knowledge of God due to come to the nations. *Because amongst all the sages of the nations and amongst all their kingdoms whence could anyone be like you, O Lord?* Then in turn he parades the gods of the nations, and shows them to have their being from craftsmanship and materials. And he proceeds once more to the praise of God: *But the Lord is true God, God of the living and eternal king* (v. 10). The idols, he is saying, are not alive; it is rather God who is the source of life, God of the living and eternal king. *By his wrath the earth will be shaken, and nations will not sustain his rebuke.* Blessed David also speaks in similar terms, "He who looks on the earth and makes it tremble."[2]

He next bids him say to the so-called gods, *May gods who did not make heaven and earth perish from the earth and from under this heaven* (v. 11): it belongs to God to create, not to be created by someone else. So if (568) the Son is created, he is not God; but if he is creator and maker of all things, he is truly God.[3] Of him the prophet speaks in what follows: *The Lord, who made the earth in his power, is the one who restored the world in his wisdom and stretched out the heaven in his understanding* (v. 12). It belongs to God to do these things – not for them to be formed by someone else – namely, *providing rain, producing crashes of thunder and bringing clouds from the end of the earth* (v. 13): he raises sea water at will, and from it forms the clouds. *He turns lightning flashes into rain*: they betoken rain. *He brought out winds from his storehouses. His storehouses* are his will. "He spoke," remember, "and it was made; he gave orders, and it was created," and "Whatever the Lord willed he did in heaven and on earth."[4] So while the true God is creator of all these things, most people fell victim to illogicality, some making up gods and others adoring the ones made by them.

He foretells also the cessation of the error, saying that *their vain works are objects of ridicule* (v. 15) – namely, the idols – and going on, *In the time of their accounting they will perish*: the apostolic preaching completely wiped out memory of them, and we see the fulfillment of the prophecy. *Not like this is the portion of Jacob, because the one who formed everything is its inheritance, and Israel the rod of its inheritance; the Lord of Hosts is his name* (v. 16). It was not you who were taught this error, he is saying: I chose you from of old, and in a particular manner I vouchsafed you my care.

From beyond he gathered your substance when it was dwelling among the elect (v. 17): having called the patriarch from Chaldea he transferred him to Palestine, and when his progeny were freed from their slavery in Egypt, he led them out – such is the meaning of the inspired statement, *From beyond he gathered your substance when it was dwelling among the elect*, in other words, having chosen you from the other nations I made a gift to you of the chosen land.[5] *Because the Lord says this, I am rooting up the inhabitants of this land in distress, and afflicting them so that they may be censured* (v. 18): if their course was right, (569) they would be given guidance; but since their direction is astray, they are kept in darkness so as to stop them heading for disaster.

Woes are visited upon your bruise, your wound is distressing (v. 19). By *bruise* he refers to sin, and by *woes* to retribution. Punishment followed upon your wickedness, he is saying, and you sustained a distressing wound. Then he composes a lament on the part of the city to bring out what words it had to use in deploring its failings: he says, *Truly this is the wound, and it caught hold of me*, that is, the wound of sin proved responsible for my troubles. *Your tent has worn out, it perished and all your coverings are scattered* (v. 20). By *tent* he refers not only to the divine Temple but also to the houses, towers and ramparts. *My children and my sheep have left me, and are no more; there is no place for my tent, no place for my coverings*: I am bereft of everything at once. He mentions also the teachers of wickedness: *Because the shepherds lost sense and did not seek out God* (v. 21). By *shepherds* he refers to the kings and the priests: both groups proved a source of error. Now, the story of the Kings and the Chronicles brings this out more clearly. *Hence all their pasture lost understanding, and was scattered.* Here by *pasture* he refers not to the feed but to the flocks, and implies that the shepherds' lack of sense was the cause of the error of the sheep.

Lo, the sound of noise is heard, and a great shaking from the north to bring the cities of Judah to destruction, a bed for sparrows (v. 22). He calls *sparrows* those huge Libyan creatures people generally refer to as ostriches: this creature also likes the desert.[6] The prophet next explains who brings Nebuchadnezzar. *I know, Lord, that people's ways are not their own: a man will not make progress, direct his own path or guide his own going* (v. 23): that man would not have launched himself at us without your willing it, Lord; had he done so, he would not have achieved what he wanted if your right hand had been caring for us, knowing as I do what fate Sennacherib met. We implore you, however, not to let him exact of us (572) the penalty for our impiety, and instead that you correct us and impose fatherly correction. He says as much, in fact, in what follows: *Correct us, O Lord, but with judgment and not with anger lest you reduce us to small numbers. Pour out your anger on nations that do not know you and on kingdoms that did not invoke your name. Because they devoured Jacob, brought him to an end and devastated his pasture* (vv. 24-25). It is clear, therefore, from what was said at first and what was added that the verse *I know, Lord, that people's way are not their own* neither subjects our free will to nature's enslavement nor submits our affairs to an ordained necessity. Instead, it expressly teaches us that the Lord God keeps his hand on the tiller of the universe and wisely directs it; he provides good things, and he also corrects justly whenever he perceives that despite his extended longsuffering we persist in evildoing.[7]

Chapter Eleven

After this he bids him say to the whole people, *The Lord God of Israel says this, Accursed be the person who does not listen to the words of this covenant, which I enjoined upon your fathers on the day I led them from the land of Egypt, from the iron furnace* (vv. 3-4). This was an addition he also made to the Law when laying it down, saying, "Accursed be everyone who does not abide by the complete letter of the book of the Law so as to observe it;"[1] there too he promises, and again here, that he will accord those observing the divine commandments complete care. He reminds them also of what was said to their fathers and of their own disobedience: *They turned their ears away and traveled each man in the direction of his evil heart* (v. 8). By *direction* here he means not straightforwardness but the wickedness committed consistently through vice; instead of turning from it, they unceasingly traveled that path. *I brought to bear upon them all the words of this covenant which I commanded them to observe, but they did not observe*: he gave them over to various punishments, enslaving them at one time to Ammonites, at another to Moabites, at another to Philistines.

The Lord said, A conspiracy has been discovered among the men of Judah and among the inhabitants of Jerusalem. They turned back to the iniquities of their ancestors in the past, who refused to hear my words (vv. 9-10). The phrase *a conspiracy has been discovered* (573) means, They have conspired and are implicated with their ancestors and travel by their path. He indicates as much, in fact, in what follows. *Lo, they go after foreign gods to serve them*: they do this by transgressing the covenant given them – hence I shall invest them with a range of calamities, and when they grieve I shall not grant them pardon, nor do they enjoy any assistance from the gods worshiped by them. He mentions also the great number of the gods: *Because your gods were as numerous as your cities, Judah; and as numerous as your exits, Jerusalem, were the shrines you erected in your shame, altars for sacrificing to the Baal* (v. 13).

On account of the extraordinary degree of their impiety he forbids the prophet to offer intercession for them. *Do not pray for this people, and do not make requests for them in supplication and prayer, because I shall not heed you at the time they invoke me, at the time of their affliction* (v. 14). They make appeals in the very time of punishment, note; this is the reason blessed David also makes this recommendation, "Let us take the initiative in coming into his presence with confession."[2] At this point he brings out their unparalleled impiety: *Why has my beloved committed abominations in my house?* (v. 15) Both aspects suggest the gravity of the godlessness, the fact that she is called *beloved* and the placing of images of the false gods inside the divine Temple. *Surely prayers and consecrated flesh will not remove your evil from you, nor will you escape by these means?* The inspired norm and word clearly taught us that the Lord looks for good behavior, something the divine David also shouts aloud: "Sacrifice and offering you did not want, but a body you have prepared for me,"[3] and again, "For if you wanted sacrifice, I would have given it; with burned offerings you will not be pleased, a contrite spirit a sacrifice to God, a contrite and humbled heart God will not despise."[4]

After calling her *beloved* he calls her in turn by another name. *The Lord gave you the name comely olive tree, fair in appearance* (v. 16). He gave her this name to prompt her to fruitfulness; likewise he often gave her the name vine as well. *At the sound of circumcision itself fire was enkindled against it.* Since he had called it *olive tree,* he also mentions its purification, calling the purification *circumcision;* in similar fashion the Lord also says in the divine Gospels, "Every branch in me that does not bear fruit will be cut off and thrown into the fire."[5] *Great the distress affecting you,* (576) *its branches were rendered useless.* They were not prepared to offer good fruit, you see; and to make clear that it was not the powerful Babylonian but he himself who inflicts the punishment on her, he adds this, *The Lord God of hosts, who planted you, has had evil things to say against you in return for the evil of the house of Israel and the house of Judah, because they brought this on themselves in provoking me by their sacrificing to the Baal* (v. 17). The vinedresser himself, he is saying, cut off your branches; but it is you who are responsible, producing fruit that is not useful but harmful.

The prophet brings out through what follows the kinds of things committed against him and against Christ the Lord; in him the latter, too, were foreshadowed. *Lord, make it known to me, and I shall know* (v. 18). The fact that he mentions not only what happened to him the prayer testifies. There was no need of revelation to see what was happening at that time; rather, revelation makes clear in advance what is going to happen. *At that time I saw their exploits. But like an innocent lamb being led out to be sacrificed I did not know* (vv. 18-19). The phrase *I did not know* relates to the prophet as though not expecting troubles. He did not heed carefully the Lord's promises; instead, after hearing, *I set you today as a fortified city, as an iron column and as a bronze wall* (1.18), he thought he would in no way be tried by difficulties. The divine word, however, promised not that, but that he would be superior to the troubles: *They will war against you but will not prevail over you, because I am with you to deliver you, says the Lord* (1.19). The verse is applicable to Christ the Lord, however, in a different sense: as the lamb led out to slaughter does not know what it will suffer, he in accepting the passion follows those leading him. *Because they devised a scheme against me, saying, Come, let us put wood on his bread, and wipe him out from the land of the living, and let his name be no longer remembered.* This is not completely applicable to the prophet: how could wood be put on his bread? By contrast, the verse bears very closely on Christ the Lord: he called his own body bread, remember, "The bread that I shall give is my flesh, which I shall give for the life of the world."[6] This bread they nailed to the wood, thinking to snuff out his memory.

Then the prophet, *But you, Lord of Hosts, who makes righteous judgments and tests entrails and hearts, let me see vengeance from you upon them, because to you* (577) *have I revealed my plea* (v. 20). He calls thoughts *entrails*, as we have often remarked, since concupiscence, which resides in the entrails, often stirs thought. It was not without purpose that God allowed the prophet to be tested by troubles; instead, since he had often tried to offer intercession for the transgressors, in his wish to convince him to consider himself not compassionate but the harsh treasury of goodness, he allowed the rebellion to happen. In his deep grief, however, he implores God to judge justly and exact penalties of the unholy. The Lord accepts his petition, gives a reply, threatens punishment and says some will be slaughtered in war and others destroyed by famine.

Chapter Twelve

Once more, however, on perceiving the prosperity of those given to wickedness the prophet implores that the reason for it be demonstrated. *You are too righteous, O Lord, for me to speak in defense against you, but I shall discuss judgments with you* (v. 1). I know well, he says, the righteousness of your verdict; yet it would not be out of place for me to think of putting a question to you. *Why is it that the way of impious people pros-*

pers, that all those who engage in illegality flourish? You planted them, and they took root; they had children and brought forth fruit (vv. 1-2). In this way he indicated their prosperity, whereas in what follows he indicated their godless attitude. *You are near in their mouths but far from their hearts*: they parade your name in word only, driving out memory of you from their thoughts.

You, Lord, know me, you understand me, you tested my heart (v. 3): you understand not only appearances but also thoughts that escape detection. *Gather them together like sheep for slaughter, and purify them for the day of their slaughter*. The word *purify* means set apart: the ones wanting to be purified set themselves apart – hence the Syriac also put "prepare" for *purify*.[1] *How long will the land grieve and the grass of the field wither at the evil of the inhabitants of the land? Cattle and birds were destroyed because they said, God will not see our ways* (v. 4): the land has remained desolate because of their lawlessness, Lord; they presume you are not observing them nor looking at what they commit. (580)

Your feet run towards evil, and they will enfeeble you. How will you prepare for horses, and trust in a land of peace? (v. 5) The Syriac put it this way: "You were defeated when you ran on foot," and how will you manage to resist horsemen? What he means is something like this: The neighboring enemies – Moabites, Ammonites, Idumeans and Philistines – waged war on foot, and many times you were defeated in battle with them; so how will you manage to resist Babylonians arrayed on horseback? The meaning to be taken from the Greek version, on the other hand, is this: Your course enfeebled you on account of wickedness and robbed you of strength; deprived of health and strength, how will you manage to resist and enter battle against those campaigning with great numbers of horses? I have cited both senses, leaving the choice of the better one to the readers. *How will you cope with neighing in the Jordan?* The Syriac put it this way, "How will you ford the

Jordan in flood?" By the flooding river he referred metaphorically to the size of the enemies' army, and reminded them of the events in the time of Joshua, son of Nun, namely, When I was taking care of you, you crossed that flooding river.[2] *Because they are your father's house, and they spurned you and shouted out behind your back, and they were the ones to assemble against you* (v. 6). It is likely, you see, that even some from the ten tribes, already made captive, joined forces with the enemy in attacking them. *Do not believe them, because they speak evil of you.* Rabshakeh was such a person; he used the Hebrew tongue in blaspheming against God.[3]

After this interjection the prophet resumes the prophecy about the Lord and foretells the ruin of Jews, saying on God's part, *I have abandoned my house, I have dismissed my inheritance, I have given my beloved soul into its enemies' hands* (v. 7). He reveals his characteristic goodness and makes clear their brutality by way of accusation. While he uses loving words and calls what is hostile his *beloved soul*, it is involved in matters of hostility and deceit, as emerges from what follows. *My inheritance became for me like a lion in a thicket* (v. 8): she became a wild animal instead of a bride and devoured the bridegroom. *She lifted her voice against me.* The Gospels bring out the truth of the prophecy: we learn there that they shouted, "Away with him, (581) away with him, crucify him."[4] *Hence I hated her.* He brought out the justice of the punishment.

Surely my inheritance has not become for me a hyena's lair, or what is around it a lair? (v. 9) In what was commented on above, he called the Temple a brigands' lair on account of the lawlessness of the celebrants,[5] whereas here he refers not only to the city as *a hyena's lair* but also what is round about it, that is, Judea; and again he accuses it of lawlessness committed against him. It has become for me a hyena's lair, he is saying. Then he prophesies its ultimate ruin: *Go, assemble against her all the wild animals of the field, and let them come and eat her.* The Romans gained control of the world, assembled the army of different nations, slaughtered some and took others into captivity. Now, he says the teachers of the Law were responsible for the impiety, going on, *Many shepherds destroyed my vineyard, they defiled my portion, they turned over my cherished portion into a trackless waste; it became a ruinous dispersion* (vv. 10-11): the chief priests, the scribes and the pharisees by deceiving the people and crucifying the Lord brought on the Jews those celebrated calamities. He emphasizes this more clearly: *On account of me all the land is dispersed in dispersion.* He means the whole land of Israel: on account of what was done to him their country at that time was left desolate by the enemy, while today they are completely bereft of their famed mother city.[6] *Because there is no man who takes it to heart*, that is, they do not have recourse to pious thoughts.

To every track of the wilderness they came, suffering distress in the wilderness (v. 12). The Syriac rendered *track* as pathway: they filled the whole desert with pathways, suffering distress and running from the enemy, it being typical of fugitives not to use set thoroughfares. *Because the Lord's sword devours from one end of the land to the other; all flesh is without peace.* He is referring to what happened to Jews from one end of the land of Israel to the other. He foretells also what was inflicted on the nations at various times; at the end of the prophecy as well he prophesies against them. *You sowed wheat and reaped thorns* (v. 13). He urges them to rely not on fertile soil (584) but on the soil's good performance: the person employing evil gathers thorns from the soil. *Your lots will be of no benefit to you.* By *lots* he referred again to their prosperous situation, in which he advises them not to trust. *You have been confounded in your boasting, in your reproach before God*: the things you believe to be to your credit – wealth, influence – will fill you with shame when you appear before God as judge; after receiving the gifts from him you repaid him with the opposite.

The Lord says this about all the evil neighbors, the shepherds laying hands on my inheritance, which I allotted to my people Is-

rael (v. 14). Idumeans, Moabites, Ammonites and Philistines were always estranged and hostile to the Jews; so they were pleased to see what befell them. This is surely the reason he brings out in advance the future recall of the Jews, referring to their leaders as *shepherds. Lo, I shall pluck them from their land and expel the house of Israel from their midst. And it will happen after my expelling them that I shall turn about and have mercy on them, and shall make them dwell each one in their own inheritance and each one in their own land* (vv. 14-15). After prophesying in these words the return that happened under Cyrus and Darius, he brings out in advance also what would happen later. *And it will happen that if they really teach my people my way so as to swear by my name, The Lord lives, as they taught my people to swear by the Baal, they will be built in the midst of my people. But if they do not turn about, I shall banish that nation with banishment and ruin, says the Lord* (vv. 16-17). He mentioned also the complete expulsion of the race of Jews: *I shall banish that nation with banishment and ruin, says the Lord.*[7]

Chapter Thirteen

After this the prophet is bidden to buy a linen loincloth, wrap it round his loins and hide it near the river Euphrates, and he immediately carried out what he was bidden. After the passing of many days, he was ordered in turn to recover the loincloth; he likewise did what the Lord had ordered him. Taking it in his hand he found it spoiled and useless for any purpose. Then he listens to the Lord's words, *I shall likewise spoil the pride of Judah and the pride of Jerusalem, this great pride.* (585) *This wicked people, unwilling to heed my voice, walking in the obstinacy of their wicked heart and following foreign gods so as to serve them and worship them – they will be like this loincloth, which will be of no further use to anyone* (vv. 9-10). In this way he signals the period in Babylon; the Euphrates runs through that city, and in a hole in the rock by the Euphrates he was ordered to hide the loincloth (by *hole in the rock* referring to Babylon). While there the people were useless, no longer styled God's people, not living by their own laws, nor performing worship according to the Law; instead, they were useless, like that spoilt loincloth.

In what follows, he comments on the use of the loincloth. *As the loincloth clings to a person's loins, you see, so I made the house of Israel and the whole house of Judah cling to me, says the Lord, so that they might be to me a celebrated people, a boast, a glory; but they did not listen to me* (v. 11). In these words he indicated the extraordinary degree of his goodness, and brought out the manner of the relationship, and the fact that while he for his part wanted them to appear conspicuous and famous, they brought shame on themselves by lawlessness.

Having in this way performed a prophecy also through actions, he foretells what is to befall them through another image as well.[1] *The Lord God of Israel says this: Every wineskin will be filled with wine. It will happen, if they say to you, Surely we shall know that every wineskin will be filled with wine? you will say to them, Thus says the Lord, Lo, I shall fill all the inhabitants of this land and all the kings, David's sons, seated on his throne* – then adds – *the prophets and the priests and all the people with drunkenness* (vv. 12-13). And to explain what the drunkenness is, he went on, *And I shall scatter them abroad, a man and his brother, his fathers and his children alike, says the Lord* (v. 14). And to bring out also the unalterable character of his rage, he went on, *I shall not have longing, I shall not spare and I shall not show mercy in their destruction*, that is, their ruin. So by *drunkenness* he referred to the punishment: people falling afoul of the worst calamities are like drunkards, unable to lament on account of their extreme condition.[2]

Hear and give ear, and do not be puffed up, because the Lord has spoken (v. 15): put an end to your audacity (568) and insane arrogance; take what is said as from God. *Give glory to the Lord your God before he brings darkness and before your feet tremble on mountains in the dark* (v. 16): anticipate the time of punishment. The divine apostle also gives this advice, "So, then, as we have the opportunity, let us do good."[3] *You will await the light, and the shadow of death is there, and you will be plunged into darkness* (v. 16): in the very moment of punishment you will beg for lovingkindness but will not attain it. *If you will not listen, your soul will grieve in secret in the face of insolence, it will weep tearfully and your eyes will let loose tears, because the Lord's flock has been crushed* (v. 17). The phrase *will grieve in secret* suggests the excess of calamities: enslaved to the enemies, you will not be bold enough to weep openly, but will do so in hiding.

He bids both the king and the rulers to deplore the change in fortunes, and he reminds them of what has gone before. *The cities are closed towards the south, and there is no one to open them. Judah has been deported, it has gone through total deportation* (v. 19), that is, slavery, Sennacherib having taken off into slavery many cities of Judah. They endured this, he is saying, to pay the penalty for their sins. He also bids Jerusalem look at the multitude of enemies coming from the north, and goes on, *Where is the flock that was given to you, sheep of your glory?* (v. 20), that is, the huge number of colonists.

What will you say when they take account of you? (v. 21), that is, the enemy. *You taught them lessons in ruling over you*. When they were under attack from the Syrians, they called on the Assyrians for help, even though they should have looked to God for care. *Pangs will seize you like a woman in labor*. He indicated the magnitude of the pangs. *And if you say in your heart, Why have these things come upon me? it is on account of the greatness of your iniquity that your rear is exposed to make an example of your heels* (v. 22). Such stripping shames those subjected to it. So his meaning is, are not your sins responsible also for these calamities befalling you, your being stripped naked?

If an Ethiopian changes his skin and a leopard its spots, you too will be able to do well after learning evil (v. 23). The saying, of course, is true, that habit is second nature: voluntary actions become part of natural actions by long habit.[4] For this reason he threatens to scatter them like embers borne hither and yon by the hurricane. (589) He refers also to its multitude of sins, its intemperance, audacity and worship of idols, calling it *deviance of fornication* (v. 27). He went on from there, *On the hills and in the fields I saw your abominations.* Then in lament, *Woe to you, Jerusalem, that you were not purified behind me. How long yet will it be?* After committing many transgressions, he is saying, you were not prepared to have recourse to repentance; I shall no longer show longsuffering, and shall instead inflict punishment.

It is better, therefore, to live according to the divine laws; but since we are human and falling is likely, we ought to have recourse to the remedies of repentance, and through them placate the judge and escape the experience of the threatened punishments.[5] May we for our part continue to have no experience of them, thanks to the grace and lovingkindness of our Lord Jesus Christ, to whom with the Father and the all-holy Spirit be glory and power, now and forever, for ages of ages. Amen.

Chapter Fourteen

The word of the Lord came to Jeremiah concerning the drought (v. 1). He inflicts on them various chastisements so as to halt the course of evil. The prophet describes the wailing and lamentation for the lack of rain, mentioning that springs, wells and pools of rainwater had dried up. Infertility of the land followed, and not only domestic animals but also wild animals shared in the suffering. *Deer gave birth in the countryside and abandoned their young because there was no green to eat. Wild asses stood in valleys drawing breath like a serpent* (vv. 5-6). Human beings also act like this when they are thirsty, gaining respite from the heat with a breath of air.[1]

The prophet then offers supplication, reminds them of their joint sins and with the following remark placates God: *We have sinned against you. Expectation of Israel, you will save in the time of trouble* (vv. 7-8): we all await mercy from you. (592) *Why have you become like a sojourner in the land, and like a native turning aside to a resting place?* The phrase *like a native* the Syriac rendered *like a traveler*. Why on earth do you ignore us, he is saying, and why act like a sojourner spurning the dwelling in which he lives as though it was not his own, and like a traveler not interested in what lies along the way?[2] *Surely you are not like a person asleep, and a man incapable of saving?* (v. 9) A sleeper does not hear those calling, and the victim of weakness cannot offer assistance; in other words, do not delay your mercy: you are able, you are awake, you are everywhere and stand by everyone. In fact, he added as much: *You are amongst us, Lord, and your name has been invoked upon us; do not forget us.*[3]

He cites also the reply given by God, *They loved to move their feet, and did not desist* (v. 10) – that is, on the road of wickedness. What follows confirms it: *God was not well pleased with them.* He says that he will also make mention of their iniquities and exact penalties of them for their impieties. He also urges the prophet not to offer prayers for them, and insists he will neither heed their fasting nor accept the sacrifices they offer, but will consign them to famine, pestilence and slaughter. Hearing this, the prophet brings forward the predictions of the false prophets and says they foretell the contrary, promising them peace and abundance of good things. The Lord in reply, however, tells the prophet that they predict falsehood, not serving the divine words or acting as instruments of grace but uttering what they please. *I did not command them or speak to them, because it is they who prophesy to you false visions, hallucinations, divinations and preferences of their own heart* (v. 14). By *visions* he refers to dreams, by *divinations* auguries, by *hallucinations* the works of demons, and by *preferences of the heart* the deceit arising from their own ideas. Then he threatens them with both death from ill-health and slaughter in war: *They will die a death from illness and will meet their end by the sword and by famine* (v. 15), and with them those who followed their words; they will not even be granted burial, all alike falling victim to the same evils.

The loving Lord in turn, however, after forecasting the calamities, urges them to have recourse to the remedies of repentance. *Shed tears from your eyes day and night* (v. 17) on account of the magnitude of the evils inflicted upon you. The prophet describes the tragedy of the events: (593) *If I go out into the countryside, lo, victims of the sword; and if I go into the city, lo, a hunger plague* (v. 18). To these words he adds as well the evils of captivity: *Because prophet and priest went into a land which they did not know.* Blessed Daniel the prophet, the divine Ezekiel, priest and prophet, and a great number of other priests in addition to them were involved in the adversities; in his providential care for those unholy people God sent prophets also to accompany them as supervisors and teachers lest they lapse completely into godlessness.

After describing this, the prophet shifts his address to God. *Surely you have not utterly rejected Judah, nor has your soul departed from Zion?* (v. 19) – that is, your providence: he used *soul* in human fashion for a clearer meaning of the prophecy. He mentions also the incurable blow inflicted, and proceeds as follows: *We know our sins, Lord, our fathers' iniquities, that we have sinned in your sight. Stop, for your name's sake* (vv. 20-21) – that is, cease being angry with us; consider not us but your name, as we are styled your people. *Do not destroy the throne of your glory.* This is the name he gave Jerusalem; the Lord also said in the sacred Gospels, when forbidding oaths, "Do not swear by Jerusalem, because it is the throne of the great king,"[4] as it was there he made his characteristic appearance. He reminds them also of the covenant made with their fathers and of the fact that no help comes from the idols; rather, he is the one who is the source of rain falling from on high, creation not being able to govern itself. He says as much, in fact: *Will heaven give satisfaction of itself? Is it not you, Lord, and do we not wait upon you? You bring about all these happenings* (v. 22).

Chapter Fifteen

After this the Lord replies again, *Even if Moses and Samuel were to stand in my presence, my soul would not be with them* (v. 1). By these words he comforts the prophet: Do not think (he is saying) that in not admitting your intercession I am despising you; I would not yield even to the appeals of those who worked such marvelous wonders. He made mention of those men both as ambassadors and as people who had often won him over to the people's cause. The mighty Moses, remember, at the time of the making of the calf, when God said, "Leave me be, and in my anger I may destroy them,"[1] offered earnest supplication, and reconciled the Lord to the sinners. (596) Samuel did the same, and brought down a lot of rain in summer time.[2]

Then he bids the prophet dismiss the people, who were standing by. *If they say to you, Where shall we go? you will say to them, The Lord says this: Those for death to death, those for the sword to the sword, those for famine to famine, and those for captivity to captivity* (v. 2): I subject them to these four fates, and in addition to them the dead will become food for animals and birds. *I shall subject them to the oppression of all the kingdoms of the earth* (v. 4). He forecasts what would happen after the return, what would befall them under the Macedonians and the destruction that would be inflicted on them by the Romans. He brings out that the first fate would befall them owing to the impiety committed by Manasseh. Yet he is not an unjust judge, nor does he require an account of them for others' faults; he submits them to the evils prophesied as sharers in impiety and enthusiastic supporters of the wicked king.

Who will spare you, Jerusalem? And who will have fear on your account? Or who will turn aside to inquire after your welfare? (v. 5) – in other words, to all people you will seem to have got your just deserts. People are accustomed, in fact, when they see someone extremely vicious being punished, not only to have no sympathy for them but even to be pleased for the wronged in being rid of that person's vice. *You turned away from me, says the Lord, you will go backwards* (v. 6): you will suffer for what you have done. He used the phrase *you will go backwards* to mean, you will be humbled. *I shall stretch out my hand on you and destroy you, and shall no longer make allowances for them*: I shall no longer exercise my former longsuffering.

Then to bring out that he is forced against his will to punish, he says as though in sympathy, *In the gates of my people they were made childless; I destroyed my people on account of their evils, and they did not relent* (v. 7): they brought ruin upon themselves, unprepared as they were to put a stop to their wickedness. He says that on account of the loss of the men the widows have increased in number, and likewise for the same reason mothers have been deprived of children. *I have brought upon the mother the misery of young people at midday, I inflicted on her trembling and anxiety unexpectedly.* (597) *The bearer of seven children is empty, her soul is distraught* (vv. 8-9). He represents the disaster in various ways so as to give a lesson to the stubborn and persuade them to abandon their former impiety. *The sun went down in the very middle of the day*: for the grieving even the light is called darkness.[3]

After saying this and similar things, the prophet mourns and laments. *Woe is me, mother, that you bore me, a man bringing the whole land to face trial and judgment; I earned no benefit, nor did anyone benefit me; my strength failed me before those cursing me* (v. 10). The phrase *I earned no benefit* the Syriac rendered "I owed nothing," meaning, I neither owed nor lent anything; I acquired many enemies, who unremittingly abuse me and shout imprecations at me, since conspiracies generally tend to breed hostility. The meaning to be taken from the Greek version, on the other hand, is this: I deserve laments, being brought into this life to no purpose, having benefited no one or taken a benefit from the hands of others; curses are my only reward from those hearing my prophecies.[4] *So be it, Lord, when they were at the helm, if I did not stand by you at the time of their troubles and the time of their distress for the good of the enemy* (v. 11): listen to their curses; I frequently offered supplication to you for them.

Then in turn in God's person: *If iron will be recognized and a bronze covering. I shall give your might and your treasures as booty, as compensation for all your sins in all your territories* (vv. 12-13): have no trust in bronze or iron coverings; I shall give all your wealth to the enemy, and it will be in repayment for your sins. He adds to this also the captivity that was happening. For prophesying this the prophet runs a risk on the part of those reluctant to listen and attempting to do away with him; he implores the God of all in the words, *Be mindful of me, O Lord, and take account of me, and protect me from those persecuting me* (v. 15), that is, Do not hand me over to those persecuting me: an innocent person is set free. *In your longsuffering do not take me.* Some manuscripts[5] have *cast me*, that is, Exercising your tolerance and postponing the punishment of the wrongdoers, do not bring distress upon us the wronged. *Know that I was the object of reproach on your account* (600) *on the part of those who set aside your words* (vv. 15-16): for your sake, O Lord, I am beset by the current distress; I was alienated when I transmitted your words. *Put them into effect, and for me your word will mean happiness and joy of my heart because your name has been imposed on me*: since they think I prophesy falsehood, and instead they give credence to the promises of the false prophets, confirm your words with deeds, and thus console me.

He next says that instead of sharing either their table or their laughter, he preferred to them fear of God; on account of their wickedness and on account of its punishment, he continued to suffer grief. But at once the Lord consoles him in the words, *If you turn back, I shall restore you, you will stand in my presence; and if you separate the worthy from the undeserving, you will be like my mouth* (v. 19): no slight reward has been kept for you by me for undertaking this; if you convert any of the deceived, you will enjoy great confidence with me (the force of *you will stand in my presence*); if you change any of the unholy and convince them to opt for the better, you will be likened to my mouth, as I made what exists by a word, and you with a word brought to virtue the evildoers. He likewise promised he would be invincible and insuperable, and reminded him of the promises made from the beginning.

Chapter Sixteen

He urges him not to marry or to have children, for the reason that both parents and children will be consigned to famine and pestilence, to slaughter and slavery. He also exhorts him not to rejoice with the rejoicing, nor grieve with the grieving. *I have taken my peace from this people, says the Lord, my mercy and my compassion. Great and small will die in this land* (vv. 5-6). He says that they will not be vouchsafed burial, nor will the customary laments be raised for them, nor will the mourners be vouchsafed any consolation. He threatens the city with deprivation of all forms of happiness, so that no sound is raised of weddings or banquets or anything else that provides people with a satisfying life.[1]

When they inquire and ask (he is saying), For what cause did we fall foul of these troubles? remind them of the ancestral impiety and bring out what was committed by them and the fact that they sinned worse than their fathers, not living according to my Law but following their own ideas. For this reason (601) *I shall cast you out of this land into a land which you and your fathers did not know, and day and night you will serve other gods there who will not give you mercy* (v. 13): since you love the false gods, I shall expel you from the ancestral land and hand you over to the enemy so that along with them you may be in thrall to error. He also promises the return, however, and says that at that time they will not sing the praises of God by parading his former kindnesses, nor will they recount the deliverance from the slavery of the Egyptians; instead, all will marvel at the return from Babylon.

Lo, I shall send many fishermen, says the Lord, and they will catch them; and after that I shall send many hunters and they will hunt them atop every hill and from the holes in rocks (v. 16). By this he indicated the ineluctability of the retribution, that in the manner of fishermen and hunters the enemy would sweep them all away, and bring under their control even those endeavoring to escape detection in the mountains. *Because my eyes are on all their ways, they are not hidden from my sight and their iniquities do not lie hidden before my eyes* (v. 17): I see everything, nothing of what is done escapes me. *And first I shall doubly repay their iniquities and their transgressions by which they have befouled the earth with the carcasses of their abominations* (v. 18). Out of love he spoke of double retribution for sins: according to the letter of the law they did not pay the punishment they deserved. By *carcasses of the abominations* he refers to the slaughter of their sons and daughters, which they committed as an offering to the idols.

Having thus brought out the people's impiety, he prophesies the conversion of the nations. *O Lord, my strength and my help, and my refuge in the day of troubles, to you nations will come from the end of the earth, and will say, How false the idols our ancestors had; there is no benefit in them* (v. 19): those accorded such wonderful care and enjoying teaching of Law and Prophets persisted in their impious practices and transgressions, whereas the nations, who did not enjoy such providence and heard only the apostolic preaching, shunned the error and made their approach to the light of the knowledge of God.[2] Reminiscent of the former proverb I cry aloud to you,[3] *Will one make gods for oneself that are not really gods? For this reason, see, I shall reveal my hand to them at that time,* (604) *and let them know my power, and they will know that my name is Lord* (vv. 20-21): I am foretelling well in advance what is to come, and teaching them in advance my might, the fact that through a few insignificant people I shall bring about their conversion.

Chapter Seventeen

Having thus prophesied the conversion of the nations, he once more accuses Jews of impiety. *Judah's sin is recorded in writing, with an adamantine gem, on the breast of their heart and on the horns of their altars* (v. 1).[1] Nothing is more potent than conscience: letters inscribed on it are indelible. I mean, even if everybody should present their conscience with favorable evidence, conscience cannot tolerate the wickedness of falsehood: it is pricked and goaded, and delivers its verdict incorruptibly.[2] He says this here, too: The facts accuse you, and conscience joins in testimony against you. He reminds them also of the groves, the altars, and what was done on them, and he threatens to give to the enemy all their wealth along with the idols.

He foretells also the devastation of the city; after that he mentions out-and-out misery, and subjects to curses the one who forsakes God, on the one hand, and on the other trusts in human influence, and he likens them to some kind of fruitless and mean bushes growing in the desert and given no attention. *They are like the tamarisk in the desert, and will not see when good things come. They will inhabit salty places in desert land, on brackish soil which is uninhabited* (v. 6). The phrase *in salty places* the Syriac rendered "in caves."[3] In all statements he indicated the uselessness of this sort of thing. By contrast he compared the person trusting in God to a plant constantly watered and unharmed by the severest heat, always bearing fruit in season.

Now, he said this not without purpose but to exhort them not to trust in the help of Egyptians,[4] and instead to win the divine favor by transformation of their life. *Devious is the heart above all else, as are human beings – who will know them? I am the Lord, who examines hearts, tests entrails, giving to each according to their ways and according to the fruits of their exploits* (vv. 9-10): the designs of the neighbor are incomprehensible to people, the motions of the heart remaining hidden, whereas to me their maker even these are obvious; I rule not only (605) on their doings but also on their thoughts, and the verdict I deliver is fair and just. Then he shifts his attention to the Babylonian. *The partridge uttered its call, it gathered what it did not lay, amassing its wealth without justice* (v. 11). Partridge hunters domesticate partridges, and by using their call they attract the creatures of this kind, which run together and fall into the traps. He used this as a comparison for the Babylonian in his efforts to gain control of all people and assemble unjust wealth. He forecasts also what will befall him: *At the midpoint of their life they will abandon him, and at his end he will be foolish.* The divinely-inspired Daniel also told us of this: he contracted insanity, turned savage and was driven from his kingdom.[5] *Throne of glory uplifted* (v. 12). He was deprived also of his throne.

Our exalted sanctification from the beginning, place of our sanctification, expectation of Israel (vv. 12-13): you, Lord, are our sanctification, the splendor of our place, you have everlasting power.[6] So we look forward to you: you will provide us with release from distress; those who forsake you will be filled with utter shame. *Heal me, Lord, and I shall be healed, save me and I shall be saved, because you are my boast* (v. 14): I throw myself on your providence, and beg to attain salvation from you. *Lo, they say to me, Where is the word of the Lord? Let it come. But I have not tired of following behind you, I have not hankered after a day of doom for humanity, you understand. What proceeds from my lips is before your face* (vv. 15-16): they find fault with the delay in retribution, and think the prophecy false, since you postpone retribution; for my part, though seeing this insensibility of theirs, I did not want them to fall victim to troubles, saying as much: *I have not hankered after a day of doom for humanity. Do not turn out to be alienated from me; spare me on the evil day* (v. 17). By *the evil day* he refers to the resistance offered to him. He asks to enjoy God's care, and that they fail in their endeavors and be confounded, while he emerges superior to the schemes.

After this the prophet is bidden to take up a position in the palace gates and urge everyone, prince and peasant, not to transgress the Law about the sabbath, but to honor that day by resting (608) and imitate the obedience of the ancestors. If this is done, he says, you will enjoy the fruits of peace, and there will come in haste from all quarters those who offer to God sacrifices in peace, whereas if you transgress the Law of rest and carry loads on the sabbath day, I shall consign to the flames not only the gates but also the whole city.[7]

Chapter Eighteen

Having thus concluded this address, he bids the prophet go into the potter's lodgings. The prophet does what he is bidden, and notices the potter making some kind of vessel, then refashioning it when it crumbled and fell apart. *The jar he was making out of clay came apart in his hands, and in turn he made another jar out of it just as it pleased him to do* (v. 4). Having thus shown the potter with power over clay and shaping it as he wished, he said to the prophet, Say to them, *Can I not do to you, house of Israel, says the Lord, just as the potter has done? Lo, like clay in the potter's hand, so are you in my hands, house of Israel* (v. 6): just as he can mix the clay and shape it as he wishes, so it is easy for me to consign to punishment, grant salvation, consign those in prosperity to misfortune, and in turn grant those in difficulties success.

What follows, in fact, says as much. *At last I shall speak against nations and kingdom to lift them up and bring them down so as to destroy them. If that nation turns away from their evil, I shall repent of the evils I planned to inflict on them* (vv. 7-8). Do not despair of salvation, he is saying: even if I condemn a nation and threaten ultimate punishment, and if I see their repentance, instead of inflicting punishment I extend mercy. On the other hand, if I promise an abundance of good things, but they scorn me and embrace wickedness, I shall not fulfill the promise of good things. Knowing this, then, do not despair of better things, but apply repentance and reap salvation.

Lo, I am shaping evils against you, and plotting plots against you. Let each of you turn from your evil way, and (609) *improve your behavior and your ways* (v. 11). But being full of love he offered remedies of that kind, whereas they did not accept the physician's advice. *But they replied, We shall put on a brave face because we shall travel in the path of our defaults, and each of us will do what is their heart's desire* (v. 12). By *defaults* he refers to the retrograde way.

Hence the Lord says this, Ask the nations, Who has heard of such frightful horrors which the virgin daughter Jerusalem has committed? (v. 13) He refers to her as *virgin* not because she is not immodest but because she titivates herself and takes pride in her appearance. *Surely breasts do not fail from the rock, or snow from Lebanon? Or water violently driven by the wind change its course?* (v. 14) Springs gush without ceasing, he is saying,

Lebanon constantly has snow, water driven by force travels a well-worn course,[1] whereas they abandoned the way of the Law, and they retain no memory of my commandments. What follows, in fact, suggests as much. *Because my people have forgotten me, they burned incense to a nonentity, and they lose heart for their eternal ways so as to enter upon a path that offers no way to tread* (v. 15): they set their minds upon paths not trodden from the beginning and made them eternal ways – in other words, they continue to use these forever – and hence I shall give over their land to desolation. He went on, in fact, *to reduce their land to destruction and to eternal hissing* (v. 16). The *hissing* suggests the desolation of the city: people who saw the city in its heyday normally hiss on seeing it devastated, and by this means highlight the disaster.

Like a burning wind I shall scatter them before their enemies (v. 17): they will enjoy no mercy from the foe; instead, they will hate them, like someone turning from the heat. *I shall show them my back and not my face on the day of their destruction.* It is usual with captives and slaves to bow to the ground so that their back rather than their front appears. It can also be taken another way: we see not the face but the back of those who turn away; so the verse suggests God's turning away.[2]

While the threats made to them were of this kind, then, let their sufferings prove remedies for us, (612) so that chastened by others' sufferings we may live according to the divine laws and keep the lawgiver propitious forever. Amen.[3]

They said, Come, let us make plots against Jeremiah, because the Law shall not be lost to the priest, or counsel to the sage, or a word to the prophet (v. 18). They bring the three highest institutions to testify against him[4] – priesthood, prophecy and wisdom – and they know the power and reliability of each gift. Since there was no gainsaying their words, they not only opposed him but also made plans for his death. *Come, let us make our assault on him by word, and not heed all his pronouncements*, so aghast were they also at the very words of God. The phrase *let us make our assault on him by word* means, Let us concoct calumny against him. Aware of this the prophet beseeches God to turn judge, and reminds him of the representations he frequently made on their behalf. Then he expresses his thought in the form of a prayer, and foretells the death that would occur through famine, the slaughter that would be inflicted by the enemy, and the other disasters occurring in the wars.

Chapter Nineteen

After saying these things and others like them, he is bidden to take an earthenware jug and go out to the cemetery in the company of the priests and the elders of the people, and in turn threaten the city with ruin and remind them of their worship of the idols. He foretold also the troubles that would be produced by the siege and the dearth of necessities. After this he was to smash the jug and say, *Thus shall I smash this people and this city, just as an earthenware jar is smashed, and cannot any longer be repaired* (v. 11). He threatens both the end of the royal house and the desolation of the whole city since they had offered libations and sacrifices to the idols not only in the open but also in their very homes. The very place of the idols would become a grave for those killed. *They will bury in Topheth because of there being no room for burial.* (613) By this he indicated the vast number of those killed. The Lord then bade the prophet on his return to make his prophecy in the hallowed court and prophesy desolation to the whole city and all the subject cities and towns.[1]

Chapter Twenty

On hearing this speech, Pashhur, who was chief priest, not only assaulted the prophet but also detained him. *Pashhur struck the prophet Jeremiah, and threw him into the dungeon* (v. 2). He refers to some underground place; the Temple built by Solomon had many such quarters. When he brought him up on the next day, he heard him saying further, *The Lord has named you not Pashhur but a roaming refugee* (v. 3).[1] He means that not only he but also his friends would become captives and be done away with after the captivity. He also threatens, of course, to surrender the whole people to Nebuchadnezzar.

Having said this in many ways, therefore, the prophet shows irritation with the resistance constantly shown him; and trusting in the purity of his conscience he adopts forthrightness towards the Lord, saying, *You deceived me, Lord, and I was deceived; you overpowered me and you prevailed* (v. 7): I shunned the role of prophecy, I claimed I was too young and not up to this ministry; you promised to make me superior to the adversaries and to give me the appearance of a bronze wall and iron pillar. Now I have become a laughingstock. He said as much, in fact: *I am a joke all day long, I am constantly sneered at. Because I shall be mocked by my harsh message, I shall call down devastation and misery, because the word of the Lord has become for me reproach and mockery all day long* (vv. 7-8). What galls the prophet are not the miseries and abuse happening to him but the mockery made of the divine oracles. *I said, I shall not mention the name of the Lord, and shall not speak in his name* (v. 9), that is, I shall not prophesy or offer God's prophecy to the unbelievers. *In my heart there was a burning and flaming fire affecting my bones, and I am made completely weary and cannot bear it.* The divine Paul also endured this in Athens (616) when he kept silence: "Seeing the city full of idols, Paul's spirit was afflicted."[2] This is what the prophet also feels: the prophetic charism afflicted him when he was unwilling to speak out.

He then describes how they not only abused and tormented him, but also stitched up another plot in an attempt to deceive him and separate him from God. They said, in fact, *Let all his friends conspire against him, observe his intentions in case he makes a mistake, and we shall get the better of him and take our revenge on him* (v. 10). Who could adequately deplore this wicked intention? Far from trusting in himself, however, the prophet praises the divine assistance, saying, *The Lord is with me as a strong warrior* (v. 11). He brings out also the victory of the divine assistance: *Hence their persecution, but they were unable to prevail; they were utterly confounded because they were unable to understand their disrepute, which will never be forgotten.* He then begs once more for God to turn judge and for penalties to be required of them that match their crimes.

Distressed, however, extremely sorrowful and dissatisfied with the present life, he first praises the God of all, and then curses the day of his mother's birth pangs. *Sing to the Lord, sing to him, because he has rescued the life of the needy from the hands of evildoers* (v. 13). He gives pride of place to the hymn of praise so as to remove any occasion of blasphemy. Then he says, *Cursed be the day on which I was born, the day my mother bore me. Cursed be the one who brought this news to my father, A boy child is born to you; let him not be happy* (vv. 14-15).[3] People who are in deep grief are accustomed to take hold of those nearby and press their hands, and sometimes when under pressure of the distress to strike their hands. The prophet also felt like this: in his surpassing pain he latched upon the day, something inoffensive, and the person who reported the birth to his father – a person of no particular importance: he probably could not even mention the name. And he goes on to say, It would even have been better for me to die in the womb and emerge dead than fall victim to the various calamities.

Chapter Twenty-One

The word that came to Jeremiah from the Lord when King Zedekiah sent to him (617) *Pashhur son of Malchiah and the priest Zephaniah son of Maaseiah* (v. 1). This is a different Pashhur: he was the son of Malchiah, whereas the one who was cursed was the son of Immer. It is necessary to realize, however, that the prophecies do not now occur in order:[1] in this case he is prophesying events in the time of Zedekiah, whereas a little further on events in the time of Jehoiakim and Jeconiah, who ruled before Zedekiah. In any case, Zedekiah, besieged by Nebuchadnezzar, exhorts the prophet to beg God's help, while the prophet is bidden to make this prophecy: *The Lord God of Israel says this, Lo, I am turning aside the weapons of war in your hands with which you will do battle against the king of Babylon and the Chaldeans, who have enclosed you from outside the wall. I shall lead them into the middle of this city, and I shall fight you with hand outstretched and arm uplifted, with anger and rage and intense indignation* (vv. 3-5): weapons will be of no use to you with me leading the enemy and taking a position with them against you.

Then he says that he will give everything over to famine, death and captivity, and along with them King Zedekiah himself to the foot-guards and lancers, and some they will slay and others they will take off into captivity. To the people in their turn he urges him to make this pronouncement: *Lo, I have set before you the way of life and the way of death* (v. 8). He then explains that the person staying in the city and resisting the enemy will be traveling the way of death, whereas the person willingly going out to them will enjoy life. This is the sentence I have delivered against the city, he is saying, that it is given over to the enemy's flames.

After making this threat he exhorts the king and the rulers to give attention to the demands of justice, deliver a verdict in keeping with justice and come to the aid of the wronged, and by this means to forestall the imposition of the punishment. *Lo, I am against you, inhabitant of the valley Sor in the plain, says the Lord* (v. 13), that is to say, lying between mountains in a hollow, which is the way the Syriac also rendered it. He is referring to Jerusalem: it has this situation. *Sor* means constraint, and likewise rock;[2] this city was constrained by mountains. *Those saying, Who will strike us? Or who will come into our dwelling?* He brings out their boldness and false confidence. Then he threatens to consume its wood with fire, by wood referring to its buildings and the great number of its inhabitants. (620)

Chapter Twenty-Two

After this he further bids the prophet occupy the palace and bring the king and the rulers around to judging justly and delivering impartial verdicts, looking carefully after those mourning their widowhood and deprived of parents, refraining from bloodshed and avoiding their former impiety. To those doing this he promises peace and prosperity, and to the king length of rule. *But if you will not act in keeping with these words, I swear by myself, says the Lord, this place will become a wilderness* (v. 5). He included the oath by way of confirming his words; the phrase *I swear by myself* brings out the preeminent status of the one swearing. The divine apostle, remember, says, "Since he had no one else greater to swear by, he said, I swear by myself, says the Lord."[1]

He makes this addition to the threat: *The Lord says this against the house of the king of Judah. Gilead, you are to me height of Lebanon* (v. 6). He calls Jerusalem *Lebanon* and the palace in it *Gilead*. There is a place in Lebanon with this name; but there is also another Gilead in the territory of Israel. Our view, however, is that here the palace is compared with the one in Lebanon on account of the impiety committed in it. Hence he threatens them also with utter desolation. *I shall consecrate destroyers against you* (v. 7). The phrase *I shall consecrate* means *I shall assign*; he says this also in Isaiah, "They are consecrated and I lead them," that is, assigned; we cited this explanation of it in many places in the Commentary on the divine Isaiah.[2] *A man and his axe, and they will cut down your chosen cedars and throw them into the fire.* Since he had mentioned Lebanon, he persisted with the metaphor, by *cedars* referring to the rulers, those conceited about their strength.[3]

Then he foretells the desolation of the city, and that the onlookers will marvel, and on learning the cause of the disasters they will grasp the wickedness of the inhabitants and the fact that it was on their account that the city received this sentence from God. He bids him to mourn not for the dead but for the living for being deported and handed over to harsh servitude. *The Lord says this on Shallum son of King Josiah of Judah, who reigned in the place of Josiah his father: he left this place, never to return; in the place* (621) *where they deported him he died, and he shall not see this country again* (vv. 11-12). Shallum, in the view of some, means not Jehoiakim but Jehoahaz, who reigned in the place of Josiah his father. The pharaoh Neco took him as a captive to Egypt, Jehoiakim being put to death in Jerusalem. The prophet himself explains this, along with the fourth book of Kings and the second book of the Chronicles.[4]

Like the man who does not build his house in righteousness or his upper rooms in justice (v. 13). He finds fault not with building but unjustly building; what follows brings this out. *His neighbor works for him gratis, and he does not give him his wages. You built for yourself a modest house* (vv. 13-14). He cites the modesty not in respect of its small size but for its being well-proportioned in length, breadth and height; the fact that he attributes size to the house is indicated by what follows: *spacious upper rooms, equipped with windows, paneled in cedar and painted red.*

Surely you are not a king by the fact of competing with cedar?

(v. 15) By *cedar* he referred to Josiah, who had held the throne for a lengthy period; and he blames Shallum, also called Jehoahaz, for aspiring to the height of the cedar but not emulating its incorruptibility, and instead having presumptions about the kingship. To bring out that God faults not the building but the impiety, he went on, *Did not your father eat and drink and do justice and righteousness, and then it was well for him? He gave just judgments in favor of the lowly and poor, and it was then well for him. Is not this to know me? says the Lord* (vv. 15-16).[5] This resembles the Gospel verse, "Not everyone who says to me, Lord, Lord, will enter the kingdom of God – only the person doing the will of my father in heaven."[6] This, in fact, he said here, too, that hating wrongdoing and helping the wronged are a sign that the one so doing knows me. *Lo, your eyes are not upright or your heart sound* (v. 17). He next accuses him of greed and bloodshed, and actually in addition to them of calumny as well, through which he was responsible also for the murders. (624)

For this reason the Lord says this to Jehoiakim son of Josiah king of Judah (v. 18). Here the prophecy adheres to the order: after Jehoahaz, Jehoiakim became king, who was likewise son of King Josiah; and he foretells his ruin as well. *They shall not mourn him, crying, Alas lord, or Alas brother, nor will they weep for him, O brother, Alas brother. He will not be given a proper burial: rotting like a dunghill he will be cast outside the gate of Jerusalem* (vv. 18-19). From this it is clear that Shallum is not Jehoiakim: of the former he said that instead of seeing this land he would die in exile, whereas of the latter that he would be thrown outside the gate like dead birds. The histories, however, will recount it more clearly.[7]

He next urges the city to make haste to Lebanon and to Bashan (these are mountains) and likewise to the seashore, and cry aloud and lament its own misfortune in not enjoying any help from the idols (calling them *lovers*).[8] *I spoke to you in your misfortune, and you said, I shall not listen* (v. 21): I urged you in your sin to be rid of the error, but you did not accept the advice. *This has been your way from your youth, not listening to my voice*: you fell into disobedience in the past from the very outset. *The wind will shepherd all your shepherds* (v. 22), the wicked kings and also the false prophets. *Your lovers will go into captivity.* The enemy seized the very idols, probably made of silver and gold. *Then you will be dismayed and dishonored at the hands of those loving you*: you will not get help from them. Then he reminds them of their former prosperity. *Inhabitant of Lebanon, nesting in the cedars* (v. 23) – that is, famous and illustrious though you were, and celebrated by all – *you will groan at the onset of pangs like a woman in labor.*

Having associated this with the prophecy about Jehoiakim, he makes a similar prediction to Jeconiah as well, son of Jehoiakim and grandson of Josiah, who reigned only three months, was taken off into captivity with his mother and ended his life in Babylon. *As I live, says the Lord, even if Jeconiah, son of Jehoiakim king of Judah, were a signet ring on my right hand, I would pull you off it and give you into* (625) *the hands of those seeking your life and into the hands of those whose presence fills you with awe, in the hand of Nebuchadnezzar king of Babylon and in the hand of the Chaldeans* (vv. 24-25). Since they did not imitate the piety of their ancestors, though taking pride in their kinship with them, making much of Abraham, Isaac, Israel, David, Hezekiah and Josiah, men conspicuous for virtue, for this reason the God of all rejects the arrogance of Jeconiah in the words, Even if he were a ring and were placed on my right hand, I would pull it off and hand it over to the enemy. So let him not trust in his forebears' virtue without emulating their virtue. *I shall cast you and your mother who bore you into another land, into a land where you were not born, and you will die there* (v. 26). He added that they would not return to the land for which they longed.

He mentions also the cause of the punishment. *This man is a mouth despised and cast off.*[9] He criticizes his levity and facile attitude to lawless words. *Jeconiah had become disreputable, like a pot which is of no use. Hence he and his offspring were thrown out and banished to a land he did not know* (v. 28). Then, as though the recipients of his address were not listening, he directs his words to the land, lifeless though it is. *Land, land, land, listen to the word of the Lord. The Lord says this, Register this man as a banished man, someone not prospering in his time, because no one of his progeny will go on to sit on the throne of David, ruling over Judah* (vv. 29-30). He highlighted the end of the Jewish monarchy, and the statement is not erroneous. I mean, let no one cite Zerubbabel: he was not the people's king – only popular leader and general. The Lord, in taking his ancestry from him according to the flesh, did not take his seat on the Davidic chair – rather, "above all rule, authority, dominion and every name that is named, not only in this age but also in the age to come."[10] So the prophecy is without error. (628)

Chapter Twenty-Three

At this point he accuses these shepherds – namely, the kings themselves – of being responsible for the scattering of the sheep, and threatens them with destruction while promising the people recall. *I shall welcome the remnants of the people from all the land whence I expelled them in their pasture, and they will experience increase and be multiplied* (v. 3). He also promises greater benefits. *I shall raise up for them shepherds who will shepherd them, and they shall no longer fear or be dismayed or be in disagreement, says the Lord* (v. 4).[1] This happened as a type in the time of Zerubbabel and Jeshua son of Jozadak, though in fact not everything that was prophesied: many rebelled against them, not only neighboring peoples but also at a later time Macedonians and finally Romans, whereas the prophecy forecasts the duration of grace. Clearly, then, some things happened in their time and some in the time of the holy apostles, the latter alone having the gift of the Spirit.

Lo, the days are coming, says the Lord, and I shall raise up a righteous dawning to David, and he will rule as a righteous king, he will understand and exercise judgment and righteousness upon the land. In his time Judah will be saved, and Israel will dwell securely. This is the name which the Lord will call him, Jozadak; he is in the prophets (vv. 5-6).[2] The stupid Jews shamelessly endeavor to apply this to Zerubbabel; but they need to understand that he was no king – just a popular leader – and he was not called *Jozadak*. Neither is the meaning of the name appropriate to him, the word meaning "Lord our righteousness" or, in the Syriac rendering, "Lord, make us righteous," neither of which applies to Zerubbabel. Since, however, he was a type of Christ the Lord and brought back the captives from Babylon to Judah, just as the Lord transferred those enslaved by the devil to truth, anyone applying this to him in the manner of a type would do nothing beyond reason. There is need to understand, however, that it is the Lord Jesus Christ, a descendant of David according to the flesh, who is proclaimed by the prophets "righteous dawn," "righteous king" and "Lord of righteousness."

At this point he shifts his criticism to those prophesying falsehood, and he classes them *adulterers* for adulterating and corrupting the divine word.[3] He also calls them authors of the people's wickedness, and says the priests have also become sharers in their impiety. He foretells also the troubles that will befall them, and compares them to the prophets of Samaria, who were openly known as prophets of Baal; they wrongly promised the people peace, and so proved responsible for each person's failure to turn aside from their evil way, and on account of them the people imitated the wickedness of Sodom and Gomorrah. *Lo, I feed them pain and give them bitter water to drink, because from the prophets of Jerusalem defilement went out for all the land* (v. 15). By this he indicated to everyone the various disasters.

He urges the people also not to accept the words proposed by them. *From their own heart they speak, and not from the Lord's mouth. They guarantee peace, which I did not promise. To all those walking in their own desires, and to everyone walking in the error of their heart they said, Troubles will not befall you. Because who has been part of the substance of the Lord, and known and heard his word? Who has given ear to his word and heard?* (vv. 16-18): by saying this they encourage the evildoers, cause them to persist in their lawlessness and prevent their giving ear to the prophetic words. *Lo, a shaking from the Lord, and rage issues forth, whipped up into shaking* (v. 19). By this he indicates successive disasters, and the fact they are sent by God; he it is who inflicts the punishments. Then he mentions also the sufferers, *It will come upon the unholy. The Lord's anger will not turn aside until he puts into effect the endeavors of his heart* (vv. 19-20): what he prophesied will come to pass. *In the last days they will come to an understanding of it*: whenever they see the fulfillment, they will recall the promises.

Then he says that those prophesying falsehood of their own accord and not under orders proposed contrary advice to the people. *If they had been part of my substance and heard my words, they would have instructed my people and turned them aside from their evil way and from their evil exploits* (v. 22): I clearly forbade in the Law the forms of wickedness; so if they had followed my words, they would have criticized (632) the people's transgressions and led them to the straight and narrow.

He explains to them that he is ignorant of nothing that is hidden. *I am a God who is close and not a God who is far off. If anyone hides, will I not see them? says the Lord* (vv. 23-24). Then he brings out his being uncircumscribed. *Do I not fill heaven and earth? says the Lord*: if I am present everywhere, therefore, how will people think I am ignorant of anything that happens? He intensifies still further the charge against the false prophets for recounting dreams, deceiving the people and presuming to do things similar to the prophets of Baal. Then he bids the distinction be drawn between the prophet and the false prophet. *Let the prophet who has the dream recount the dream, and the one to whom my word has come recount my word in truth* (v. 28). He brings out the distinction in figurative manner: *What has straw in common with grain? says the Lord. Are my words not like fire? says the Lord; and like an axe striking rock?* (vv. 28-29) Through the figures he brought out the power of the divine word.

Then he explains the difference with the false prophets: some of them, like thieves, steal some prophetic words and spoil them by distortion, while others concoct false prophecy, and others recount dreams they have not had and by beguiling the people in their utter misery cause them to persist in their wickedness. He then gives this direction to the prophet: *When this people, priest or prophet asks, What is the pledge of the Lord? you will reply to them, You are the pledge of the Lord, and I shall throw you away, says the Lord. As for the prophet and priest, whoever say Pledge of the Lord, I shall take vengeance on that person and their house* (vv. 33-34). The godless referred to the prophets as light-fingered, and to their prophecy as *pledge*; so God urges them not to use that term, and threatens the unresponsive with punishment.[4] He bids them make their inquiries in these terms, What has been the Lord's reply, what has the Lord said? and not to keep using the term *pledge of the Lord*.

Those who infringe his commands he threatens in the words, *Lo, I take you as a pledge and cast you out* (633) *from my presence along with the city I gave to you and your fathers. And I shall bring on you everlasting reproach and everlasting dishonor which will not be forgotten* (vv. 39-40). The Lord God ordered this to strike down the habits of superstition and to explain that, far from being demented, the prophets were ministers of the divine sayings. Having threatened them with captivity, he promises also the return, and says it will be so remarkable that the exodus from Egypt will be consigned to oblivion on account of its splendor. May we for our part, I beseech you, follow both the Old Testament and the New Testament words,[5] worship the one who spoke through the former and the latter, and keep his life-giving laws so as to enjoy the promised goods, thanks to the grace and lovingkindness of our Lord Jesus Christ, to whom with the Father and the all-holy Spirit be the glory, now and forever, for ages of ages. Amen.

Chapter Twenty-Four

Once again he delivers the prophecy through figures and symbols, and by some kind of revelation he sees two baskets of figs lying in front of the divine Temple.[1] He mentions also the time of the prophecy: he says it was after the deportation of Jeconiah and the reign of Zedekiah that he saw this, one basket with good, ripe figs, the other with very poor figs, no good at all for eating. Then, on receiving a divine inquiry about them, he explained the difference in what was shown him. Finally, the significance of the figs is brought out: the God of all compared those already made captive to the ripe figs, and promises them return from that place, care on his part and prosperity along with godliness. To the unsightly figs, on the other hand, he likens not only those left in Judah but also those who had fled to Egypt and with them King Zedekiah and the rulers, and he threatens them with the army of the Babylonians and the hardships stemming from war – famine, pestilence, slaughter and captivity.

Chapter Twenty-Five

After thus prophesying these things, he cites the prophecy made beforehand.[1] The former, you see, was uttered after Jeconiah, (636) whereas what he is about to say is from the time of King Jehoiakim, who was father of Jeconiah. He also mentions the time clearly. *The word of the Lord that came to Jeremiah concerning all the people of Judah in the fourth year of Jehoiakim son of Josiah king of Judah, the first year of Nebuchadnezzar king of Babylon* (v. 1).[2] In this year Nebuchadnezzar conducted his campaign against Jerusalem, enslaving some and imposing tribute on others, and returned home.

So he mentions also what these words were. *In the thirteenth year of Josiah son of Amon king of Judah (and for twenty-three years to this day) the word of the Lord came to me, and I rose betimes to speak to you, but you did not listen* (v. 3). He mentions the great number of years to bring out God's longsuffering in putting up with unbelievers for so long. I sent my servants the prophets to you, he is saying; I urge you to abandon the road to ruin and travel by the other road that is productive of life, and I promised you good things for doing this. But you did not listen, and instead chose the worship of the idols. And to censure the purpose of this unbelief he went on, *So that you might provoke me by the works of your own hands to your own misfortune* (v. 7): to provoke me you committed those things, but in the past you actually reaped harmful effects.

This is the reason, he is saying, that along with Nebuchadnezzar I shall assemble the kings serving under him against you and against your neighbors from whom you learned the worship of the idols, and I shall give your land and theirs over to utter devastation and rob you of every happiness, including *the sound of the groom and the sound of the bride, sound of the mill and light of the lamp* (v. 10). He specifies the time of desolation as seventy years: after seventy years he says that he would require penalty for ungodliness and lawlessness of the king of Babylon himself and of his subordinates and put into effect the whole prophecy of Jeremiah.[3]

So he (637) bids him at once take the cup of pure wine from the hand of the Lord, and give a drink to all the nations *to whom I send you. They will drink and vomit and go insane at the prospect of the sword which I shall send in their midst* (vv. 15-16). By *cup of pure wine* he refers to punishment; the divine David likewise said, "In the hand of the Lord there is a cup of pure wine well mixed."[4] By *they will drink and vomit* he indicates satiety, and by *go insane* he hints at the severity of the punishment. Then the prophet describes how he gave it to Jerusalem to drink and the cities serving under her, along with the kings and rulers; and he explains what is meant by the cup, *to make them a trackless waste, an object of hissing and cursing to this day* (v. 18), that is, at this time. By *trackless* he suggests desolation, and by *hissing* he signifies the astonishment of the onlookers, since we normally hiss when seeing a turn for the worse; following on this *cursing*, since some people are in the habit of saying, May you suffer what so-and-so suffered.

He proceeds to say that he gave it to Pharaoh king of Egypt, his commanders and all his subjects to drink, and to migrants as well as residents, referring to them as *mixed*, and by this term suggesting that the fugitive Jews would also fall victim to the same troubles. He says he gave it also to the kings of the Chaldeans to drink, and the whole of Arabia and all the kings of the land of Uz, referring thus to the Idumeans, the prophet himself bringing this out more clearly in what follows: he gave it to *the Philistine kings, Moabites, Ammonites, from Tyre and Sidon, Dedan and Tema* (vv. 21-23), which are cities of Arabia, as we explained also in the commentaries on the other prophets.[5] *Buz* , the Persian nation, *and all who have shaven temples*, meaning the Saracens, *all the kings of Arabia, all the kings of the mixed peoples inhabiting the desert, all the kings of Zimri* (we found Zimri in the Hebrew and the Syriac, a son of Keturah;[6] they inhabited the desert), *all the kings of Elam*, a Persian nation, *all the kings of Medes and Persians, all the kings of the east*, (640), *near and far, each against his brother* – that is, to pay the penalty for godlessness through one another – *and all the kingdoms of the earth that are on the face of the earth, and King Sheshach will drink as the last of them* (vv. 24-26). Our view is that the Babylonian was called this:[7] through him those mentioned in the prophecy also came to drink it, and it says that after a while he was the last to drink it – in other words, following the punishment inflicted on the others by him, he himself had to pay the penalty.

He then threatens those unwilling to drink, that they will drink willy-nilly. *I shall begin with the city named after me; with it I begin the abuse. You will be purified with purification, and you will not be pure* (v. 29): I am handing over the city set apart, and will you escape punishment? It is impossible. *You will prophesy against them all these words, and will say to them, The Lord will make a pronouncement from on high, and from his holy habitation he will give voice* (v. 30). He indicated two things, that he delivers his verdict from heaven, and that he will make his appearance in his dedicated Temple. *He will make a pronouncement from his place, and like those treading the grapes they will reply to all those residing in the land* (v. 30). By the *reply* he means the effect, since on the divine word there follows also the effect. *Ruin will come upon a portion of the land, because the Lord has a judgment on the nations. He is entering into judgment with all flesh, and the ungodly will be given to the sword, says the Lord* (v. 31). Once again he reveals his ineffable goodness: he did not say, He will judge all flesh, but *He is entering into judgment,*[8] bringing out his characteristic kindness and reproving the ingratitude of the recipients.

In what follows he mentions both the evils coming from the wars and the fact that the killed will lie unburied and will be like dung on the land. *Wail, you shepherds, cry aloud and lament, you rams of the sheep, because your days and your dispersions have culminated in slaughter and you will fall like chosen rams. Flight will fail the shepherds, and safety the rams of the sheep* (vv. 34-35). By *shepherds* he referred to the kings, by *sheep* to their subjects, and by *rams of the sheep* to the rulers; he threatens flight and deportation to all. And he forecasts the lamentation of both kings and rulers. (641) *Because the good things of peace have come to an end in the face of the wrath of the Lord's anger* (v. 37). *The good things of peace* are farming, planting, trading, use of skills, exchange of contracts, marriages, gatherings, festivals, pleasant times and everything like that.

Chapter Twenty-Six

After this prophecy he cites a different one in turn,[1] which in the time of King Jehoiakim he was ordered to deliver to the people. He was ordered to stand in the divine court, deliver an oracle to the people, and transmit all the divine sayings: *Do not remove a word* (v. 2). He next brings out the reason for what is to come. *Perhaps they will listen, and each of them turn from their evil ways, and I shall put an end to the troubles I am considering bringing upon them on account of their evil pursuits* (v. 3). He did not use the word *perhaps* out of ignorance, aware as he was of their disobedience; instead, he expressed the uncertainty to avoid their taking note of the divine sentence and despairing of salvation. It resembles also what was was said by Ezekiel, "If then they hear, if then they see;"[2] in other words, it was not a result of ignorance – instead, it was to prevent their saying, He foretold our disobedience, and he is trustworthy, so how is it possible for us to be changed? Now, in these words he brings out that it is possible to undergo a change in behavior if they are willing. For this reason he also adds the threat, *If you do not listen to my words that I deliver to you through the prophets, I shall make this house like Shiloh and turn this city into a curse for all the nations of the earth* (vv. 5-6).

On hearing this, the priests, the false prophets and the people threaten the prophet with death. The leaders learned of it and ran from the palace to the divine Temple. The priests for their part along with the false prophets accused the prophet of blasphemy in making a prophecy against the city and the divine Temple; so the prophet said that he had been sent by the God of all and that the words uttered by him were divine oracles. He also offered them exhortation, *Reform your ways and your actions, listen to the voice of the Lord God, and the Lord will put an end to the troubles he threatened against you* (v. 13). But if you do not obey and adopt your customary attitude, (644) *Lo, I am in your hands: do with me as suits and what seems best for you* (v. 14). Then he gives a glimpse of the fruit of homicide. *Only be perfectly clear that, if you do away with me, you bring innocent blood upon yourselves and upon this city* (v. 15). In delivering these words, he is saying, I was bidden by God.

On hearing this the leaders and the people accused the priests and the false prophets of an unjust sentence, claiming the prophet was innocent for ministering to the divine words. Then some of the elders remind them of prophecy in former times, and say that Micah of Moresheth once prophesied that Zion would be ploughed like a field, Jerusalem would be like a shed, and the mountain of the house like a forest grove,[3] and that despite saying this, he came to no harm. On the contrary, they claimed, in that situation they were in dread of the threat, and by changing their life they escaped the wrath – whereas you committed awful crimes. Uriah son of Shemaiah, they went on,[4] delivered similar oracles at one time, but in dread of the king fled to Egypt, and with our connivance was put to death by King Jehoiakim, who brought him back and cut him down.

He also makes clear the one who used pious words, saying, *But the hand of Ahikam son of Shaphan was with Jeremiah to prevent him being handed over to the people and done away with* (v. 24).[5]

Chapter Twenty-Seven

After completing this narrative, he shifts to a different one previous to it.[1] *In the beginning of the reign of Jehoiakim son of Josiah this word came from the Lord to Jeremiah in these terms* (v. 1). He then says he was bidden to put bars on his neck and send them to the neighboring kings, whose names he also supplies. He was ordered also to dispatch these words through ambassadors,[2] *It was I who made the earth, human beings and all the cattle on the face of the earth with my great power and my raised arm, and I shall give it to whomever is pleasing in my sight* (v. 5). He used the phrase *with my great power and my raised arm* on account of the magnificence of the elements and the limitations of the listeners, this phrase being equivalent to saying he willed it and everything he willed came into being.[3] (645)

Now I am the one: I have given this land into the hand of Nebuchadnezzar, king of Babylon, my slave, I have given the beasts of the countryside to work for him and serve him (v. 6). By *beasts of the countryside* he means the savage nations. I am creator and master, he is saying, I govern as I wish. *All the nations will serve him and his son until the time of his own land comes* (v. 7).[4] He clearly conveyed that, having employed the Babylonians as executioners and brought the other nations to account by means of them, he will later hand them over as well to destruction. To those objecting and resisting the yoke he makes the threat of famine, slaughter and captivity. He urges them not to trust in soothsayers, seers, augurs and diviners, but to yield and accept the yoke of Babylon; and to the compliant he promises peace.

Now, these things he said to King Zedekiah, and urges him not to trust the false prophets, who promise peace and the restoration of the divine vessels carried off to Babylon: they are telling lies. *If they are prophets, and if the word of the Lord is in them, let them approach the Lord of Hosts to prevent the vessels left in the house of the Lord, in the house of the king of Judah and Jerusalem from being taken to Babylon* (v. 18). The phrase *approach the Lord* means "impede," overturn the divine prophecies and reveal the divine prophecies to be of no value. In other words, you will see all the sacred vessels secretly removed and taken to Babylon, and after a period of seventy years sent back from there and returned to the house dedicated to me. Now, the stands are mentioned in the third book of Kings; they were required for the bowls, and were made of bronze.[5]

Chapter Twenty-Eight

After this he recounts that, while Zedekiah was king, in the fourth year Hananiah the false prophet presumed to say in the presence of the people and the priests, *The Lord of Hosts, the God of Israel, says this, I have broken the yoke of the king of Babylon. In two years the sacred vessels that were removed I shall restore, and shall bring back Jeconiah with all the captives* (vv. 2-4). In his wish (648) to show that he prays for this to happen, for his part the prophet Jeremiah said to all the listeners, *May the Lord fulfill the word you prophesy for the return of the vessels of the house of the Lord from Babylon to their place along with all those deported* (v. 6). He did not actually allow the prophecy to be endorsed with his approval,[1] saying in fact, *Only listen to this word that I speak in your ears and the ears of all the people. The prophets previous to me and those previous to you from olden times delivered prophecy of many lands and great kingdoms, of war and troubles and death. The one who prophesied peace, when the prophet's word comes to pass, will be known as the prophet whom the Lord sent in truth* (vv. 7-9). The outcome in events, he is saying, will demonstrate the truth of the prophecy; so we shall see if for one thing we are given over to the Babylonians according to my prophecy.

That false prophet, however, gained nothing from this; rather, he smashed the bars the prophet was carrying, claiming this was the way he would smash the yoke of Nebuchadnezzar in two years. But the God of all urged the prophet to say to Hananiah, *You have broken bars of wood, and in their place I shall make bars of iron* (v. 13). He calls the yoke of the Babylonians *iron* as a form of punishment that would be heavier on account of disobedience.[2] Then when the prophet was disappointed to learn precisely that the oracle of Hananiah was false, he said, *Listen carefully, Hananiah, the Lord did not send you, and you made this people trust in something wrong* (v. 15). He also forecasts his death within a few months *because you recommended rebellion against the Lord* (v. 16) – that is, you caused the people to rebel against the divine sayings and trust in the falsehood. He then recounted both the death of the false prophet and the extraordinary degree of the divine longsuffering, as he did not at once deprive him of life, waiting for his repentance;[3] when he persisted in wickedness, he handed him over to death after seven months.

Chapter Twenty-Nine

At this point he switches to a different narrative, and explains that at God's decision he wrote to the captives in Babylon after the capture of Jeconiah the king.[1] He mentions also the names of those who took the letters. Now, their contents were to the effect that the God of all bids those now in captivity to have children, build houses, (649) give their daughters in marriage, get wives for their sons, have a care for the increase in their race, and pray for their captors *for the reason that in their peace will be your peace* (v. 7). To this advice corresponds also the requirement of the apostle that urges, "Offer prayers and supplications for kings and all in high station and authority so that we may live a quiet and peaceful life in all piety and seemliness."[2] The God of all gave these directions, of course, to teach them not to trust in the false prophets but to await the appointed time; he indicated as much, in fact, in what follows, saying, *Do not let your false prophets among you mislead you, nor your seers deceive you, and do not heed the dreams you dream, because they prophesy wrong things to you in my name. I did not send them, says the Lord* (vv. 8-9).

He brings out also the time of the return, saying, At the completion of seventy years I shall visit you and fulfill the good promises. He also promises to vouchsafe them total care and provide good things in response to their prayers: *Whenever you seek me with all your heart, I shall make myself known to you, says the Lord* (vv. 13-14). Know this, too, that those who escaped the former captivity *I shall consign to famine and slaughter: I shall make them like souarim figs which are too bad to be eaten* (v. 17). What he described above as "vile" he called here *souarim; souarim* in the language of the Hebrews is what grows on trees – that is, wild, uncultivated, not worth growing, useless for eating.[3] *I shall make them a trouble to all the kingdoms of the earth* (v. 18): all who hear of the disasters befalling them will be in dread. *And an object of cursing, of mockery and of insult amongst all the nations where I scattered them.* Many people are in the habit of saying, May I not suffer what so-and-so suffered[4] – hence his saying here *an object of cursing*. The meaning of *an object of mockery* we have often explained; and *insult* blessed David also refers to, "We have become an object of insult to all our neighbors, to be mocked and scorned by those round about us," and again, "You made us an object of insult to the nations."[5] They will meet this fate, he is saying, *because I sent them my servants the prophets, rising early and sending them, and they did not listen, says the Lord* (v. 19). By *rising early* he indicated his assiduity: (652) instead of treating it as a secondary interest, he even made it his most urgent concern.[6]

He then foretells also the ruin of the two false prophets,

Ahab and Zedekiah: *I shall give them into the hands of Nebuchadnezzar, king of Babylon, and he shall strike them down before your eyes. On their account they will adopt a curse in the whole colony of Judah and in Babylon in the words, The Lord do to you as he did to Zedekiah and Ahab* (vv. 21-22). From this we learn clearly the meaning of the curse. He mentions also the manner of retribution, *whom the king of Babylon roasted alive. On account of the iniquity they committed in Israel* (v. 23). He brings out as well the form this took: *They committed adultery with the wives of their fellows, and gave false expression in my name that I did not express to them. I am the one who knows and bears witness, says the Lord.* Nothing that happens escapes me, he is saying; I see even what is done in hiding.

He threatens also Shemaiah the Elamite for presuming to give contrary oracles and send a letter to the priest Zephaniah and the priests serving under him.[7] This is what he sent, *The Lord made you a priest in place of Jehoiada the priest* (v. 26). Jehoiada was the celebrated high-priest; so, intending to repress Zephaniah's pride, he mentioned the other's time of office. *For you to preside in the house of the Lord over anyone prophesying and anyone out of his mind so as to put him in the confinement of Sinoch and in the dungeon.* As we said before, they referred to the prophets as deranged, and it is clear from this: he linked the prophet to the madman. Now, Syriac renders *Sinoch* as "prison;"[8] he means, You have the responsibility of constraining and punishing those prophesying troubles. He suggests as much, in fact, in what follows. *So why did you not rebuke Jeremiah for presuming to write this, You are to build buildings and plant gardens?* (vv. 27-28) The high-priest Zephaniah read this letter out to the prophet. Immediately the God of all bade the prophet write in reply and indicate to the people in Babylon that Shemaiah had prophesied falsely, not having been sent by the God of all. For this reason I shall consign him utterly with all his family to death, and he will not see a reversal of the distress.

On learning this, then, let us dread falsehood, trust in the truth, expel uncertainty from our souls (653) and follow the divine sayings so that we may see the good things of the Jerusalem on high, thanks to the grace and lovingkindness of our Lord Jesus Christ, to whom with the Father and the Holy Spirit be the glory, now and forever, for ages of ages. Amen.[9]

Chapter Thirty

Wishing to bring out the truth of the prophecy, the Lord God bids the prophet consign to writing both the prophecies made about the captivity and those about the recall. First, however, he foretells the sad things. *Thus said the Lord, You will hear a sound of fear; it is fear, not peace. Ask and see if a man gave birth* (v. 5-6). He clearly indicated the extremity of distress, comparing the extent of the disaster with the pangs of a woman giving birth, indicated by the phrase *Ask and see if a man gave birth*. What follows is also in harmony with this. *About fear in that they will hold their loins; hence I saw everyone, and their hands were on their loins like a woman in labor.*[1] To bring out the pain at this stage he presents the image of the woman in labor, whereas elswhere to convey grief he said each person had their hands folded on their head. *All the faces were like a suppliant*, this suggestive of dread.

Because that day is awful, and there is nothing like it; it is a time of anguish and distress for all of Jacob (v. 7). On the basis of the extent of the retribution he called the day *awful*. Then he links consolation to the sadness, saying, *and he will be saved from it*. He promises to break the yoke of slavery. He foretells also the change in behavior, *They will no longer work for foreigners, they will work for the Lord their God* (vv. 8-9). He used the name *foreigners* of the idols: knowing that he is the Lord God, and that he both supplies good things and inflicts correction (he is saying), they will give prior importance (656) to his prophecy. *I shall raise up David their king for them.* Christ the Lord brought fulfillment to the prophecy: he sprang from David according to the flesh, and he shepherds no longer Israel alone but all the nations. The prophecy had a kind of outcome by way of shadow and type in the time of Zerubbabel as well.

Having made this pledge he consoles them in turn by promising the return. While he threatens the Babylonians with ruin – *I shall bring an end on all the nations to whom I despatched you* (v. 11) – to them he offers promises of good things: *You I shall not bring to an end, I shall correct you for judgment, and shall not leave you untouched,* that is, I shall correct, console, I shall not let you off uncorrected, nor shall I leave you without help, the clause *I shall not leave you untouched* suggesting this, meaning, I shall not leave you without experience of trouble.[2] On the other hand, in his wish to change their wickedness by the extent of the threat, he proceeds to say this as well, *Violent is your wound, painful your affliction. There is no one rendering you judgment* (vv. 12-13): no living person charged Nebuchadnezzar with injustice. *Your cure comes with pain,* that is, with pangs. *There is no improvement for you;* in this case he used *improvement* not of the soul but of human assistance.

What follows, in fact, suggests as much, *All your friends have forgotten you, they will not inquire after you, because I struck you a hostile blow* (v. 14): instead of adopting the customary longsuffering, I delivered a deep incision. A physician likewise, on seeing the seriousness of the complaint, does this. To bring out the justice of the retribution, he went on, *Harsh correction for all your iniquity – hence your wounds are multiplied.* What follows is also in harmony with this. *Why do you cry out at your wound? Sore is your distress* (v. 15) – that is, severe yet still just. *On account of the number of your crimes, because your sins abounded, I have done this to you.* Nevertheless he threatens the enemy attacking them with slaughter and servitude:

those escaping death became the slaves of the victors. He continues consoling her with good promises. (657) *Because I shall begin your healing, I shall cure you of the painful wound, says the Lord* (v. 17). He used incision, sponge and medicines of both the harsher and the milder kind. *Because Zion, who was scattered, has been called*: the neighboring nations mocked her, citing her captivity and servitude. *This is your prey, that there is no one seeking her out*: when I passed her over and did not assist her, she was vulnerable to those attacking her, like a ready prey.

After the correction of slavery, however, I shall liberate them so that they will return, build cities, raise the Temple and perform in it the worship according to the Law. He said as much, in fact, *The Temple will take its place according to his judgment* (v. 18).[3] He proceeds to add as well what is typical of prosperity. *They will depart from them singing, and there will be the sound of dancing* (v. 19). He promises also increase in numbers and many children: *I shall pour them forth, and they will not be diminished. Their children will enter in as before, and their testimonies will be established in my sight* (v. 20). For *testimonies* the Syriac put "synagogues."[4]

I shall call to account all those afflicting you. Those stronger than they will be against them (vv. 20-21). By *those afflicting* he means Babylonians, and *those stronger than they* Medes and Persians, these latter destroying their prosperity. *His rule will depart from him*. At the time of the captivity they had for ruler the king of the Babylonians; but after the return they first had Zerubbabel and the son of Jozadak, and after this they were led by the high priests. *Who is this who has given his heart to turn to me? says the Lord*. He says this elsewhere as well, Ask the generations coming after you, Who trusted the Lord and was confounded?[5] He then attributes the sorrows befalling them to God's wrath; and to bring out its justice he goes on, *It will fall upon the impious* (v. 23). To bring out its possibility he adds, *The wrath of God's anger will not turn back until he implements and until he fulfills the intentions of his heart* (v. 24) – in other words, who resisted his purposes? Charging them with unbelief he says, *You will know this in the last days*: since you do not believe the words, you will learn from experience of the events themselves. (660)

Chapter Thirty-One

Once more he mingles satisfaction with trouble, and brings out their cause. *Thus said the Lord, I found warmth in the desert, those traveling in the way of Israel's concerns along with victims of the sword* (v. 2). For *warmth* the Syriac and the Hebrew put "pity"; and the translation in the Greek language bears a relationship to it, a person who experiences warmth being inclined to mercy. By *desert* he refers to Babylon, and he brings out that the Lord had pity on those enslaved there. What follows is also in harmony with the Syriac version, too.[1] *I loved you with an everlasting love; hence I enveloped you in pity* (v. 3): it is not your behavior but my mercy that is responsible for your salvation.[2]

He foretells that once again they will dance and use drums and other instruments, they will attend to agriculture and observe the divine festivals. He foretells also the union of the tribes. *Because there is a day of calling to give an account on the mountains of Ephraim. Arise, let us go up to to Zion, to the Lord our God* (v. 6). Those who worshiped calves in olden times, he is saying, will give an account of their former sins, will run to Zion and adore the God of all. He bids them sing God's praises with joy, on the one hand, and on the other laud it over the neighboring nations; he says as much, in fact, *Whinny at the head of the nations*, and in this way suggest the divine assistance.

He mentions also the time of the return. *For I shall gather them on the festival of Phasek from the ends of the earth* (v. 8). The term *Phasek* is rendered Pasch in Greek. And to signal their great number, he says, *Among them lame and blind, pregnant and in labor, a great assembly of one mind*. In the densely-populated cities, in fact, it is possible to find all such things. He mentions also the lamentation of captivity, and he foretells the pleasure of the return and the consolation of the journey. *I shall lead them back with encouragement, spelling them at springs of water, by a straight path, and on it they will no longer go astray* (v. 9). He proceeded to bring out the reason for the care. *Because I am like a father to Israel, and Ephraim is my firstborn*. By *Ephraim* he refers not to the son of Joseph but to the ten tribes; Reuben was the firstborn among them,[3] and Simeon the second, (661) but the ten tribes were called Ephraim since they built the palace in the portion of Ephraim. And just as today we are all called Romans after the city of the Romans, so at that time the ten tribes were named after Ephraim.

He bids this be broadcast to the nations as well, and the return be brought to the attention of all members of the people. The announcement was not made in words; instead, all heard of it when the events bruited it abroad more clearly. He promises as well the land's productivity, fertility of cattle and joy of spirit. The verse *I shall intoxicate the soul of the priests, the sons of Levi* means, I shall fill them with good things of all kinds. What follows, in fact, also suggests this, *And my people will be filled with good things, says the Lord*.

Thus said the Lord, A sound was heard in Ramah, wailing and weeping and lamentation, Rachel weeping for her children, and she refuses to be consoled because they are no more (v. 15). Ramah belonged to the tribe of Benjamin, and the tomb of Rachel is in the hippodrome of Chaphratha on the way to Ephrath.[4] While the prophecy had its fulfillment in the time of Herod the Great, who did away with the babies in the hope of doing away at the same time with the newborn savior,[5] the prophet put it here in the context of the promise of good things so as to bring out that the birth of our Lord and savior according to the flesh was the real good and the summit of salvation, though on account of it the babies met that unjust end. *Thus says the Lord, Give your voice a rest from wailing, and your eyes from crying, because there is a reward for your efforts, says the Lord, and your children will return to their mountains* (vv. 16-17).

To bring out what are the works for which he promises reward, he gives him a glimpse of the repentance in Babylon. *When I listened, I heard Ephraim lamenting* (v. 18). He brings out also the words he used. *You corrected me, Lord, and I was not corrected; like a calf I was not trained.* The prophet had said this in what preceded as well, "You flayed them and they were not distressed, you reduced them to extremes and they were unwilling to accept correction."[6] And the prophet Hosea said, "Ephraim a heifer trained to love trouble" – that is, it is contrary, and does not accept the yoke of the Law – and again, (664) "Ephraim is like a frenzied heifer."[7] He cites also what he said in his loud howling, *Bring me back, Lord, and I shall be brought back, because the Lord is my God*: if you do not wish it, I shall not be freed from slavery. *Because after my captivity I repented, and after coming to knowledge I struck my thigh and groaned at my days of shame* (v. 19). After experience of trouble, he came to a sense of sin. Blessed David also said this, "Before I was humbled, I sinned; for this reason I kept your word," and again, "It was good for me that you humbled me so that I might learn your ordinances."[8] Slapping the thigh is a mark of people grieving and doing penance. *I was ashamed and contrite before you because I incurred reproach from my youth*: from the very outset I persisted in transgressing your commandments. The Lord also gives a glimpse of lovingkindness in the words, *If Ephraim is my beloved son, if a spoilt child* (v. 20), that is, dainty and pleasant. If you continue to adopt this attitude, he is saying, and remember my care, you will enjoy good things (including the promise in what follows). *For the reason that my words are in him, I shall still remember him*: since he has had recourse to repentance and remembers my commandments, he will attain my providence. *For this reason I shall visit him, in my mercy I shall have mercy on him.*

Then he urges her to apply the remedies of repentance. *Set yourself up as sioneim* (v. 21). The Syriac rendered the word *sioneim* as "signs" – in other words, You need to indicate on the one hand what fruits you reaped from lawlessness, and on the other of what good things repentance proved the source. Hence he exhorts her to have recourse also to voluntary correction. *Practice retribution on yourself, give your heart to your shoulders*, that is, Impose on yourself the burden of repentance, keep to the good choice you have made. He went on, in fact, *the way you are traveling*. He then bids her turn back and return to her own cities, and not to desist from her grief. *Go back* (665) *grieving to your cities*. This kind of grief is not inconsistent with happiness. You need, he is saying, even while enjoying good things, to remember your own failings and lament them. *How long will you turn away, despised daughter? For the Lord has created you for salvation, as new growth; people will come round in salvation* (v. 22). Here he brought out clearly also the reason for the recall, prophesying there would be new growth through her. The apostles that sprang from her offered it to the world, and the inspired word clearly said as much, *people will come round in salvation*: the apostles visited the nations and offered them salvation through the knowledge of God.[9]

Then he forecasts once again the good things following the return and the joy stemming from it. The verse *I shall sow the house of Israel and the house of Judah with the seed of human beings and the seed of cattle* (v. 27) suggests their great number. *In those days they will not say, The parents ate sour grapes, and the children's teeth were set on edge. Instead, everyone will die for their own sin, and the teeth of the person eating sour grapes will be set on edge* (vv. 29-30). The Lord put this more clearly through the divinely-inspired Ezekiel as well, and we conducted the commentary by reference also to the many versions.[10] Now, what it means is something like this: As it is impossible to eat sour grapes without the teeth of the eater being set on edge, so it is impossible for the children to be called to account when the parents sin.

He cites the following by way of confirmation of that statement. *Behold, days are coming, says the Lord, and I shall make a new covenant with the house of Israel and the house of Judah, not in terms of the covenant I made with their ancestors on the day when I took them by the hand to lead them out of the hand of Egypt, because they did not adhere to my covenant, and I ignored them, says the Lord* (vv. 31-32). It is likewise impossible, he is saying, for the children to be called to account for ancestral sins, because I promise to the children the greatest goods even when the parents sin.[11] He conveyed to us, of course, many prophecies on the same point – firstly, that there is one lawgiver for the two covenants; then, the incompleteness of the former covenant, as there would have been no need for the second one if the former had been adequate; and in addition to these, that the only-begotten (668) Word of God was the source of the evangelical goods for us, he being the one who freed Israel from the slavery of the Egyptians. He was therefore the one who in speaking to Moses said, "I am he who is."[12] The verse is sufficient, not only to establish the Jews' lawlessness, but also to lay bare the heretical blasphemy. *Because this is the covenant that I shall make with the house of Israel and the house of Judah after those days, says the Lord: I shall give my laws into their minds and write them on the breast of their hearts, and I shall be their God and they will be my people* (v. 33).[13] God made this clear to us through the facts themselves: on leading the sacred apostles up the mountain, instead of giving them stone tablets he inscribed the divine laws on their hearts and proposed the Beatitudes to those who practise virtue.

They will no longer teach one another, each one their neighbor and each one their brother, saying, Know the Lord, because all will know me, from the least to the greatest of them (v. 34). The future life achieves the fulfillment of these words: in it we shall no longer need instruction from one another, things being patently obvious, sufferings at an end, bodies incorrupt, souls immune to change. Now, it is customary with the divine Scripture to mix the prophecies together:[14] it connects those about the recall with those about the captivity, and the Lord in the sacred Gospels cites at the one time the sayings about Jerusalem and those about the consummation. *Because I shall be merciful to their iniquities, and shall no longer remember their sins.* The grace of all-holy baptism grants this favor: after forgiveness, he does not remember the former sins.[15]

After this, having shown that he is creator of sun, moon and stars, that it was he who gave orders to the one to determine the day and the others to give light to the night, that it is at his direction that the sea is stirred and enjoys tranquillity, he went on, *If these laws were to cease to operate on the face of the earth, says the Lord, the race of Israel would also cease to be a nation in my sight for all time* (v. 36). This should be compared with what is said in the prophet Isaiah, "If (669) the number of the sons of Israel were like the sand of the sea, the remnant would be saved." So both prophecies contain the truth. "For not all those from Israel are really Israel – just those believing in God and accepting the saving message."[16] From them and through them the Church is constituted throughout the whole world. *The Lord says this, If heaven is lifted on high and if the earth is depressed to the depths, I too will find fault with the house of Israel, says the Lord* (v. 37): as it is impossible for heaven to be higher and earth to be lower, so it is impossible for Israel to be totally rejected.[17]

Lo, days are coming, says the Lord, and a city will be built to the Lord from Hananel to the Corner Gate (v. 38). The Syriac says this, "From the tower to the corner of Hananel." *The measuring line will go still further out of their sight to the hill of Gareb* (v. 39). He cites place names around the city. *And it will be encircled with choice stones*, that is, large and strong ones. *And to all the valley of the Phagarim and in the direction of Spodia, and to all Asarimoth to the brook Cedron, to the Corner Gate of horses of the east will be a sanctuary to the Lord* (v. 40). By *Spodia* he refers to the place where they threw the ashes of the sacrifices, and by *Phagarim* to the places of the sacrificed goats. Having mentioned above the circle of the city, he brought out by these references the perimeter of the Temple. *It will never be uprooted, and will not be destroyed forever.* The ambiguity in these words he removed in what was said before, "Eventually I shall speak to nations and kingdoms of rebuilding and replanting. And if that nation, once converted, commits evil, I shall not accord it the good I had spoken of."[18]

Chapter Thirty-Two

At this point, then, he made these promises. Since, however, they raged against our God and savior and brought condemnation on their own heads, he moved from here to a different prophecy, which had its actual delivery in the tenth year of King Zedekiah, (672) the eighteenth year of King Nebuchadnezzar.[1] The city was under siege by the latter at that time, and the prophet was in prison, having been put there by King Zedekiah since he had prophesied the capture of the city and the enslavement of the king and the people – hence the text's saying, *he was in prison* (v. 2).

Still, he was ordered by God to buy his relative's field: "The purchase is your right on the grounds of degrees of kinship." The one selling it came to me, I bought it as instructed, received the receipt for it in the presence of everyone, the seller and the witnesses. He gave the receipt to Baruch, saying God had ordered it to be placed in an earthenware jar so as to last a long time. Now, God ordered this to be done to convince the people through the actual events that they would really be recalled from captivity, and would repossess their homeland, the prophet actually saying as much, *Because the omnipotent Lord, the God of Israel, said this, Houses, fields and vineyards will still be acquired in this land* (v. 15).[2]

When this had happened in this fashion, I offered supplication to the Lord (he says) in these words, You are creator of heaven and earth, you survey everything, nothing escapes you of the present or the future, you have immeasurable treasures of mercy and you require an account of sins. If the children imitated their fathers' wickedness, you would inflict worse punishments on them for not learning from their fathers' example. He added many other such recriminations and reminded them of the marvels worked in Egypt and the favors granted after release from there and of course the ingratitude for the favors. Then he inquired, Why on earth, when the enemy are encamped at the gates and the city under siege and those within wasting away with famine and pestilence, did you order me to buy a field and get a receipt for it when the city was in the process of destruction?

To this God replies, *I am the Lord, the God of all flesh: surely no explanation will be hidden from me?* (v. 27) Can the creator and Lord of all be ignorant of anything that happens? *Hence the Lord says this, This city will be given into the hands of the Chaldeans and into the hands of Nebuchadnezzar king of Babylon, and he will take it* (v. 28). Then he describes how they will go in and burn it along with the houses in which they made offerings to Baal and poured libations to other gods. He criticizes also the purpose of these practices, (673) *to provoke me* (v. 29). I am handing the city over on account of the inhabitants' lawlessness: they ceaselessly continued provoking me, from the day I built it to this very day. Hence I decided to take it out of my sight on account of all the evil of the children of Israel and children of Judah, since the kings, the priests, the leaders and those prophesying falsehood along with all the people turned their back to me, not their face; abandoning me, they served the idols; blessed Ezekiel also reports that they turned their back on the Temple and adored the sun.[3] I did not abandon them, however, he says, instructing them in the truth through the prophets; but the impiety in their houses was not sufficient for them – instead, they set up images of the idols even in the very house dedicated to me. *They built the altars to the Baal in the valley of the son of Hinnom, the towers in Geb* (v. 35). From this it is clear that the name of the idol is Thapheth, *Baal* being the generic name of the idols; he means that in these places they murdered their sons and daughters.[4] Hence, he says, I gave up the city to famine and pestilence, slaughter and slavery.

Still, after the determined period I shall allow the enslaved to enjoy freedom, I shall bring them back to their ancestral land and accord them their former care. The verse *I shall give them a different heart and a different way so as to fear me all their days* (v. 39) should be taken to mean that through the correction and through the freedom after it they will know I alone am truly God, and they will be freed from their former error. *I shall make an eternal covenant with them, which I shall not put behind them* (v. 40). They would have attained this promise as well had they been willing; but they rebelled and were deprived of the grace. This and similar things he said in various ways, and went on, *Properties will be acquired in this land which you claim is untrodden by human beings or cattle, and will be given into the hands of the Chaldeans. They will acquire properties for money, receipts will be signed and sealed* (vv. 43-44). This was the reply he gave to the prophet's inquiry, bringing out that it was for this reason he bade him buy the field, that even by the events he might demonstrate the truth of the prophecy. *They will buy properties in the land of Benjamin, around Jerusalem, in the cities of Judah, in the hill cities,* (676) *in the cities of the Shephelah and in the cities of the Negeb.* By *Shephelah* he refers to the open country, and by *Negeb* to the south.[5]

Chapter Thirty-Three

Then once more the prophet, while still confined to prison, sees a different revelation. God says to him, *Call to me, and I shall hearken to you, and announce to you great and mighty things of which you are unaware* (v. 3). After revealing the siege, he foretells also the liberation. *Lo, I am bringing to it healing and curing, and I shall cure it* (v. 6). *Healing* suggests the complete cure.[1] He next recounts how, on seeing the return, the nations will sing the praises of the one responsible for the liberation: while those living a good and honest life will marvel, those embracing wickedness will be chagrined to see the city enjoying prosperity and constantly performing the divine festivals.

In those days and at that time I shall raise up a horn for David, a righteous dawning; he will perform judgment and righteousness in the land (v. 15).[2] We remarked before that while in the time of Zerubbabel these things were realized as a type, the Lord instructed us more precisely in the truth of the prophecy. *In those days Judah will be saved, and Jerusalem will dwell in confidence, and this is the name by which it will be called, The Lord is our righteousness* (v. 16). He conferred this name also in what went before, referring to her as Jozadak in the Hebrew. *Because the Lord says this, A man sitting on the throne of the house of Israel will not be lacking to David* (v. 17). The patriarch David also foretold this, "A ruler will not be missing from Judah, nor a leader from his thighs, until he comes to whom it belongs, the expectation of the nations."[3] But after Zerubbabel we know of no one as a leader from the tribe of Judah. Nevertheless we do discover the truth of the prophecy: a combination occurred of the royal and the priestly, and the priests ruled up to the foreigner Herod. Hence the present prophecy associates what relates to the priests with what relates to David. *Of the priests and Levites a man will not be missing to offer holocausts in my sight, present a gift and offer a victim for all time* (v. 18). We see (677) the fulfillment of this prophecy, too: when the new covenant was given in keeping with the divine promise, a priesthood was also given according to the order of Melchizedek, and those vouchsafed it offer the spiritual sacrifice to God continually.

Then he says, As it is impossible for day to become night, so it is impossible for the Davidic monarchy to be destroyed. The fulfillment of this prophecy is also clear: Christ, who is of David according to the flesh, does not occupy the throne here below; seated with the Father, however, he governs all things. This very thing, of course, he says also of the priests and the Levites, that their line will be compared with the host of heaven and the sand of the sea. The facts confirm what is said: the whole land and sea are full of high priests and the deacons performing the Levitical liturgy.[4] Now, after citing what had been said by the impious, that he had completely rejected the two tribes which he had chosen, the kingly and the priestly, he once again promised what he had previously foretold.

Chapter Thirty-Four

Having thus completed this prophecy, he shifts to a different one.[1] With the enemy in position he is bidden to say to King Zedekiah, The city will be taken and will be put to the torch; they will seize you and bring you to the king of the Babylonians, and while you will escape death, you will be led away as a captive, you will dwell in a foreign land, meet your end in peace and be accorded due obsequies by your kith and kin. I said as much to the king, he says, with the enemy besieging not only Jerusalem but also the surviving cities of Judah.

Now, to this prophecy he attaches another, bearing the same sense. In keeping with the divine Law, Zedekiah gave the order for the Hebrew slaves to be set free, the Law clearly proclaiming that after their serving for six years they should gain their freedom in the seventh year.[2] After responding, however, and allowing them to enjoy freedom, everyone reduced them once again to their former slavery, having malicious second thoughts. The God of all, accordingly, in his anger reminds them of the slavery in Egypt, the acquisition of freedom and the giving of the Law afterwards, and finds fault with them for loving the observance of the Law, on the one hand, and on the other for having second thoughts and trampling on it. *You were brought around to doing what is right in my eyes*, the text says, *each of you announcing release of their neighbor. You observed a covenant before me in the house where my name was invoked* (v. 15): within the house dedicated to me you made an agreement on release in my sight and immediately broke it. So since you were not prepared to effect the release, *Lo, I announce a release for you, says the Lord – to the sword, to death and to famine. I shall allow you to be scattered to all the kingdoms of the earth* (v. 17).

He also makes the charge of violation of the oath. *The people who broke my covenant, those who did not keep the words of my covenant they made in my sight, I shall make like the calf which they divided into two and passed between its two parts – the leaders of Judah and the leaders of Jerusalem, the powerful, the priests and all the people of the land, who passed between the two parts of the calf* (vv. 18-19). That was the way they normally took an oath in olden times. The God of all also in making a treaty with Abraham, of course, ordered a three-year-old ram, a calf and a goat to be divided into two, and the parts to be placed opposite one another together with a smoking pan and a lamp alight, and had him pass between the two parts, making a treaty with him according to the custom in force.[3] This is what they also did in making the promise of the freeing of the Hebrew slaves and wanting to confirm the freeing with an oath; but they immediately broke it. For this very reason he threatens to hand them over to their foes for their bodies to be given as fodder to wild animals, and the yoke of slavery to be imposed on the king and the leaders.

Chapter Thirty-Five

On completing this prophecy, he recalls an older prediction. In the time of Jehoiakim, son of Josiah king of Judah, he was ordered to take the sons of Rechab into the divine Temple and in one of the courts to offer them wine. I carried out the command, he says, I set before them vessels full of wine, inviting them to drink. But they refused, saying, *We will not drink wine, because Jonadab, son of our ancestor Rechab, instructed us in the words, You and your children are never to drink wine. You are not to build houses, sow seed, or plant vines, and you are not to own them; instead, live in tents all your days so that you may live many days on the earth where you spend your lives* (vv. 6-7). We heeded these words, they said, and observed the commands, along with our wives and children: we did not build houses (681) or attend to farming; instead, we continued living in tents to the present day. Now, with the assault of the Babylonians, we were obliged to take refuge in this city.

Deserving of admiration are both the ancestor's stipulation and the obedience of both sons and descendants: they preferred a life free from cares and possessions, and – most remarkable of all – though having children, they scorned possessions, leaving themselves to rely on divine hope . Now, if in the time of the Law, which lacked perfection on account of the limitations of the lawgivers, these people exemplified the highest values, what would they have been like if they had heard the evangelical law?[1] The God of all, however, bids the prophet say to all the inhabitants of Jerusalem, Whereas these people kept their ancestor's command and refused to drink wine, you by contrast, despite being in receipt night and day of the prophetic teachings, do not live according to my laws – hence I shall inflict on you manifold calamities. To the descendants of Rechab, on the other hand, who kept the ancestral command, he promises the finest of good things: *A man will not be lacking from the sons of Jonadab to stand in my presence all the days of the earth* (v. 19). It should be understood, of course, that everyone keeping those laws is styled a son of Jonadab son of Rechab.[2]

Chapter Thirty-Six

After this he says that he was ordered to write down the whole prophecy.[1] By *chapter of a book* he means the volumes, which Jews have preferred to use to the present day. It is likely, he is saying, you see, that on gaining a precise knowledge of the threatened troubles, they will through repentance attain salvation. The prophet carries out the order: while he, inspired by divine grace,[2] delivered the oracles, Baruch wrote them down. And since he was prevented from entering the divine Temple, being in prison, he urges Baruch to read out to the people what was written down. With the lapse of a long period of time and the celebration of a general fast, Baruch read out the prophecy. Now, one of the listeners, of a very pious inclination, informed the leaders of the threatened troubles; they sent for Baruch, ordered him to read it out, and, filled with dread, they were anxious to learn of its writer. Baruch told them: Jeremiah, inspired by divine grace, urged me to write it. The rulers gave the book to the royal scribe, recommended Baruch to make himself scarce, and communicated the contents to the king. He summoned the scribe and bade him read it out, but being impious and lawless he cut up the pages as they were read out (684) and consigned them to the flames, there being a stove on hand owing to the winter season. *They did not seek the Lord*, the text goes on, *nor did the king and all his servants, who heard all these words, rend their garments* (v. 24).[3] As he accuses these men of extreme insensitivity, however, so he commends Elnathan, Delaiah and Gemaria: they suggested to the king not to burn the book, but he took no notice.

The impious king, however, was not satisfied with committing this lawlessness: he ordered Baruch and Jeremiah to be apprehended. But the God of all bade Jeremiah to write the former oracles in a different book: whereas the writing matter was consumed by fire, the divine Law remained intact; likewise also the Word, when the body that was assumed suffered, remained immune to suffering.[4] The prophet was also bidden to say the following to Jehoiakim: *The Lord says this, You burned this book with the words, Why have you written in it the statement, The king of Babylon will truly come and destroy this land, and man and beast will disappear from it? For this reason the Lord spoke thus to Jehoiakim king of Judah, He will have no one to sit on the throne of David, and his corpse will be exposed to the heat of the day and the frost of night* (vv. 29-30). The prophecy did not lie: even if his son did reign, yet after three months he was taken off into captivity.[5] He also threatens him and all his house with destruction, the city with desolation and the people with the predicted calamities. Once again the prophet carried out the order and wrote down the prophecy once more with Baruch's assistance: *And there were included in it as well many other words than these* (v. 32) – that is to say, since the impious king was upset on hearing the threats, the Lord ordered them to happen many times over.

For our part, I beseech you, let us be in dread of the divine threats, believe the good promises and walk in a manner worthy of the calling in which we are called so as to avoid the experience of the threats and enjoy the promised good things, thanks to the grace and lovingkindness of our Lord Jesus Christ, to whom with the Father and the all-holy Spirit belongs the glory, now and forever, for ages of ages. Amen. (685)

Chapter Thirty-Seven

On the point of describing the events of the capture of the city, the divinely-inspired prophet brings out first at what age King Zedekiah took the throne, the length of time he reigned, and the fact that at the time of the siege, on learning of the prophecies spoken by the prophet against himself and the city, he sent some people and exhorted him to offer intercession on his behalf.[1] At that time he was not in prison, living instead untroubled in the city. With the Babylonians besieging the city, the Egyptians came to the aid of the Jews – that is to say, when the king called on them for assistance. When they heard of this, the Chaldeans desisted from the siege.

Accordingly, the Lord God urged the prophet to tell the king and the leaders not to trust in the help of the Egyptians nor to set the Chaldeans at naught: the Egyptians would make for home as quickly as possible, and the Chaldeans would return, besiege the city and consign it to the flames. And to bring out that he personally had delivered a sentence against them, he adds the following: *But even if you struck down all the might of the Chaldeans who attack you, and only some wounded were left of them, each in his own tent, they would rise up and put this city to the torch* (v. 10). In other words, Do not think you will prevail over the strength of the Chaldeans: even a few wounded, left in their tents on account of weakness, are sufficient for your overthrow, sin having made you weak.[2]

He then reports that when some respite had been given them on account of the Chaldeans' withdrawal, he left to visit his family, intending to buy bread. But a certain Irijah suspected him of fleeing to the enemy and reported him to the leaders, and they detained him, not in the public prison – *this being full*, it says – but in the house of Jonathan the scribe.[3] After the lapse of many days Zedekiah secretly sent for him and asked if there was a word from the Lord, and the prophet foretold to him his capture; and after the prophecy he complained of the injustice done him. *What wrong did I do you or* (688) *your children for you to put me in this house under guard? Where are your prophets who prophesied to you in the words, The king of Babylon will not attack you in this land?* (vv. 18-19) With events demonstrating the truth of my prophecy, he is saying, and the falsehood of your prophets, you ought to judge fairly and call the liars to account, not the one making true predictions. Then he begs to be released from the house of the scribe. Zedekiah brought him out from there, but committed him to the public prison and ordered bread to be supplied to him every day.

Chapter Thirty-Eight

Now, some of the leaders were displeased with the prophecies delivered by the prophet against the city. He had, in fact, said that those deserting to the Chaldeans would enjoy safekeeping, whereas those putting up with the siege would be dispatched to destruction. So they swayed the king against the prophet, claiming that by his oracles he undermined the enthusiasm of those capable of fighting. The foolish king handed the prophet over to his traducers, who took it on themselves to vent their anger against him and lower him into a smelly and muddy pit. But the eunuch Ebed-melech, an Ethiopian, reproached the king and forthrightly protested, You have done wrong in causing the man of God to die of hunger because there is no bread left in the city. Zedekiah accepted the accusation, and made Ebed-melech the means of the prophet's rescue; he took others to help, tossed old rags to the prophet, told him to put them in his armpits under the rope, and pulled him up from the pit Chereth, calling the pit Chereth. After he had been brought up and was living in the prison, again the king sent for him and brought him to him in the house Asalisael, *which was in the house of the Lord* (v. 14), which the Syriac rendered "inside the meeting of the three paths;" he asks the prophet to inform him of a divine oracle, and not conceal the truth.[1]

The prophet answered, *If I tell you, will you not put me to death? if I advise you, you will not listen* (v. 15). As prophet, you see, he knew what would happen, having experience as his teacher. When the king swore he would definitely not surrender him to the impious, he said again, (689) *If you will actually go out to the general of the king of Babylon, your soul will live, the city itself will not be consumed by fire, and you and your house will live. But if you will not go out to the leaders of the king of Babylon, the city will be surrendered into the hands of the Chaldeans, and they will put it to the torch, and you will not be saved from their hand* (vv. 17-18). He had often foretold this; but it is necessary to inquire why on earth he promises salvation to those leaving, but threatens destruction to those not leaving.[2] Zedekiah had given an oath to Nebuchadnezzar when he put him on the throne that he would pay tribute and keep on good terms with the one who appointed him; but after the lapse of a short time he broke the agreement by not paying the levy and having recourse to the Egyptians. The Lord God accordingly, since he swore not by lifeless idols but by the very creator of all things, and presumed to break them, bade him go out to the Chaldeans and in this way make up for the breaking of the oaths.

Zedekiah, however, said to the prophet, *I have a concern lest the Jews who have deserted to the Chaldeans give me into their hands and mock me* (v. 19). I am afraid of becoming a figure of ridicule to the deserters. The prophet for his part nonetheless exhorts him further, and delivers a threat to him in his reluctance. *Lo, all the women, those left behind in the house of the king of Judah, are brought out to the leaders of the king of Babylon, and they say, They deceived you, your men of peace[3] prevailed over you, and they will overcome you as your feet slip* (v. 22): you are afraid of being an object of malicious joy to the deserters; you will see later, when the city is taken, women dragged out from the palace, reminding you of the deceit of the false prophets, and saying, Responsible for this were those promising peace, enjoying respect from you, and for this reason causing you to slip from the divine laws. *They will lead out all your wives and your children to the Chaldeans* (v. 23). The city will be set alight, he is saying, and you will be taken off into captivity.

In his stupidity, however, the king remained unresponsive. All the same, he urged the prophet not to mention what was said to any of the leaders, but to say, I begged the king not to dispatch me to that awful dungeon. He then described that they arrived and tried to find out what was said to the king, and that he convinced them by telling the story about the dungeon. (692)

Chapter Thirty-Nine

From this point he goes on to the capture, and says that in the ninth year of Zedekiah's reign the Babylonians attacked; on the ninth day of the fourth month of the eleventh year of Zedekiah they toppled the wall, and the enemy poured into the city. When this happened, Zedekiah and all those with a name for strength took to flight; the Chaldeans pursued and caught up with him, and apprehended him by the city of Jericho. Now, by Jericho he means Arabah, to the west of Jerusalem. *They took him to Riblah, in the land of Hamath* (v. 5). Now, it was under the control of Emesa, so it is clear that by *Hamath* here he refers to Emesa.[1] *He passed sentence on him*, that is, he accused him of breaking the oath, of disloyalty and ingratitude to his benefactor who had made him king. After charging him with wrongdoing, he imposed the penalty, firstly executing before his eyes his children and all those in office and of some standing; and after punishing him in this way by the distressing spectacle, he deprived him of his eyesight. He recounts how they burned the palace and all the other buildings, and destroyed the ramparts of the city; Nebuzaradan the king's lieutenant enslaved the rest, leaving some few who lived in poverty with instructions about farming.

Nebuchadnezzar king of Babylon gave instructions about Jeremiah to Nebuzaradan in these words, Take him into custody, keep your eye on him, and do him no harm; instead, treat him as he tells you (vv. 11-12). King Nebuchadnezzar and Ebed-melech the Babylonian increased the charge against the Jews:[2] though foreigners, they respected the prophet, whereas Jews raised on prophetic statement were not prepared to give heed to the divine oracles and subjected the prophets to manifold punishments. God's promise, of course, had its fulfillment: in appointing the prophet, he had promised that he would emerge unscathed like an iron column and a bronze wall, and that though they would show hostility to him, they would not prevail.[3] Nebuzaradan, in fact, and all the company of the leaders sent for Jeremiah from the dungeon and handed him over to Gedeliah, who had been appointed to govern those left in Judea.

Now, the prophet vouchsafed also a written account of what had been prophesied by God about Ebed-melech and had reached its fulfillment: nothing goes unnoticed or unrewarded by him. At that time, he says, God made this promise, (693) *Lo, I am bringing to effect my word of evil, not of good, against this city, and they will be before your eyes on that day. I shall save you on that day,*[4] *says the Lord, I shall not give you into the hands of human beings of whose presence you are afraid. Because I shall really save you, and you will not be a victim of the sword; your life will be a bonus for you because you trusted in me, says the Lord* (vv. 16-18). "Truly blessed is the one whose helper is the God of Jacob," and "Blessed the people whose God is the Lord."[5] After all, what good did kingship do for Zedekiah? what harm did servitude do Ebed-melech? In other words, while one met that awful fate through impiety, the other through piety did not experience trouble.

Chapter Forty

Then the prophet recounts what Nebuzaradan the lieutenant says to him. *The Lord your God prophesies these calamities for this city. The Lord proceeded to do as he said, because you sinned against him and did not listen to his voice, and this threat befell you* (vv. 2-3). It is clear from this that God chose Israel from the beginning by way of kindness to the other nations: the wonders worked in their favor astonished everyone and clearly brought out that their God is the only true God; and likewise the disasters befalling them accused them of lawlessness, on the one hand, and on the other proclaimed God's just sentence. So Nebuzaradan began by saying that they deserved to pay the penalty and that God had acted justly.

Then he gives the prophet a choice, and guarantees him safekeeping in Babylon if he chose to reside there, and on the other hand he promises to leave him behind if he chose that. *Lo, all the land lies before you: in whatever direction it is good and pleasing to you to go, go. Before I take my leave, set out and betake yourself to Gedeliah son of Ahikam son of Shaphan, whom the king of Babylon put in charge of the land of Judah, and dwell with him amidst your people; but if not, to any place it is favorable in your eyes to go, go* (vv. 4-5). You are your own master, he is saying, you are beyond my authority, you are under divine lordship, do what you decide. Employing these and similar words, and plying him with many gifts, he let him go. The (696) prophet in fact went off to Gedeliah.

The prophet next recounts that those leaders who had fled heard of the developments with Gedeliah and hastened in a body to him. Gedeliah assured them in an oath that they would come to no harm at the hands of the Chaldeans, and urged them to harvest crops from the land and enjoy in peace the goods of peace. As well, those who had taken refuge with Idumeans, Moabites and Ammonites came back on hearing that Gedeliah had been made ruler. Then he mentions that Johanan along with the other leaders reported a plot hatched by Ishmael; but though reporting it they did not convince him that they spoke the truth. Johanan sought permission in secret to assassinate Ishmael *lest he take your life, and all the Jews who have come in a body to you will be scattered and the remaining Jews will perish* (v. 15). But even on hearing this Gedeliah did not budge, forbidding the proposal and calling the accusation calumny.[1]

Chapter Forty-One

After the lapse of seven months Ishmael came back. Being of the royal line he shared his table; he slew Gedeliah and all who were left with him, both Chaldeans and Jews. Two days passed; *men came from Shechem, from Salem and from Samaria, eighty in number, with beards shaven and clothes torn, grieving, carrying grain and incense to present at the house of the Lord* (v. 5). The Hebrew and the Syriac call *Salem* Shiloh.[1] He recounts that Ishmael slew these as well, and threw their bodies into a cistern; but some ten survived and implored Ishmael to halt the slaughter, promising to tell him of the whereabouts of certain storehouses. After committing all these crimes, he took all the survivors and made off, seeking refuge with Ammonites. On learning of these doings, Johanan with the other leaders assembled a throng and did battle with Ishmael; witnessing those attacking Ishmael, those who had been enslaved by him rejoiced and joined them. Ishmael, however, fled with eight men to the Ammonites. The divine sentence brought this upon the Jews: just when they thought they had escaped the enemy, they were surrendered into one another's hands.[2]

In the event, Johanan assembled a large number and got as far as a town near Bethlehem with the intention of fleeing to Egypt, in fear of the Chaldeans on account of the killing of Gedeliah. (697)

Chapter Forty-Two

At all events everyone, leaders and people alike, besought the prophet in these words, *Let pity for us come upon you so that you will pray to the Lord your God for this remnant, because we few remain from many, as your eyes behold us. Let the Lord your God announce to us the way we should take and the word we should follow* (vv. 2-3). While they beg him correctly and desire to know what to do, out of habit they are unresponsive and resist the divine laws. The prophet for his part, however, promises to make intercession and report the instructions; they promised to respond to everything, and ratified their promise with an oath. *May the Lord be to us a righteous and faithful witness that whatever word the Lord God sends you for us, we shall do, good or bad, and we shall listen to the word of the Lord our God to whom we are sending you so that it may be better for us for listening to the word of the Lord our God* (vv. 5-6).

While their speech oozed devotion, their behavior did not correspond to the words. After the lapse of ten days, you see, the prophet received the reply; in my view the delay in the reply was for the benefit of the petitioners, for them to know that God reluctantly received the prophet's supplication.[1] The prophet, then, says that God ordered them to abide in the land: I will accord you every care, he says, *I shall build you up and not destroy you, plant you and not root you up. Because I have desisted from the evils which I said I would cause you* (v. 10). He expels their fear and urges them to have confidence. *Do not be afraid of the king of Babylon, of whom you are in fear, because I am with you to rescue you and save you from his hand*

(v. 11). He promises also the recall of those made prisoner. But if you oppose my words, he says, and make for Egypt in an endeavor to escape the enemy there, I shall send to that place the enemy you dread. *The sword of which you are in fear will find you there in the land of Egypt, and famine likewise* (700) *which you abhor will fall upon you in that land* (v. 17).

After developing this at greater length, he adds the following as well. *Just as my anger and my rage dropped down upon the inhabitants of Jerusalem, so my anger will drop down upon you when you enter Egypt; you will be in a trackless waste, subservient, a curse and a reproach, and you will no longer see this place* (v. 18). He made clear that it is possible for people to see the greatness of his might, referring to the evils befalling the Jews as *drops of anger*, that is, the process of retribution.[2] *It was you, remember, who sent me to the Lord your God with the words, Pray for us, and whatever the Lord our God says to us, tell us and we shall do it. I have told you today, and you have not listened to the voice of the Lord your God in all he sent to you. Now you are finding out that by sword, by famine and by death you will perish in this place which you insisted on entering to dwell there* (vv. 20-22). In other words, what you are trying to escape you will find in Egypt.

Chapter Forty-Three

On hearing this, those in charge of the people gave way to audacity and arrogance, and forgetful of the exhortations and the oaths they presumed to say to the prophet, *It is a lie you are telling: the Lord our God did not send you to us with the words, Do not go into Egypt. Instead, Baruch son of Neriah advised you against us so that you would give us into the hands of the Chaldeans for them to kill us and move us to Babylon* (vv. 2-3). After saying this to the prophet, and openly breaking the oaths taken, they set off for Egypt with all the assembled people; they also took with them the prophet and Baruch.

In Taphanhes, accordingly (it is a city in Egypt), the prophet is ordered to get some stones and bury them in front of the palace gates, with the Jews looking on, and to make the following prediction. *Lo, I am sending and am bringing my servant Nebuchadnezzar king of Babylon, and he will erect his throne on these stones and will raise his weapons over them. Some of the Egyptians he will put to death, of others he will make slaves;* (701) *he will also burn the temples of the idols, and them he will take captive* (vv. 10-12). To bring out that, far from idly making war against Egypt, he will deliberately destroy it, he compares it to a shepherd collecting lice from his cloak, shepherds doing this when they have plenty of time on their hands. *He will delouse Egypt as a shepherd delouses his cloak, and he will leave there safely. He will smash the pillars of Heliopolis and those in On, he will consume with fire the houses of the gods themselves* (vv. 12-13). The city had two names, being called both On and Heliopolis; the Exodus also taught us this, saying that the sons of Israel built for the Pharaoh the cities of Pithom, Ramses and On, which is Heliopolis.[1] God calls Nebuchadnezar his *servant*, of course, not because he was such in condition and disposition, but because he was one by nature, the creature being the servant of the creator; he also makes clear at the same time that it was with his permission that he did these things.

Chapter Forty-Four

To the Jews, though they were suffering from disobedience, the loving Lord again offers exhortation, using the prophet as his minister. He first reminds them of the troubles that occurred in Judea on account of the inhabitants' lawlessness, then he blames them in their own persons for committing the same crimes and drawing down the divine anger.

Lo, you are doing great evil to your own selves, cutting off man and wife, babe and infant from the midst of Judah so that no one will be left. You provoke me by the works of your hands, sacrificing to other gods in the land of Egypt where you went in to dwell so as to be cut off and become a curse and a reproach amongst all the nations of the earth (vv. 7-8). He reminds them, as though they had recent recollection, of the evils committed both by their ancestors and the kings, and of course by the high and mighty, and of the manifold calamities befalling them on that account.

He also levels a threat at them, calling himself *Lord of Hosts and God of Israel* (v. 11),[1] so that on hearing of the greatness of his authority and learning of his care for the forebears they might feel shame and dread. *Lo, I set my face to bring troubles upon you.* It is characteristic of angry people to adopt a grim look, have a fixed stare, and glare at length at those irritating them; so he expresses the threat in human terms, *I set my face* (704) *to bring troubles upon you so as to devastate the whole of Judah.* Then he says they will be handed over to famine and sword and utterly annihilated, they will become an object of execration and ruin, a curse and a reproach, and will suffer the same things as the besieged in Jerusalem. *Yet none of them will escape or return to the land of Judah* (v. 14).

None of this, however, put fear into the miserable and thrice-miserable men. Instead, they all cried out openly, men and women, and especially the Babylonians,[2] *We cannot bear your words* (v. 16); worse than that, though believing they came from God, they blatantly opposed them. *The word you spoke to us in the name of the Lord we shall not heed. We shall make a point of putting into effect every word that will come from our mouth, sacrificing to the queen of heaven and pouring libations to her as we have done along with our fathers, our kings and our leaders, in the cities of Judah and in the streets of Jerusalem* (vv. 16-17). By *queen of heaven* they refer to Aphrodite, and the Greeks call her Urania. By doing this, they claimed, we enjoyed an abundance of good things, whereas by abandoning her service we would be consigned to death and starvation. Then the women cried out more brazenly, *If we sacrificed to the queen of heaven and poured libations to her, surely it was not without our husbands that we made sponges for her and poured libations to her?* (v. 19) While the action was irreverent, the statement was true: in what was commented on before the God of all said, "Do you not see what they are doing? Their children are gathering wood, their fathers kindling a fire, their wives grinding suet to make sponges for the heavenly host."[3]

The prophet, of course, made this reply to them all: On account of this superstition and the error about the idols the Lord God inflicted on you manifold punishments, the fruits of transgression of the Law. For your part, however, though you observed them, your frenzy for the error continued. *Persist, then, in your admissions, and go on making your vows. But hear the word of the Lord: Lo, I swear by my great name, said the Lord God, if my name is ever again invoked by the mouth of any Jew* (705) *in the land of Egypt, saying, The Lord lives* (vv. 25-26). Once again the oath suggests that nothing is more important to the one who took it. He threatens the Jews living in Egypt with destruction, indicating this by these words, with which what follows is in harmony: he threatens them with famine and the sword, and with migration for those who escape it. *All the surviving Jews residing in the land of Egypt will know whose word abides, mine or theirs* (v. 28): by very experience they will come to know the truth of my words.

This will be a sign to you, says the Lord: I shall visit trouble upon you in this place so that you may know that my promise of trouble for you will surely come to pass (v. 29). The outcome of the events demonstrates the truth of the words: just as I surrendered Zedekiah to the king of the Babylonians, so Pharaoh Hophra I shall surrender to Nebuchadnezzar. Now, he refers to the Pharaoh as Hophra to bring out that he had this as his proper name, while the term Pharaoh is indicative of royal rank. Likewise we also call our emperors Tiberius Caesar and Claudius Caesar, the former a proper name, the latter implying royal rank.[4]

Chapter Forty-Five

Having thus completed this story interwoven with prophecy, he recalls an earlier prediction which he was ordered to deliver to Baruch in the days of Jehoiakim. *The Lord the God of Israel said, Since, Baruch, you said, Alas for the Lord's piling hardship on hardship, I laid myself down with groaning and found no rest, tell him this. Thus said the Lord, Lo, it is I who built, it is I who shall lay waste, and what I planted I shall root up – the whole land.*[1] *Do you seek great things for yourself? Do not seek them, because I am bringing trouble on all flesh, says the Lord, and I shall give your life as a bonus in every place* (708) *you go to* (vv. 2-5). The Lord consoles Baruch, who ministered to the prophet and wrote down the oracles, though querulous and upset; he urges him to bear nobly his life, full of pain though it was. In other words, he is saying, if I planted in this land all the people I led out from Egypt, and shall now pull them up, cut them down and consign them to such awful punishments, are you grieving because you alone are not living in contentment? You should not be like this: I shall take care of you nonetheless, and while inflicting punishment on them, I shall offer you consolation, and wherever you are living you will be the beneficiary of care from me.

It behooves us on learning this, therefore, not to be upset whenever tribulation befalls us, but to request a better lot from God, and at the same time to put up with the present. The Lord, after all, on seeing our patience will not let us be tried beyond our capacity; instead, along with the trial he will provide the way out so that we may be able to endure it.[2] To him belong the glory and the magnificence, together with his only begotten Son and the all-holy Spirit, now and forever, for ages of ages. Amen.

Chapter Forty-Six

The word that came from the Lord to Jeremiah the prophet against all the nations (v. 1). After bringing to an end the prophecies about the people,[1] he predicts what will happen to the other nations, bringing out that he is creator and God and Lord of all. He outlines first of all the fate of Egypt, and conveys also the time of the prophecy: the prediction happened after the death of Pharaoh Neco; he killed Josiah by the river Euphrates,[2] but was killed himself by the king of the Babylonians. *Take up weapons and shields and proceed into battle. Load up horses, mount horses, take your position with your helmets on, raise spears and don your breastplates* (vv. 3-4). After exhorting them to equestrian skills and armor, he bids them use them, he brings out their futility, the sequel suggesting this. (709) *Why is it that they are terrified and move back? Because their champions will be cut down, they have taken to flight and have not turned back, surrounded on all sides, says the Lord* (v. 5). Then, by way of command, *Let the lightly armed not flee, nor the champion find salvation to the north; what is by the Euphrates has weakened and fallen* (v. 6).

He next reminds them of their former prosperity. *Who is this that rises like a river, whose waves swell like rivers, Egypt, rising like a river and, like a river, agitating its waters?* (vv. 7-8). He gives evidence also of its arrogant words. *It said, I shall rise up, flood the earth, destroy a city and the inhabitants in it.* And to bring out that events did not happen as imagined in its thinking, he says ironically, *Mount the horses, prepare the chariots, go forth, warriors* (v. 9). He mentions the Egyptians' allies, *Ethiopians,*

Libyans equipped with weapons, and Ludim, go up, draw the bow. Then he explains that it is by God's will that the audacity of the Egyptians is overthrown. *That day is a day of retribution for the Lord God, for exacting retribution on his enemies; my sword will eat meat and be filled, and will be intoxicated with their blood* (v. 10). In this he indicates the vast number of the slain. *Because there is a sacrifice to the Lord Sabaoth in the north land on the river Euphrates.* Since the Egyptians paid the penalty for impiety and were slain with God's concurrence, for this reason he used the word *sacrifice* for their slaughter.

Go up to Gilead and take balm to virgin daughter Egypt (v. 11). The brothers of Joseph took balm and gum to Egypt;[3] balm is a liquid from trees that is suitable as a medicine, and Gilead in particular produces it. He said this by way of irony to show the incurable nature of the complaint, as emerges also from what follows. *In vain you multiplied your remedies; they are of no use to you.* To highlight the gravity of the disease he went on, *Nations heard your voice, and the earth was filled with your cry, because warrior in combat with warrior has failed, both have fallen at the same time* (v. 12). In this he predicted also the future destruction of the victors.

These, then, (712) were the prophecies the prophet delivered on the former defeat, whereas in what follows he foretells Nebuchadnezzar's campaign into Egypt, and urges him to convey it to Migdol, Memphis, Tahpanhes and of course the whole kingdom of Egypt in the words, *Take your post and prepare yourself, because the sword has devoured your yew tree* (v. 14). The Syriac rendered *yew tree* "the things surrounding you," and *yew tree* implies the same idea: it is a tree that is intertwined with plants growing nearby; so in figurative manner he spoke of the Egyptians' allies in this fashion, foretelling their defeat and flight.[4] *Why has Apis, your chosen calf, fled and not held his ground?* (v. 15) He called Apis *a chosen calf*: it was a bull, raised and adored by them. So the inspired word is bringing out the reason for the defeat:

having made a god of a calf and put their faith in it, they got no help from it.

Your vast numbers have failed and fallen (v. 16). He refers both to the dread encompassing them and the fact that they urged one another to flight, terrified of the enemy and their allies. *Let us arise and return to our people and our own country before the Greek sword.* Though it is likely there were also some Greeks fighting with the king of the Babylonians, I think that he is foretelling the power of the Macedonians against him; Alexander, remember, after destroying the kingdom of the Egyptians, forced them to serve the Macedonians.[5] *Give Pharaoh Neco, king of Egypt, the name Saon eebeir emoed* (v. 17). The Syriac rendered it this way, "Give him the name Disturber who missed his opportunity": formerly the kingdom of the Egyptians was strong and caused alarm in the neighboring nations, and changed many people's prosperity into misfortune.[6]

I live, says the Lord God, whose name is king of hosts (v. 18). He taught us at the one time both his eternity and his might. *Because like Thabor among the mountains and like Carmel by the sea, so will he come* – in other words, do not (713) delay: just as everyone admits without qualification that Thabor is a mountain and Carmel borders the sea, so the prophecy contains the truth. *Make vessels of exile for yourself, sheltered daughter of Egypt* (v. 19), that is, get ready for captivity. He refers to the desolation of the royal city: Memphis at that time had been a royal city; the divinely-inspired Isaiah informed us of this: "The rulers of Tanis have disappeared, and the rulers of Memphis have been carried away with themselves."[7] *A beautiful heifer all adorned is Egypt* (v. 20). In this he indicated her indomitability, inexperience with the yoke and daintiness; and in accusing her of the great handicap of these faults he brings out that they could not resist the assault of even a foe of small numbers, the meaning of *a fragment from the north came upon her.*

Her mercenaries in her midst are like fatted calves (v. 21). He indicated the weakness of the allies: the fatted calf does not work the soil, but is eaten by others. He refers also to their flight: *They turned and fled of their own accord, they did not hold their ground.* He adds the cause as well, *Because the day of ruin came upon them, and the time of their retribution*: they had to pay the price of impiety. In this he brings out, of course, that while exercising longsuffering, the Lord later imposes punishment. *Their sound like a snake hissing* (v. 22). It is typical of the unfortunate to groan and hiss, and to expel breath heated by their discontent. *Because they move on sand.* In this he suggested their decadence: the Lord compared the person hearing his word and not acting on it to a stupid man who builds the house on sand.[8] *They will come against her with axes, like woodchoppers.* Then by way of command, *Chop down her forest, says the Lord God, because God will not be appeased because she is more numerous than locusts* (v. 23), that is, the vast number of the inhabitants; *there is no numbering them.* He compares her to a forest and the enemy to foresters.[9] *The daughter of Egypt has been ashamed, given into the hands of the people from the north, said the Lord of Hosts, the God of Israel* (v. 24). The prophet also predicted this to the Jews who had gone down into Egypt (716) when he buried the stones in the forecourt of the palace.[10]

Lo, I shall take vengeance on Amon her son (v. 25). The Egyptians call Jupiter Amon, and hence the region, too, is called Amonian; they built a very big shrine to him. He calls Amon *her son* for being made into a god by her, the statue being handmade. So he is threatening to hand over the Amon idol also to the Babylonians, and of course their other gods as well, which is the meaning of *on Pharaoh, on Egypt, on its gods, on its kings, on Pharaoh and on those trusting in him.* The enemy, he is saying, will prevail over all together – the king, the rulers, the idols and the allies – but after being surrendered to the king of the Babylonians she will regain her former influence:[11]

After this she will be at peace as in her former life, says the Lord (v. 26). Next he foretells contentment also for Israel, and prophesies the return to Babylon. He predicts also the overthrow of Babylon. *Do not fear, my servant Jacob, says the Lord, because I am with you, because I shall bring to an end every nation where I shall lead you. But you I shall never cause to disappear, I shall correct you justly and shall not declare you innocent* (v. 28): I shall inflict healing correction on you (the meaning of *I shall correct you justly*) and I shall not let you pass as unstained (the meaning of *I shall not declare you innocent*).

Chapter Forty-Seven

At this point he directs the prophecy to the Philistines, by *Philistines* referring to the inhabitants of Ashkelon, Gaza, Ashdod, Gath and Ekron. Now, he says the prophecy had been delivered before the Pharaoh struck Gaza,[1] and he likens the Babylonian army to an overflowing torrent; the cities were overwhelmed by it, the inhabitants were destroyed and fell to wailing, unable to put up with the din of the weapons and chariots. He mentions that parents for fear were even unmindful of nature, and lost interest in their children: *Parents did not turn back for their children, so feeble their hands* (v. 3).

On the day that is coming for the destruction of all Philistines (v. 4). He foretells also destruction for the inhabitants of Tyre and Sidon for coming to their aid: (717) *I shall wipe out Tyre and Sidon and their remaining allies, because the Lord will annihilate the remaining Philistines from the island and Cappadocia*. In commentary on the other prophets we showed that settlers from Cyprus and Cappadocia formerly occupied Palestine.[2] *Baldness comes upon Gaza* (v. 5), that is, it will be bereft of its splendor; this often suggests grief as well: "Cut off your hair," remember, "and take up lament on your lips."[3] *Ashkelon is cast away and the rest of the Anakim*. Its descendants dwelt in the region of Ashkelon.[4] *How long will you be converted? How long will the sword of the Lord leave a mark?* (vv. 5-6) By *sword of the Lord* he referred to Nebuchadnezzar: it was with his permission that he did those things, and the impious had one another to blame for paying the price of impiety. *Put yourself into your scabbard, be at rest and uplifted.* And to make clear who it is who ordered the action, he went on, *The Lord gave it instructions to proceed against Ashkelon, against coast dwellers and against the remainder* (v. 7). He is using personification to bring out more clearly that instead of creation being ungoverned, its creator presides over everything, at one time supplying them with an abundance of good things, at another allowing them to fall foul of calamities.

Chapter Forty-Eight

The prophet switches the prophecy to Moab. *Thus said the Lord of Hosts, the God of Israel, to Moab, Alas for Nebo, because it is destroyed, it has been captured* (v. 1). It was an idol, and the prophet Isaiah mentions it, speaking this way, "Bel has fallen, Nebo been crushed."[1] It is also a city named after the idol. *Kiriathaim has been captured, Misgab has been shamed and defeated. There is no further healing, rejoicing in Heshbon* (vv. 1-2). They were famous cities of which the Moabites were proud. *They plotted evil against her, Come, let us let us cut her off from being a nation, and she will rest in repose.* Then he states that not even the fugitives will enjoy salvation. *A sword will come after you,* this clause suggesting the pursuers. (720)

Because there is a noise of those crying aloud from Horonaim (v. 3); it is another city. He says that Zoar also received bad news, and that the other cities were filled with lament. He bids them flee, and live in the wilderness like wild asses; and to instruct them not to trust in ramparts but in the incorruptible creator and Lord, he went on, *Because you trusted in your strongholds, trials will come upon you, and not only will you be taken by your enemies but also Chemosh will go into exile* – it was an idol of the Moabites – *its priests and its leaders with it. Destruction will come upon the whole city* (vv. 7-8). He says that the valley and the plain will undergo the same suffering.

He foretells also utter devastation by the enemy. *Give signals to Moab* (v. 9). By placing signs made out of stone in the desolate and completely deserted places, they will make a path, and by noticing them people will travel securely. *Because it will be set alight with kindling*, that is, it will be torched. *Its cities will become a trackless waste* to the extent of no one living there: *how could anyone live there?* In what follows the God of all bids this happen. *Cursed is the one who does the works of God carelessly, and cursed the one who withdraws his sword from blood* (v. 10). If the inspired word puts under a curse those slaughtering carelessly when God bids, what awful penalties shall we pay for making light of spiritual work?[2]

Moab took its rest from its youth, rested on its laurels, and did not pour from vessel to vessel (v. 11), that is, did not change its habitation or turn migrant. *It did not live in exile; hence it kept its taste, and its fragrance did not fail.* He persisted with the metaphor, and since he mentioned a *vessel*, he had to mention also *taste* and *fragrance*.[3] For this reason, he is saying, it continued in prosperity and did not experience misfortune, as though always living in the same places. *For this reason, lo, the days are coming, says the Lord, and I shall send it tilters, and they will tilt it, and empty its vessels, and smash its drinking horns* (v. 12). He expresses this in parabolic and figurative fashion: (721) he spoke of *tilting* in regard to a vessel in the sense of emptying: it will not be enough for them to take what is in the vessels – instead, they will also smash them. By *vessels* he refers to the cities, and by the contents of the vessels to their wealth: the enemy had created both, laid them waste and incinerated them. *Moab will be ashamed of Chemosh, as the house of Israel was ashamed of Bethel, their hope* (v. 13). Jeroboam set up the calf in Bethel;[4] so the inspired word explains that, just as Israel gained no help from the idols, so Moab got no benefit from Chemosh.

Then he presents them as glorying in their strength and suffering ruin, since the God of all ordered it. After mentioning that the time for retribution had come, he bids its neighbors stir it up to bravery and stimulate its former strength; and he urges them to say, *How is the famous scepter broken, the rod of magnificence?* (v. 17) These imply both your strength and your pride in your strength. He also lists the cities,[5] which once were splendid and famous, and he conveys the change in their prosperity and brings out the reason. *Make him drunk, because he grew in importance against the Lord* (v. 26), that is to say, when the Moabites learned of the fate of the Jews, they mocked them on the grounds of the weakness of the God of all. What follows also brings this out: *Moab will clap its hands,* that is, dance and rejoice. *It, too, will be a source of merriment.* Then more clearly, *Israel was truly a laughingstock for you: was it found in your secret places because you warred against it?* (v. 27) For what wrong inflicted, he is saying, did you completely subdue it? Did you come across burglars and robbers? *Because of it you will migrate,* that is, on account of the injustice done to it.

He mentions also their flight. *Those dwelling in Moab left the cities and occupied rocks, they became like doves nesting in rocks, in the mouth of a pit* (v. 28): they occupied caves on the summits, not withstanding the assault of the enemy. He calls it haughty, arrogant and overweening: *I was an eyewitness of this* (v. 30). And to bring out that experience of its actions belied the claims of its words, he went on, *Is not his reach beyond his grasp?* (724) *He did not go so far*: though full of bravado before the war and threatening to play the hero, it took to its heels on seeing the enemy. The Syriac rendered the phrase *shorn in squalor* (v. 31) as "their heads were shorn and their beards shaven;"[6] this is the appearance of captives, and the inspired word applies it also to Moab, *Lament for the men on the wall, shorn in squalor,* that is, for those once making use of walls and ramparts, and now shorn of their former prosperity and enveloped in squalor.

I shall weep for you like weeping for Jazer (v. 32). He recalled a certain story and implied the great amount of weeping.[7] *Vine of Sibmah, your branches crossed over the sea* (v. 32). It was a place of good and plentiful wine; so he likens the amplitude of the vine to the sea. He means its land was crossed and its vines destroyed. *Wine was in your winepresses; in the morning they did not tread them, nor in the evening did they do so* (v. 33). The Syriac rendered it this way, "No longer saying in the pressing, Ah, ah." Citing the same words *shorn in squalor,* he took them differently: *They will shave every beard in every place, and every beard will be shaved; all the hands will be cut, and sackcloth on all loins. On all the housetops of Moab and in its streets lamentation* (vv. 37-38). By all this he brings out the magnitude of the disaster. *Because I have smashed Moab like a jar, no good for anything, says the Lord.* He brought out its utter uselessness.

He shows clearly also the speed of Nebuchadnezzar. *The Lord says this, He will speed like an eagle, and extend his wings against Moab* (v. 40). The divinely-inspired Ezekiel also likens Nebuchadnezzar to an eagle;[8] it is a regal creature, the fastest and most powerful of all the birds. He foretells also Moab's fear, and likens its heart to the heart of a woman in labor. He also brings out its impiety. (725) *Moab will cease to be a populace, because it magnified itself against the Lord* (v. 42). He foretells also the successive troubles. *Fear, pit and snare are upon you who reside in Moab, says the Lord. The one fleeing before fear will fall into the pit, and the one climbing out of the pit will be taken in the snare* (vv. 43-44). He indicates in this that those taking to flight were captured and fell foul of what they did not want.[9] *Because I shall bring this upon Moab as in a year when I shall call it to account, says the Lord.* He refers to the time as a *year*. When I shall decide to punish them, he is saying, I shall envelop them in all these troubles.

He foretells their internecine warring as well. *Because fire has issued forth from Heshbon, and a flame from the city of Sihon, and destroyed leaders of Moab* (v. 45).[10] He foretells also some pleasant things for them. *I shall reverse the captivity of Moab in the last days, says the Lord* (v. 47). He revealed both through the retribution and through the lovingkindness that it is he who is Lord of all, enriching all those who call upon him, and that he is God not only of Jews but also of all people. *Thus far is the judgment on Moab*, that is, the verdict delivered against it.

Chapter Forty-Nine

The argument in the prophecy now switches to the people of Ammon, and the Lord of all says to them, *Has Israel no children, or is there no one to adopt them? Why has Milcom adopted Gilead, and its peoples settled in its cities?* (v. 1) The ten tribes occupied the region of Gilead; so when they were captured, the Ammonites took possession of it. God says to them, Was it the people you despised or me? By the one *adopting* – that is, taking over or assisting – he referred to himself. Now, Milcom was an idol of the people of Ammon. Do you believe, he is asking, that the thing which is not real prevails over me, who am ever in existence?

For this reason, lo, the days are coming, says the Lord, (728) *when I shall make the din of battles heard against Rabbah of the people of Ammon* (v. 2). Rabbah was a city of Arabia. The phrase *make to hear* means bring to their attention. *It will be a trackless waste and ruin; its altars will be consumed by fire and Israel will take control of them, says the Lord.* He continues foretelling the fate to befall the Ammonites. *Lament, Heshbon, because your force is destroyed; cry out, daughters of Rabbah, put on sackcloth, cut yourselves, run through the walls, because Milcom will go into exile, and his priests and his leaders likewise* (v. 3). He brought out also the weakness of the idols: they went off into captivity along with their worshipers.

Why do you rejoice in the plains of the Anakim?[1] *Your plains have been dissolved, daughter of ignominy* (v. 4). He accuses it of shamelessness and reliance on wealth, as the sequel also brings out, *You who trusted in your treasures and said, Who will come against me?* And since it heeded what it saw while in ignorance of the unseen God, he explains who is the one who punishes. *Lo, I bring fear upon you, said the Lord of Hosts, from all the neighborhood* (v. 5): from all sides come running those who report to you the enemies' army. *Each of you will be scattered headlong, with no one to collect the stragglers*: instead of fleeing all together, owing to the great degree of terror you will be scattered. But he also predicts a return for them lest Jews get conceited on the grounds of being the only ones to enjoy a return.[2]

He foretells disasters also for Idumea; and since they fancied themselves for wisdom, he says they will be deprived of it. *There is no wisdom in Teman, counsel has vanished from the clever* (v. 7). This was a city, and Eliphaz ruled it, Eliphaz being king of the Temanites.[3] *Its place has been trampled down. Lower yourselves and stoop, you dwellers of Dedan, because he imposed hardship; I brought it on him* (729) *at the time I called him to account* (v. 8). Dedan was another city; he bids them hide under the earth, the meaning of *lower yourselves and stoop*. He brings out that it is he who imposes the punishment; even if it happened in times past (he is saying), I exercised longsuffering. *Because grape-pickers came to you, and they will not leave gleanings* (v. 9). By *grape-pickers* he refers to the enemy, who he says rape and pillage everything. He also mentions the time of their assault. *Like thieves they will thrust their hand by night. Because I ravaged Esau, I exposed their secret things, they cannot remain hidden* (v. 10). There are large and lofty mountains in Idumea;

so by digging holes in them they took refuge in them when the enemy attacked, but their hope was frustrated, since the God of all betrayed them even there. *His offspring perished at the hand of his brother and his neighbor.* No respect was shown for nature or for proximity: Jacob and Esau were brothers and of course neighbors; no one else came between them.

There is no one to show mercy and leave your orphans behind to be saved – and shall I save them? (v. 11) On account of your great wickedness everyone is hostile to you, he is saying, and shall I, the just judge, prove your ally? *Let your widows trust in me.* He said this ironically, as the sequel shows. *Because thus says the Lord, Lo, those not obliged to drink the cup really drank it, and you though innocent will not be excepted* (v. 12): I oblige those living a life of impiety and wickedness to be punished; but both prophets and priests, Daniel and Ezekiel, were taken off to Babylon, and pious men, Hananiah, Azariah and Mishael, and probably most others, as history records. So they were not liable to punishment on account of virtue, but they became captives – and do you expect to escape? Instead, you will not attain your hope, *because you will really drink. Because I have sworn on myself, says the Lord, that you would be an object of destruction, reproach, ruin and curse. Bozrah in its midst and all its cities will be desolate forever* (v. 13). *Bozrah* means not this Bostra but another city located in Idumea.[4] (732)

I heard a report from the Lord, and he sent angels to the nations, Assemble, move against her and go into battle against her (v. 14). He used the phrase *he sent messengers to the nations* to mean "bade." It is also likely that by divine command ministering angels stirred up the enemy; the divine David also says, remember, "He sent forth on them wrath of his anger; anger, wrath and distress, a dispatch by means of wicked angels."[5] He calls them "wicked," not as such by nature, but as communicating punishment as a grace; we too are in the habit of calling calamities befalling us "evil." Likewise an angel wiped out the firstborn of the Egyptians,[6] likewise others were sent against Israel when David took a census of the people;[7] and there are many other such examples you could find in the divine Scripture.

Lo, I have made you insignificant among the nations, despicable among human beings (v. 15). Idumeans are, in fact, undistinguished; they would have been completely unknown had not the divine Scripture given them attention, drawing them to the attention not of everyone but of the studious. *Your deceitfulness entrusted you with this, and the dishonor of your heart* (v. 16). In this he charges them with idolatry, decadence and intemperance. *He lived in holes in rocks.* We mentioned previously the kinds of refuges they had. *He took over the strength of a high hill.* He means the summits; they are very big and high. *Because even if you elevate your nest as high as an eagle, I shall pull you down from there, says the Lord.*

Idumea will be a trackless waste (v. 17). He means that those traveling through it will marvel, and will indicate with a whistle the extent of the desolation; and that the cities mentioned would be like Sodom and Gomorrah and the other cities that shared their fate. The statement proved true: Dedan, Teman and Bosra are completely desolate.[8] He also says that the Babylonian will also advance against him like a lion, and will make his way by the Jordan; and he bids the picked troops be armed against it, adding, *Because who is like me? Who will resist me? Who is this shepherd who will stand up to me?* (v. 19) Neither the kings nor their idols will be able to resist when I give the word. *For this reason listen to the Lord's resolution which he formed against Idumea and the plan he had against the inhabitants* (733) *of Teman* (v. 20). He next says their sheep will be easily numbered and their land desolate, the sound of their lamentation will reach the Red Sea and dominate fortresses, the Idumeans will be seized with dread and pain, and their heart compared to a woman in labor.

Having at this point completed the prophecy about Idumea, he shifts his attention to Damascus in the words, *Hamath and Arpad are confounded because they heard bad news* (v. 23). As we remarked before, *Hamath* means Emesa; there is also another Hamath, which is now Epiphaneia.[9] Some say *Arpad* is what is now called Rephaneai. *They were stupefied by the sea, they were enraged, they could not rest* (by *sea* referring to the vast size of the army). He brought out also the first assault by Damascus, saying of them *they were enraged*. After that he accuses them of fear. *Damascus turned to water, it took to flight and was cast out, trembling seized it, and pangs gripped it like a woman in labor* (v. 24).[10] He brings out also the cause of the disaster. *How did he not abandon my cities, love my town?* (v. 25) He tried to take my cities and towns, he is saying. By his *cities and towns* he is referring to those of Israel: Damascus was always hostile to them. *Therefore your youth will fall in your streets, and all your warlike men will fall on that day, says the Lord of Hosts. I shall light a fire on the wall of Damascus, and it will consume the lane-ways of the son of Ader* (vv. 26-27). *Son of Ader* is a proper name, Baradad in the language of the Syrians; he was king of Damascus and, as the prophecy indicates, he adorned it with splendid buildings, which he threatens with incineration.

The prophet foretells calamities inflicted on the Ishmaelites as well, who are now called Saracens. *To Kedar, the queen of the court, whom Nebuchadnezzar king of Babylon struck, the Lord spoke thus* (v. 28). Kedar was one of the sons of Ishmael, and the Book of Creation informs us of this;[11] (736) at that time it probably controlled the other tribes – hence his referring to it as *queen*. By *court* he refers to the whole location of the Saracens: since they were nomads, they dwelt in tents. He bids them attack them, plunder their sheep and camels, and ravage their tents. Kedemah was also a son of Ishmael.[12] He bids them hide underground, saying as much, *Lower yourselves and stoop* (v. 30) so as to escape the enemies' assault.

Arise, go up against a well-resourced nation, residing in refreshment, says the Lord. It has no gates or bars, it lives alone

(v. 31). Victory is a simple matter for you, he is saying: you have no need of siege or blockade or length of time; they are vulnerable and easily taken. He brings out also that it is he who imposes the punishment. *I shall winnow with every wind those with shaven faces, and shall effect their overthrow from every border* (v. 32), in other words, they will be put to flight in every direction, both those settled towards the rising sun and those dwelling towards its setting. *The court will be a lair for jackals and a trackless waste forever. No mortal will settle there, nor any earthling dwell there* (v. 33). Events confirm the words: they left the totally deserted region and live close to occupied fortresses.

He prophesies also the fate of Elam, and indicated the time of the prophecy, saying it happened as soon as Zedekiah became king. *The Lord of Hosts says this, Lo, I shall break the bow of Elam, the basis of its power* (v. 35). Elam is a city situated at the mouth of the Red Sea;[13] in olden times it was a famous market, and today those sailing for the Indies set out from there. *I shall bring upon Elam four winds from the four quarters of heaven, and there will be no nation that will not come there* (v. 36). Having gained control of Egypt, the Babylonian advanced against it on his return, with an army already assembled from the northern and eastern regions, and a vast number of islanders who dwelt in the west also joined him; he gathered to himself as well Egyptians, Libyans and Ethiopians, who had been granted the more southerly region for settlement. This is what the inspired word prophesied. (737) *I shall terrify them at the sight of their enemies, those seeking their life, and I shall bring trouble upon them in keeping with the wrath of my anger, says the Lord, and I shall send my sword after them until it consumes them* (v. 37). Once again by *sword* he refers to the Babylonians: through them he brought them to account. *I shall set my throne in Elam, and destroy king and potentates from there, says the Lord* (v. 38). The phrase *I shall set my throne* means, I shall exercise justice there and deliver the verdict, employing the enemy as executioners. Now, he occupies the throne there at the present time, too, since this city is converted to piety; and so in connection with this verse, too, the prophecy is true.[14]

At the end of the ages I shall reverse the captivity of Elam, says the Lord (v. 39). In my view, the good Lord in this prophecy and in the others in which he promised the recall makes a pledge of liberation not only from physical captivity but also spiritual – the reason, surely, why he offers correction also to our bodies.[15] Accordingly, he foretells the destruction of the devil, the end of impiety and the freedom of people brought into captivity by sin. Let us who have attained this sing the praises of its author, love the life of freedom and abhor the former slavery so as also to stand with confidence before the Lord's tribunal, thanks to the grace and loving mercy of the just judge, to whom with the Father and the all-holy Spirit belong glory and magnificence, now and forever, for ages of ages. Amen.

Chapter Fifty

After prophesying what would happen to the other nations, he then forecasts the ruin of Babylon. *Announce to the nations, make it known and raise a sign, let it be heard* (740) *and do not conceal it; say, Babylon has been taken* (v. 2). Since the king of the Babylonians had overthrown the other kingdoms and forced them to serve under his control, he bids him declare to the nations its overthrow. *Bel is disgraced.* It was an idol much honored by the Babylonians; some call it Jupiter, others Kronos. He says it has been disgraced, firstly for being unable to help the worshipers, then for being completely deprived of people to honor it. *The undaunted, the effeminate.* He implied both their power and their luxurious way of life. *Merodach has been betrayed.* They called the first ruler of the Babylonians

Merodach. So here he is either mentioning the last ruler, under whom the overthrow of the kingdom occurred, or the first one, who shifted the kingship from Nineveh to Babylon.[1] You could apply the term *has been betrayed* to the second or to the first, referring to the kingdom in the case of the second; he means all the idols have been disgraced and their weakness made plain. *Nation* (v. 3) attacking *from the north* means the Medes;[2] they rendered their land desolate, he is saying, and laid waste to it.

At this time, he is saying, both the ten tribes and the two will recover their freedom, together they will return and flee to the Lord. *An everlasting covenant will not be forgotten* (v. 5), that is, the promise made to the ancestors. Then he likens them to lost sheep; the blame for the loss of the sheep he attributes to the shepherds, by *shepherds* (v. 6) referring not only to the kings but also to the priests. He also tells how they caused them to stray. *They drove them to the mountains, they misled them, they went from mountain to hill, they forgot their stall.* By *hills* and *mountains* he refers to the shrines of the idols, and by their *stall* to the divine Temple, as it was from there that they had enjoyment of good things. This error, he is saying, betrayed them to the enemy in return for the sins they committed against the Lord. *Pasture of righteousness to the one gathering their ancestors, the Lord* (v. 8). Blessed David also says, "We are his people, and sheep of his pasture."[3] He means this here, too: they were *pasture of righteousness to the Lord*, who chose their ancestors.

Separate yourselves from the middle of Babylon, and leave the land of the Chaldeans; be like young goats in front of sheep (v. 8) The Syriac rendered *young goats* as "male goats;" so he is bidding them get the better of the Babylonians, and occupy their homeland (741) – hence his comparison of them to male goats, the male goats being stronger than the sheep. Likewise the divinely-inspired Daniel had a vision of Alexander resembling a male goat, and Darius a ram.[4] He mentions also the vast number of those attacking Babylon and the fact that they would prevail and be filled with the good things stored there. He brings out also the cause of the troubles it endures. *Because you rejoiced and boasted of stealing my inheritance, and because you leaped like cattle on grass and tossed your horns like bulls. Their mother was disgraced* – namely, Babylon – *the mother who bore you was buried, for all the good she could do* (vv. 11-12), that is, she has disappeared.

This suggests the extent of the overthrow, as the sequel also brings out. *Behold, the last of the nations, desolate, desiccated. Because of the wrath of the Lord she will not be inhabited, and will be completely obliterated* (vv. 12-13). He says also that travelers will be aghast at the extremity of their suffering, indicating their astonishment with a hiss. He also bids the archers fire their arrows unsparingly, and seek vengeance for their impiety, *for they sinned against the Lord* (v. 14). He foretells also the fear of the Babylonians and the ruin of their ramparts, and supplies as well the cause of the calamity. *Because vengeance is from the Lord, take vengeance on her; as she did, so do to her. Eliminate the seed of Babylon that holds a scythe at harvest time* (vv. 15-16) – in other words, Put to death not only the fighters but also the farmers: this is what they themselves did when warring on Israel. *Each of them will return to their people in the face of a Greek sword, and each of them will flee to their own land* (v. 16). Cyrus overwhelmed the Lydians before Babylon, he subjected also the Ionians and Aeolians, and they migrated from Greece and settled in Asia; so Cyrus brought them as well and advanced on Babylon. It was not idly, of course, that the inspired word mentioned Greece;[5] instead, it was to bring out that it was a divine decree that assembled nations even from a great distance against Babylon.

Israel is an erring sheep (v. 17). The error of the idols was responsible for its troubles. *Lions drove it away*, referring thus to the kings of the Assyrians. *First the king of Assur devoured it* – Tiglath-pileser, Shalmaneser and Sennacherib,[6] and likewise later the king of Babylon Nebuchadnezzar devoured *its bones*, that is, the remains of the forefathers. For this reason, he is saying, I shall exact a penalty of them, and they shall suffer what Nineveh suffered, the former capital of the Assyrians. After punishing them, however, I shall bring Israel back to its ancestral land (referring to it as *Bashan, Carmel* and *mountain of Ephraim*). He foretells also a change for the better and freedom from the former error.

He next refers to the land of the Chaldeans as the *land of provocative people*, and to the enemy as a *sword* (v. 21), and he bids them advance on them and implement what was ordered by him. He calls the kingdom of the Babylonians a *hammer of the whole earth* (v. 23) for inflicting a blow on all the nations and destroying the other kingdoms, a hammer typically pulverizing what is struck by it. *The Lord opened his treasury and brought out the implements of his wrath, because there is a task for the Lord God of hosts in the land of the Chaldeans, because its time has come* (vv. 25-26). By *implements of wrath* he referred to the enemy, and by *its time* retribution. No longer, he is saying, will the Lord exercise lovingkindness; instead, he will wreak vengeance for impiety. Then to bring out that it is he who will inflict the retribution, he bids them search the storehouses, scatter everything and leave not a single trace of the former prosperity.

He predicts also those fleeing from there, the vast number of Jews, reaching Jerusalem and recounting the calamities besetting Babylon. Next, ordering her to suffer for what she has done, he says, *Repay her for her deeds* (v. 29); and after giving evidence of her rage against God, he directs these words to her. *Lo, I am against you, says the Lord of Hosts, against the wanton one* (v. 31). The accusation thus leveled hints at her arrogance against God, and suggests the lawlessness against all people. *Because the day of your fall has come and the time for your vengeance. Your pride will lose its force and fall, and there will be no one to raise it up. I shall set fire to its forest, and it will consume everything surrounding it* (vv. 31-32). *Forest* means the population, *the surroundings* the subjects, *failing pride* the overthrow of power. They will suffer this, he is saying, because they took my people off into captivity and refused to restore their freedom at the right time.

For this (745) reason he threatens to hand over to the enemy the city, its inhabitants, the oracles of false prophecy, those in the role of champions in it, those coming to its assistance, and the treasures stored up there. He threatens also to make its water dry up; by *water* (v. 38) he refers figuratively to the populace, and is probably forecasting what will happen to the water: while in former times the Euphrates cut the city in two, today the river has been turned back in the other direction, and the merest trickle flows between the ruins. By *islands* he refers to the city's houses, as though the water washed all around the rampart, and in turn the city had the river in its midst. By *images* he refers to likenesses of the demons, and the *daughters of sirens* (v. 39) the Syriac rendered as "ostriches," the normal way for the divine Scripture to refer to demons on account of their beguiling and deceiving human beings; both figures, of course, suggest desolation.[7] *It will never be rebuilt, and it will not be inhabited for generations of generations.* Both prophecies were fulfilled: far from being rebuilt, it has been bereft of ramparts to this day, and for long it remained uninhabited – the meaning of *for generations of generations* – and today it is only a few Jews who inhabit this land.[8] He likens it to Sodom and Gomorrah both on account of the former impiety and on account of the penalty imposed.

He gives a glimpse also of the enemies' armor, saying it is like a heaving sea and comparing their eagerness to fire. He says the hands of the Babylonians have gone limp with fear, and likens their pangs to a woman in labor. He brings out also that it is he who commands the Medes. *Who is like me? Who will resist me? Who is this shepherd who will stand before me?* (v.

44) Since he was called shepherd of Israel, and the kings of the Babylonians thought they could prevail over the God of all, he brings out that he personally imposes the punishment on them, having incomparable power. Then he orders that even the lambs of the sheep be destroyed and their pasture laid waste, by *lambs* referring to the infants and by *pasture* to the city and the land subject to it. Regarding the children, of course, blessed David also prophesies, "Blessed the one who takes hold of your babes and dashes them against the rock."[9] *Because at the sound of the capture of Babylon the earth will be shaken, and its cry heard among the nations* (v. 46). In other words, since the city was famous, report also of its misfortune sped in all directions. (748)

Chapter Fifty-One

He next refers to the enemy by various names. Firstly as *burning wind*: it normally destroys plants. Then as *wanton*, indicating by this the justice of the punishment: you will suffer what you have done (he is saying). After ordering them to show no mercy in venting their anger against them, he went on, *Because Israel and Judah have not been widowed by their God, by the Lord omnipotent, because their land was filled with lawlessness, by the holy ones of Israel* (v. 5): on account of their superstition and their lawlessness I ignored them; I did not completely deprive them of my care. *Babylon a golden cup in the hand of the Lord, inebriating all the land with its wine; nations drank it, nations staggered. Suddenly Babylon fell and was shattered* (vv. 7-8). In interpreting the dream, blessed Daniel said "the golden head" was the Babylonian himself,[1] and here he called *a golden cup* the punishment inflicted by him on the other nations. So he means that it both inflicted the punishment on the other nations and also suddenly against all expectations was captured and overthrown.

Then he tells the nations coming to her assistance, *Lament her, bring balm for her corruption in the hope of her being healed,* that is, apply remedies to assist her. The prophet also adopts a different point of view, and supplies the response from them. *We treated her, but she was not healed. Let us forsake her, and each of us return to our own land, because her judgment has approached heaven, and been lifted up even to the stars. The Lord delivered his judgment* (vv. 9-10). Blessed Isaiah also prophesied the Babylonian's conceit: "He said, I shall put my throne above the stars."[2] He identifies more clearly the one serving and the one bidding. *The Lord stirred up the spirit of the king of the Medes because his wrath was against Babylon to destroy it, because the Lord is vengeance, vengeance for his Temple, on the walls of Babylon* (vv. 11-12): what it perpetrated against the Temple I shall inflict on the ramparts of Babylon.

Next, in ironical fashion he bids the Babylonians station guards on the walls, arouse them and get their weapons ready; and to bring out that no benefit would accrue to them from it, he went on, *The Lord will execute whatever* (v. 749) *he said against the inhabitants of Babylon* – in other words, through the prophet he foretold its destruction. He says the Lord swore *by his right arm* (v. 14), that is, by his own power, adding as much, *He made the earth in his power, produced the world in his wisdom, stretched out the heavens in his understanding. He set a volume of water in the heavens for the sound of his voice to be heard, and brought clouds from the ends of the earth; he turned lightning flashes into rain, and brought light from his storehouse* (vv. 15-16).[3] He cited details of creation and details of his providence: not only did he make every single thing, but he also continues to govern it. The phrase *he set a volume of water in the heavens for the sound of his voice to be heard* brings out the crash of the thunder brought about through the clouds. He contrasts the limitations of the idols with the true teaching about God, and shows that they depend on the goldsmiths' skill and, being made by others, they are not capable even of breathing like the brute beasts. He foretells also their end. *At the time of their being called to account they will perish. The portion for Jacob is not like that, because the one who formed all things is his portion and Israel the rod of his inheritance; the Lord of Hosts is his name* (vv. 18-19): they are Babylon's gods, whereas the maker of all things is Israel's; so it is right that while the former are destroyed, the latter return home.

You scatter abroad for me implements of war, and I shall scatter abroad nations through you (v. 20). The Syriac rendered this, "Prepare for me implements of war," whereas according to the Greek version the sense is,[4] Since you used your weapons against my people, and fired arrows and spears against them, I too shall scatter abroad nations through you – which means, I shall scatter and put to flight the nations that came to your aid, the horses, their riders, of every age and each sex, rulers and ruled, pastors and farmers. You will suffer what you committed against Zion. *Lo, I come against you, corrupt mountain, says the Lord, corrupting the whole earth* (v. 25).[5] He calls it *mountain* on account of the notoriety of its power, and *corrupt* on account of its being impious and lawless. *I shall extend my hand against you, and roll you down from the rocks,* that is, (752) show you humbled. *I shall make you a burned up mountain,* in other words, completely useless, as emerges from the sequel. *They will not take from you a stone for the corner or a stone for the foundation, because you will be a waste forever, says the Lord* (v. 26). They appointed no king or ruler from the new inhabitants; foundations support the building, and cornerstones bind it together.

Raise a signal on the land, blow a trumpet among the nations. Consecrate – that is, set apart – *nations against her, summon against her kingdoms of Ararat from me and the Ashkenazi* (v. 27). By *Ararat* he refers to Armenia, and by *Ashkenazi* a different race bordering them.[6] The king of Persians and Medes assembled them all, as the sequel goes on to say, *Consecrate nations against her, the king of the Medes, his generals and all his troops* (v. 28). He mentions also the earth shaking *because the Lord's plan against Babylon has gone into effect to turn the land of Babylon into a waste and prevent it being inhabited* (v. 29). He foretells also the siege, the burning of the city, and those reporting its capture to the king. He compares the destruction of the buildings to a threshing floor trodden down and a mature harvest.

He divided me, he consumed me, he took possession of me like a fine gloom, Nebuchadnezzar king of Babylon (v. 34). The finest air penetrates our bodies further; so he means, The gloom of calamity filled even the limbs of my soul. *He turned me into an empty vessel and drank me like a dragon, he filled his belly with my daintiness.* He stripped me of all my good things, he is saying, and resembled a dragon in consuming sparrows' nests, taking all my wealth and depriving me of prosperity. He brings out that its lawlessness rendered it weak and the enemy strong. *My labors and my hardships drove me out to Babylon, Zion will say while in possession, and my blood to the inhabitants of Chaldea, Jerusalem will say* (v. 35): my blood will be avenged on them, and they will pay the penalty for their crimes (753) against me. In this way the prophet brings out the fate of Jerusalem and the just sentence imposed by God. *Hence the Lord says this, Lo, I shall judge your opponent and exercise your vengeance* (v. 36) since you know the harm coming from sin. *I shall leave her sea desolate*, that is, the multitude of subjects. *I shall dry up her fountain*, the kingdom and the power over everyone. Next he mentions the things characteristic of wilderness, which we have spoken of frequently. *It will not be inhabited at the same time.* Today it has few houses, and these scattered. He likens its champions to lions, and foretells both their dread and their defeat. *I shall give them a drink and intoxicate them so that they will get drunk and sleep an everlasting sleep and not wake, says the Lord. I shall bring them down like lambs to the slaughter and like rams with young goats* (vv. 39-40), rulers and ruled, subjects along with the king; by *lambs* and *young goats* he refers to subjects, and by *rams* to the rulers.

How Sheshach has been captured, the boast of all the earth taken (v. 41). This is the way he refers to Babylon: he called its king Sheshach in what was commented on before. It was normal in olden times for it to be given this name, and the name was changed to Babylon; what follows confirms that he is referring to the city in this way.[7] *How Babylon has become a wasteland among all the nations. The sea has risen up to Babylon, by the sound of its waves it has been overwhelmed* (vv. 41-42). Next, after foretelling its devastation, he once more focuses attention on Bel. *I shall take vengeance on Bel in Babylon, and expel from its mouth what it has swallowed; the nations will no longer come in assembly to it* (v. 44). Daniel also mentions the food offered it, and how the priests consumed it.[8]

The inspired word also foretells the end of the error; it consoles the people and bids them not to fear the impending troubles for Babylon, and explains that they had been reported much earlier. (756) *The report will arrive in the same year, and in the year after it the report and the injustice in the land: authority upon authority, and proverb upon proverb* (v. 46). In other words, despite word of the enemy a year or two before the attack, they persisted in wrongdoing and their usual lawlessness. This is the real reason that he threatens with destruction the images being worshiped and their worshipers, and says all creation is rejoicing at its overthrow. He brings out also the justice of the retribution.[9] *And of course in Babylon so that Israel's wounded may fall in it* (v. 49a). So those in Babylon, wounded by all the earth, will fall: what it did to Israel it will suffer from others.[10]

You who are returning from the land, advance, do not linger; remember the Lord, you who come from afar (v. 50). To the Jews in captivity he says, *Let Jerusalem come into your heart*: do not forget the city dedicated to God. Then on their part, *We are ashamed because we heard our reproaches; dishonor covered our face. Foreigners entered our holy places, the Lord's house* (v. 51).

With these people grieving in this way, the Lord went on, *Lo, the days are coming, says the Lord, and I shall take vengeance on its images, and in all its land wounded will fall. Because even if Babylon rises like heaven, and even if it fortifies the height of its strength, there will come from me those to destroy it, says the Lord* (vv. 52-53). It has great and very high walls; so the Lord God emphasizes that they will gain no benefit from that since he delivers his verdict against them. To the divine verdict he links the outcome, saying, *Sound of a cry in Babylon, and a great crash in the land of the Chaldeans. Because the Lord overthrew Babylon, and put a stop to the sound coming from her that rang like many waters* (vv. 54-55). In this he indicated the vast number of the inhabitants, and says no good came from bows or spears when God brought her to account. In fact, in addition to the generals and the champions *its mighty wall will be brought down and its lofty gates will become waste for the fire* (v. 58).[11]

Having thus made this prediction, he brings out that he wrote down this prophecy in the fourth year of the reign of Zedekiah under God's direction. He gave the book to (757) Seraiah, who was sent by Zedekiah to Babylon. He urged him to read this book aloud in Babylon and say, *Lord, you made a threat against this place to destroy it and not leave anyone in it, man or beast, because it will be a wasteland forever* (v. 62). After making this prayer, he says, tying the book to a stone and throwing it in the Euphrates, you will say, *Thus will Babylon be submerged and never arise in the face of the troubles that I inflict upon it* (v. 64). The Lord ordered this to happen as comfort for the captives so that they might learn of its capture and their own release, and thus have the hope of good things for consolation.

Chapter Fifty-Two

While the prophecy came to an end at this point,[1] therefore, the sequel proceeds in a more narrative vein, bringing out how Zedekiah became king, that he continued to act lawlessly, that in the ninth year of his reign Nebuchadnezzar advanced against him and conducted a siege on Jerusalem until the eleventh year, raising another wall from the outside with large stones, and how those inside were oppressed by famine worse than by the enemy. It recounts that when the wall fell, the powerful along with the king took to flight by night, that the Chaldeans pursued and overtook them, taking them off to Riblah and presenting them to Nebuchadnezzar, who charged Zedekiah with breaking his oath; first he slew his sons, then the leaders, and following that bitter spectacle he put out the king's eyes, put him in fetters, took him off to Babylon and put him in a mill.

It recounts how Nebuzaradan was sent by Nebuchadnezzar and set fire to the divine Temple and in addition to it the palace and the city's splendid buildings, and leveled the town's ramparts. He took off all the rest to Riblah, leaving some few of the poor to farm the land.[2] The huge bronze pillars that Solomon had erected and the bronze sea he melted down and carried off to Babylon along with the pots and shovels (the Syriac rendering *pots* as "foot-washing bowls"), and the other vessels he took off with them (by *sapphoth* referring to the spits). He recounts how the king of the Babylonians slew the first priest, the second and those taken off with them, and mentions (759) the number of the captives deported.[3] In addition to this he describes how after thirty-seven years of the captivity of Jeconiah (calling him Jehoiachin) King Evilmerodach released this same Jeconiah from prison, showed him benevolence, granted him a royal throne, bade him be seated as king ahead of the others and invited him to his table, supplying him generously with daily necessities.

Now, this proclaims the Lord's lovingkindness: in punishing he is merciful, in applying correction he consoles, and the justice of his verdict he tempers with lovingkindness.[4] Accordingly, let us fear the justice of his judgment, and relying on his lovingkindness let us not despair of salvation, but look forward to divine mercy and travel the straight and narrow so as to reach the blessed end, in Christ Jesus our Lord, to whom with the Father and the all-holy Spirit be the glory, now and forever, for ages of ages. Amen.

The Blessed Theodoret
Bishop of Cyrus

Commentary on the Book of the Prophet Baruch[1]

Chapter One

While the remarkable Baruch took his leave for Egypt in the company of the fugitive Jews, as we reported in what preceded, yet five years after the taking of the city he reached Babylon. The devout, in fact, displayed complete zeal in supporting the weak and leading them to the truth. On reaching Babylon, then, he read out the prophecy of the divine Jeremiah to all the captives, and of course to Jeconiah as well, who had become a captive after reigning a short time. He did not fail in his purpose: he brought them to a sense of their former sins with the result that they even admitted the cause of the calamity, shed many tears, contributed money individually, and dispatched it to the priests left in Jerusalem (761) to buy victims, sacrifice them and propitiate the Lord God (by *manna* the Hebrews referring to sacrifice). They pray for life for Nebuchadnezzar and his son Belshazzar.[2] The divine apostle likewise also required prayers for the kings still hostile to true religion and for those in high office and authority – such being the close harmony between the Old and the New.[3] They also pray for those forced into service to have their eyes enlightened lest they suffer any deceit; they also recall their former sins and admit the justice of the divine sentence.

They also urge that this letter of theirs be read out to God on the major festivals.[4] *You will say, To the Lord our God belongs righteousness, whereas to us the shame on our countenance, as it is this day to everyone in Judah, the inhabitants of Jerusalem, our leaders and our priests in the sight of God* (vv. 15-16): most just is the sentence of God delivered against us; we deserve shame, all in common having transgressed; along with the kings, note, the priests also took the wrong path.[5] *Because we disobeyed him and did not listen to the voice of the Lord our God so as to be guided by the statutes of the Lord that he set before us* (vv. 17-18). They recall also the past. *In fact, from the time when our fathers were freed from the slavery of the Egyptians to this day, we persisted in breaking the divine Law, and we showed our negligence in not listening to his voice* (v. 19). The verb *showed negligence* means "devised forms of sin," blessed Paul referring to such people as "inventors of vices;"[6] we reaped the fruits of our sins, he is saying. *The troubles have stuck fast to us, and the curse which the Lord prescribed to Moses his servant* (v. 20). The Law includes curses and blessings – blessings for those keeping it, curses for those breaking it.[7]

Chapter Two

They mention how they also scorned the prophets sent to them by God and the fact that what was prophesied by them was fulfilled. *He brought on us awful troubles which were not wreaked under all of heaven* (764) *as he wreaked them in Jerusalem* (v. 2). To bring out that even these were prophesied, they went on, *according to what was written in the Law of Moses. The result was that some people ate the flesh of their son, and some the flesh of their daughter* (v. 3): the siege caused famine, which forced them to feed on human bodies. We became an object of glee, he is saying, even to the neighboring nations. *We were brought down and not raised up* (v. 5), that is, made slaves and not masters. They then supply the cause. *Because we sinned against the Lord our God by not heeding his voice.* Once again they attribute justice to the divine verdict, and attribute shame to themselves: Despite God's frequent threats and his prophesying this through the prophets, we did not come to the Eternal in our days, instead continuing to resist. *The Lord was not tardy in inflicting evils upon us* (v. 9), by *was not tardy* referring to punishment: it is customary with the divine Scripture to refer to his longsuffering by "sleeping."[1] All the same, they once again make mention of the punishment and call the Lord just: he punished them when they had transgressed and were unwilling to be healed.

Next, they make supplication with loud cries, and call to mind the former liberation which their fathers experienced in being freed from the harsh slavery of the Egyptians. They recall also the wonders worked, and put forward their own failings, crying aloud, *We have sinned, we have been ungodly, we have done wrong, Lord our God, despite all your ordinances* (v. 12): we broke all of your commandments, we trampled on every law. *Let your anger turn away from us, because we now remain few after being many among the nations where you scattered us* (v. 13). We admit the justice of the punishment, but we beg you to halt it; formerly compared to sand, we have been reduced to a few. *Hearken to our prayer, O Lord, and to our request, and deliver us for your sake* (v. 14): we are not worthy, but you are loving; we are also styled your people. For this reason, surely, we shall receive pardon. *And grant us favor in the sight of those who have deported us* so that instead of hating us, they may let us go. *So that all the earth may know that you are the Lord our God, and that your name is borne by Israel and his descendants* (v. 15): a change in our ill fortune will prove an occasion of reverence in the others, (765) as they will learn the might of our God.

Lord, look down from your holy dwelling, and be mindful of us (v. 16). By *holy dwelling* he refers to the one in Jerusalem: in it he manifested himself.[2] *Incline your ear, Lord, and listen. Open your eyes and see* (vv. 16-17). People suffering abuse normally close their eyes when the wrongdoers are seen, and avert the pupils when the abusers call to them; so he expressed this in human fashion: the divinity is not composite but simple and uncircumscribed.[3] To this remark he adds, *because the dead are not in a position to sing your praises*, this belonging to the living instead. *The soul in grief goes on to greatness, a spirit bowed and infirm, with eyes failing, and a soul hungering will give you glory and righteousness, Lord* (v. 18): those encountering the worst calamities and despairing of better days, and then enjoying a reversal of fortunes, sing the praises of your lovingkindness sincerely.

Then they say, *Because it is not through reliance on the ancestors or on our own righteousness that we beg to obtain some mercy* (v. 19): we deserve the troubles threatened through the prophets; they urged us to accept the chastisement from your righteous judgment and serve the king of Babylon, but we continued to resist. You have fulfilled, Lord, all you predicted through them: it is not only that we the living are consigned to slavery, but also the tombs of our ancestors, and of course the kings as well, are uprooted, for their bones to be exposed to the elements and destroyed by the extremes of the weather. *They perished from awful hardships, from famine, from the sword, from banishment* (v. 25): not only did you give us up to famine, slaughter and slavery (by *banishment* referring to captivity), but the Temple, which had been famous and celebrated on account of your name, you rendered desolate.[4]

All the same, instead of inflicting this to the extent that our impiety deserved, you tempered justice with lovingkindness. *You treated us, Lord our God, with all fairness and with all your great compassion* (v. 27). They recall also the threats written in the Law; in particular he foretold in the song the troubles that would befall them, "I shall send against them teeth of wild beasts;" (768) and to show that by "wild beasts" it refers to the enemy, it went on, "Outside the sword will render them childless, and in the privacy of home there will be fear;" and again, "I shall scatter them."[5] They call to mind these threats, and they call to mind as well the promise of good things: You pledged (they say) to extend mercy to the repentant, to liberate them from captivity and to restore their former freedom.

Chapter Three

Lord almighty, the God of Israel, a soul in torment and a feeble spirit cried to you (v. 1): my eyes are on the awful extent of the calamities and the magnitude of the discouragement. *Hear, O Lord, and have mercy, because you are a merciful God; have mercy, because we have sinned in your sight* (v. 2): you have an ocean of love, you have depths of mercy, extend it to those asking for it, because mercy is due to sinners who are also repentant. *Because you are enthroned forever, and we are perishing forever* (v. 3): you are eternal, we are temporary; you are not subject to time or destruction, our life is limited by a small measure (using *enthroned forever* to this effect).

Lord almighty, the God of Israel, listen to the prayer of the dead of Israel (v. 4). The verse clearly brought out the immortality of the soul.[1] *And the children, who sinned in your sight.* His meaning is: You said, "The teeth of those eating the sour grapes were set on edge;"[2] so have an eye to the youngsters free from sin, and do not remember the sins of the ancestors. *Instead, remember your hand and your name at this time* (v. 5): exercise your customary wonderworking, and as you led us out of Egypt, so free us from Babylon. *Because you are the Lord our God* (v. 6): because you are what you are, and have undergone no change; you have the same power, the same lovingkindness. *We shall praise you, Lord, because you have put your fear into our heart for this reason, for your name to be invoked* (vv. 6-7). He brought out the benefit of punishment, saying, After being corrected we were converted. *And we shall praise you in our exile, because we put away all the iniquity in our heart of our fathers, who sinned in your sight*: we shall not follow our fathers, nor travel by their instructions; instead, we shall follow your laws. Consider our insults, therefore, and the harsh servitude we endure on account of our impiety and the ancestral lawlessness.

This is the people's prayer that the remarkable Baruch put into writing. He also cites the divine response. (769) *Listen, Israel, to commandments of life, give your ear to learn good sense. Why is it, Israel, why is it you are in the land of your foes? You have grown old in a foreign land, you are defiled with corpses, you are numbered with those in Hades* (vv. 9-11). What is unusual in this, he is saying, what is surprising? After being styled my people, famous, celebrated, you are slave and not free, living amongst foreign and impious men, and resembling corpses on account of the extent of the troubles. Then he brings out the reason for them. *You forsook the fountain of wisdom. If you had walked in the way of God, you would have dwelt in peace forever* (vv. 12-13): you became the source of the present troubles for yourself; though you should have used the Law as a guide, with which the fountain of wisdom provided you, you followed futile reasonings.[3]

Learn where it is that good sense lies, wherein lies power, wherein lies understanding, so as to know at the same time where there is length of days and life, where is light for the eyes, and peace (v. 14): now at any rate, if not beforehand, search and find out who is the source of these good things. *Who found her place, and who entered her treasuries* (of good sense, that is)? (v. 15) *Where are the rulers of the nations, those who lord it over the wild beasts on the earth, those who amuse themselves with the birds of heaven, who store up silver and gold, on which people rely and there is no end to their acquisition, who worked with silver, going to great trouble without any trace surviving of their works?* (vv. 16-18). Piety he contrasts with wealth and power, and bids them remember the most lawless kings, who could not get enough wealth. These people, he says, controlled both beasts and birds through the skill of the hunter.

He also describes their end. *They were annihilated and went down to Hades, and others rose up in their place. New arrivals saw the light and dwelt on the earth, but they did not know the way of knowledge, did not understand its paths or grasp it* (v. 19-20): they were also given over to corruption, their descendants were numbered with them when they were alive, and they shared the brightness of the light of the senses; but they did not enjoy the rays of understanding and the knowledge of God. He also lists the Canaanites, Idumeans and Ishmaelites among those boasting of wisdom, *Teman* (v. 22) being Idumea and *Hagar* (v. 23) the mother of Ishmael; (772) he refers to them as *storytellers* because they normally spoke in proverbs. Nevertheless they had no knowledge of the way of wisdom, either; they continued to be in thrall to impiety. *O Israel, how great is the house of God, and how vast the place he possesses! Mighty and boundless, lofty and immeasurable* (vv. 24-25). Do not think, he is saying, that the temple of God is the one Solomon built: God's temple is a mighty thing, immeasurable and at the same time indestructible, having no end. He next mentions the giants, celebrated for their bodily stature, and goes on, *God did not choose them or give them the way of knowledge. They perished through their senselessness* (vv. 27-28).

He conducted this survey, of course, in his wish to demonstrate that he gave them pride of place ahead of all the nations, to them alone he gave a Law in writing and appointed prophets, and vouchsafed them complete attention, and later of course he actually came to them by becoming man – something he indicates in developing what follows.[4] *Who has ever ascended to heaven, taken her* – wisdom, that is – *and brought her down from the clouds? Who ever crossed the sea, discovered her and will buy her for pure gold?* (vv. 29-30) She is not for sale, he is saying, and not simply available to merchants. *No one knows her way, or ponders her path* (v. 31): she surpasses human reasoning. *But the one who knows all things knows her, and in his understanding he sought her out* (v. 32). He used the phrase *sought her out* in human fashion, referring to him as the *fountain of wisdom*, and in the beginning of this work he called him fountain of life.[5]

In what follows he brings out the manifold power of the creative action of God, *who formed the earth for all the age and filled it with four-footed beasts* (v. 32), the present life of human beings referred to by *age*, whereas the future is ages of ages. *Who sent the light and it goes forth, he summoned it and it hearkened to him in trembling. The stars shone in their watches, and were glad; he summoned them and they replied, We are here; they gladly shone for the one who made them* (vv. 33-34). Everything yields to its maker, he is saying; each thing that is made observes its proper (773) limits (by *watches of the stars* referring to the times: each rises at its set time). *This is our God* (v. 35), creator of all, their guide and governor. *No other will be reckoned with him*. Far from comparing Father and Son, the verse is rejecting the so-called gods. *He sought the whole way of knowledge* (v. 36). Again he used *sought out* in human fashion; after all, he is the fount of good things.[6] *He gave her to his servant Jacob, and to Israel, beloved by him*, instruction in the knowledge of God, the Law given through Moses. *After this she appeared on earth, and lived with human beings* (v. 37). The verse gives a clear reference to the incarnation of the only-begotten and to the fact that he is creator of all and fountain of wisdom. He is therefore also its creator and lord; of him it says in Proverbs, "The Lord created me as the beginning of ways in his work:"[7] it is not God the Word who says this, but the wisdom of God the Word developed by him.

Chapter Four

She is the book of the commandments of God (v. 1), that is, the one given through the incarnation of the only begotten Son of God. *The Law that lasts forever*: the old covenant came to an end.[1] *All who gain possession of her will attain life, those forsaking her will die.* He made clear the end awaiting each. He then exhorts the people who bear the name Jacob. *Turn back, Jacob, and lay hold of her, move towards the brightness coming from her light* (v. 2): follow the radiance of her beam; it will enlighten you and guide you to life. *Do not give your glory to another, or your advantages to a foreign nation* (v. 3). Israel did not listen, however; hence they were isolated from the good things, while the nations enjoy the God-given benefits. *We are blessed, Israel, because what is pleasing to God is known to us* (v. 4): we do not have the excuse of ignorance, for he revealed to us what is pleasing.

He then encourages them and explains that they were consigned to slavery at that time, not that the God of all had completely rejected them, but because he endeavored to benefit them through correction. In fact, your benefactor you abandoned, he is saying, you gave preference to the worship of the demons, and thus became responsible for the devastation of the city that nourished you. By the use of personification he portrays the city in mourning, saying to her subject (776) cities, *The Lord inflicted bitter sorrow upon me* (v. 9): I saw some of the inhabitants wiped out, others given over to harsh slavery. *Let no one rejoice over me, a widow bereft of many* (v. 12). He calls her a *widow* for being deprived of divine care. *I was left desolate because of the sins of my children*, which he lists, and describes the cruelty of the enemy. *They had no respect for the aged or mercy on the young. They took off the widow's loved ones, and left the lonely woman bereft of her daughters* (vv. 15-16). She calls herself *lonely*, in my view, because in her alone was the Temple of God, or perhaps because she was left to herself when the Assyrians sacked the other cities.[2]

He then says that she cannot offer assistance, but promises God's help. All the same, she laments the present desolation. *For I have been left desolate. I have taken off the robe of peace* (vv. 19-20). He also brings out the change in those left behind. *I put on the sackcloth of my supplication, and I shall cry aloud.* It was not the walls that did and said this, but the inhabitants. Then he urges them to trust in God's lovingkindness and beg for mercy. And I await your return, he says. *I sent you out with sorrow and weeping, but God will restore you to me with gladness and joy* (v. 23). This resembles what was said by blessed David, "They went on their way and wept, casting their seed; coming back they will come in rejoicing, carrying their sheaves."[3] He mentions also the satisfaction of the neighboring nations at their captivity and their disappointment after the return. He urges them to endure the correction that was imposed, and promises the change in fortunes. *Your foe persecuted you, and you will rapidly see his ruin and will trample on his neck* (v. 25), referring by *foe* to Idumeans, Moabites, Ammonites and Philistines. *My spoiled people traveled ways of harshness; they were taken off like a flock stolen by a foe* (v. 26). By *spoiled people* he refers to those enjoying prosperity and wealth for having no experience of hardship.

He next urges them to reap salvation through repentance. Having spoken this on the part of Jerusalem, (777) he now offers encouraging words to her. *Take heart, Jerusalem, he who named you will console you* (v. 30): he has agreed on a change for the better for you; the one who gave you your name – that is, your creator, who esteemed you ahead of any other city – will transform your calamity. *Wretched those who abused you and rejoiced in your downfall; wretched the cities to whom your children were enslaved* (vv. 31-32). In fact, Babylonians paid a penalty befitting their lawlessness. He next explains that Babylon will eventually lament her own troubles. *I shall strip away her joy in her huge population, and her pride will be turned into sorrow: fire will come upon her from the Eternal for days upon end, and she will be inhabited by demons for a long time* (vv. 34-35). She sustained this retribution under the Persians. The verse brought out that he forecast that it would be uninhabited, not completely but *for a long time*: today it is inhabited by a few Jews.[4]

Lift your gaze to the east, Jerusalem, and see your joy coming to you from God (v. 36). He forecasts the return of the captives. *Lo, your children whom you sent away are coming back; they come, gathered from east to west, at the word of the Holy One, rejoicing in the glory of God* (v. 37): it was not by their own power that they prevailed over the enemy; instead, the God who surrendered them has restored their freedom.

Chapter Five

He bids her take off the garment of mourning and clothe herself in the vesture of priesthood. *Dress yourself in the double cloak of righteousness from God, and put on your head the miter of the glory of the Eternal* (v. 2). On the miter, you see, was gold leaf on which was inscribed the name of God.[1] *For God will reveal your splendor everywhere under heaven: the name given you by God will be forever Peace of Righteousness and Glory of Piety* (vv. 3-4). She has these names today; hence all betake themselves to her, the saving passion having made her illustrious and famous.

Again he urges her to see the captives returning from east and west, and explains that as they were led off in shackles, they will come back regaled with every honor. It should be recognized, of course, that when they returned from Babylon, those who had fled in time of war to west and south left those parts at that time when peace was granted to the nation and came back – hence his mention of those *from the west* (v. 5).[2]

For God ordered that every high mountain and everlasting

mounds be lowered, and valleys be filled in to be level with the earth for Israel to walk safely in the glory of God (v. 7). He put an end to all difficulty, he is saying: he overthrew Babylonians, who seemed like high mountains, and caused those subject to them, like deep valleys, to rise up; from every direction there was ease of return. *Shady forests and every tree became a fragrance for Israel at God's command* (v. 8). This resembles what was said by David, "The mountains skipped like rams, the hills like lambs of sheep."[3] So by *forests* he refers to the nations located in between which did not offer a fruit of piety to God; nonetheless, as Israel returned, they escorted them with full attention.

He mentions also the cause of the good things. *For God will lead Israel with joy in the light of his glory with mercy and righteousness that come from him* (v. 9): with God leading, everything was smooth and level. He uses *mercy* in respect of the people, *righteousness* against the Babylonians: the former, though sinners, gained benefit through correction, whereas victory made the latter more frenzied and impious. Accordingly, let us also beseech the God of all to be our leader and guide so that we may travel by the light of his countenance, according to the Davidic song,[4] not straying to right or left but treading the royal way that leads to life. May it be our good fortune to attain this by the grace and lovingkindness of our Lord Jesus Christ, to whom with the Father and the all-holy Spirit be the glory, now and forever, for ages of ages. Amen.[5]

The Blessed Theodoret
Bishop of Cyrus

Commentary on the Book of Lamentations[1]

Chapter One

While lament is a sign of sympathy and affection, it is my view that the divinely-inspired prophet (781) wrote Lamentations for the benefit not only of the people of that time but also of those to come later, so that both former and latter might learn through the text what evils sin is responsible for.[2] Now, he wrote four lamentations,[3] composing the words of each according to both the number and order of the elements. He laments the desolation of the city, recalling the formerly vast number of the inhabitants and seeing the resentment of the city that once was in receipt of tribute from the other cities. With the use of personification he says the city weeps night and day, there being no one to console her, and her friends disowning her. He brings to the fore also the deportation of the whole of Judah and its harsh slavery, and says they proved vulnerable on account of sin: *all her pursuers overtook her in the midst of her oppressors* (v. 3). He reminds her also of roads which at the time of the festivals resembled rivers: from all directions everyone came in haste to the city, and he laments. Those in anguish, in fact, have the impression that even inanimate things undergo change.[4]

He mentions also the reason for it. *Her oppressors gained control, and her enemies prosper, because the Lord humbled her to the extent of her impiety* (v. 5). Blessed Moses also predicted this for them when they transgressed the divine Law: "The enemy will be on high, and you will be below," also saying that destruction will come to sucklings along with the elders, "Suckling along with one in old age."[5] Likewise here too: *Her infants have gone off in captivity in the sight of the oppressor*. He describes how it is stripped of its former comeliness, and he likens the leaders to rams deprived of their pasture: they are bereft of their former might. He next says Jerusalem remembers her former prosperity and misfortune, and compares to them the troubles that have now befallen; she suffers more from the pleasure it gives to the adversaries.

He constantly brings out the reason for the calamities, anxious to bring some good from it. *Jerusalem committed sin, hence she has been made to totter* (v. 8). For this reason those who formerly reverenced her mocked her on perceiving her misfortune. He next calls to mind her manifold sins. *Her impurity was before her feet, she did not advert to her end, and her fall was* (784) *astounding* (v. 9): instead of trusting in her prosperity, she should even have expected a change. So since no human being is offering her comfort, he is saying, you, O Lord, behold her miserable lot and have pity.

He laments particularly the adversaries' daring to enter the sacred precincts, and says, *The oppressor extended his hand to all her precious things; she saw nations entering her holy places, though you forbade them to enter your assembly* (v. 10). Whereas the high priest alone was permitted to enter the Holy of Holies, and this in fact but once a year, the priests alone entered the holy places in front of them, the Levites the inner court, and the outer court those of the race of Israel and the circumcised proselytes, the Law preventing anyone uncircumcised entering even that area. It actually forbade Moabites and Ammonites in particular from entering: "No Ammonite or Moabite shall enter the assembly of the Lord, now or ever."[6] It is this law the lament recalled.

He then describes the troubles besetting her from famine.

All her people groaning in their search for bread; they gave their precious possessions for food to revive their spirits (v. 11). By *precious possessions* here he refers to the infants: they even tasted human flesh out of hunger.[7] He begs for divine lovingkindness, *Look, Lord, and take note that I am dishonored.* Then he invites everyone passing through her to witness her incomparable pain: the Lord inflicted this on me (he is saying) *speaking through me* (v. 12), that is, he simply gave the order and the troubles befell me (the Syriac rendering the phrase *he scarified me* as "he cooked me").[8] He describes also the blow directed at her from God. *From his eyrie he dispatched fire into my bones, and brought it down on me* (v. 13): it was he who allowed the enemy to besiege, ravage and burn the city. *He spread a net for my feet, he turned me back, he left me devastated, in grief all day long.* By *net* he refers to the inescapable nature of the troubles: those who took to flight were captured.

He brings out also the justice of the retribution. *My impiety did not escape him, he entwined me in his hands* (v. 14), that is, he bound me hand and foot, and handed me over to the foe. *He loaded the yoke onto my neck*: he harshly obliged me to serve the savage Babylonians. *My strength failed because the Lord* (785) *entrusted me with pains I cannot sustain.* He deplores also the loss of the stalwarts. *He took away all my men of strength; the Lord called down on me a time for crushing my chosen ones* (v. 15). By *time* both the Syriac and the Hebrew mean "calamity:" we are usually in the habit of deploring the difficulties of the times. *The Lord trampled the wine vat with the virgin daughter Judah. For these things I weep* (vv. 15-16). Frequently the divine Scripture likens the worst punishment to a wine vat[9] on account of all the bunches of grapes being crushed in the wine vats so that not a single grape escapes. *My eyes shed tears because the one consoling me is away from me.* And to bring out who it is, he went on, *the one reviving my spirits* – in other words, this is the reason he applied correction, to bring about benefit for my soul. He also laments the loss of the children and the control of the enemy.

He brings out also the appearance of the one grieving. *Zion stretched out her hands* (v. 17). Grieving women, you know, normally extend and withdraw their hands. He means she was actually inconsolable for the reason of God's permitting the enemy to advance against her and besmirch what was hallowed. *Jerusalem has become like a menstruating woman in their midst*. Now, according to the Law, a woman in her periods was unclean;[10] so he likens the city filled with foreign and unholy people to such a woman. The prophet, nonetheless, continually extols the justice of the sentence, offering the readers benefit from it. *The Lord is righteous, because I have provoked his word* (v. 18): I have transgressed laws made by him.

After lamenting the captivity of the maidens and young men, he brings out that the service of the idols is futile, calling them *lovers* (v. 19). He begs the one capable of relieving the untimeliness of the troubles to have pity on her for confessing her sin: *I have provoked you time and again* (v. 20). She is especially affected by the enemies' mockery; it happened, she says, with your concurrence: *You brought on the day and nominated the time, and cries of Alas, alas came to me* (v. 21). He begs that they would also fall afoul of the same calamities. *Let all their evildoing come before you* (v. 22): as you perceived my lawlessness, have an eye also to their impiety. *Scarify them in the way you scarified me* (788) *for all my sins, because my groans are many and my heart grieves*. Here the Syriac rendered the word *scarify* as "afflict them as you afflicted me." So ends the first lament.

Chapter Two

This is the opening of the second lament. *How the Lord in his wrath has enveloped daughter Zion in darkness! How he has cast down the glory of Israel from heaven to earth! How he has had no thought for his footstool on the day of his wrath!* (v. 1) It is clear from this that what the divine David calls "his footstool" is the divine Temple: "Worship at his footstool."[1] The prophet, however, likened the calamity to darkness, and says the city has been cast down from heaven to earth. *Showing no mercy, the Lord overwhelmed all the comeliness of Jacob, in his anger he destroyed the fortifications of daughter Judah, he fixed it fast to the ground* (v. 2), that is, he brought it crashing to earth. *He profaned its kings and its leaders.* Blessed David also foretold this, "You reduced his fortifications to cowardice, all who passed by plundered him."[2]

In the wrath of his anger he smashed every horn of Israel (v. 3), by *horn* referring to the leaders and men of influence. *He put behind him his right hand from the face of the foe, he lit a flaming fire in Jacob and consumed everything around it*: not wanting to assist the advancing enemy, he resembled a noble general, capable of easily destroying the enemy, who puts his hands behind him and cedes victory to the adversary. Towards me, on the contrary, you used your hands in the opposite way. *In fact, he bent his bow like an enemy, and stiffened his right hand like an adversary; he killed all my precious ones in the tent of daughter Zion. He poured out his anger like fire* (v. 4) The enemy, in fact, was guilty of slaughter in the Temple.

The verse brings out that all this happened with God's permission: since they had sinned, he promoted the fortunes of the adversaries, destroyed even the ramparts by means of the enemy, burned the buildings and brought grief on both men and women. The text says as much: *He increased the number of men and women humbled in daughter Judah.* (789) *He pulled up his dwelling like a vine* (vv. 5-6): the enemies burned the divine Temple. *He canceled his festival*: they no longer observed festivals, being obliged instead to lament. *The Lord caused Zion to forget festival and sabbath.* He went on to mention also the overthrow of the kings and the priests, the devastation of the Temple, the polluting of the altar, the destruction of the wall and – most grievous of all – *they uttered the voice of the enemy in the house of the Lord* (v. 7) like a song of the Levites *on a feast day*: instead of the customary hymn-singing, the hooting of the enemy burst forth.

The Lord planned to destroy the wall of daughter Zion, he extended a measuring line (v. 8), that is, the fair and just sentence, a vision blessed Zechariah also had.[3] After mentioning again gates and walls and rulers, he went on, *There is no Law* (v. 9). In other words, before the enemy's assault, they transgressed without scruple, whereas after the capture of the city and the burning of the Temple, they were unable, even if willing, to perform the worship according to the Law. *For their part her prophets were not granted a vision from the Lord*. He means the false prophets, those predicting false things to her. He depicts the old people lamenting and clad in sackcloth, and the prophet himself cries aloud, *My eyes failed through weeping, my innards were upset, my glory was poured out on the ground at the crushing of the daughter of my people* (v. 11).[4] He brings out also the suffering that is most pitiable of all, *with the fainting of babes and sucklings in the city streets*: famine got the better even of natural affection. He added as much, in fact, *They said to their mothers as they fainted, Where is bread and wine?* (v. 12) He says he finds no comparison adequate for the suffering. *What testimony shall I give you, and to what shall I liken you, daughter Jerusalem?* (v. 13).

He reminds them also of the false prophets, who made attractive predictions. *Your prophets had futile and foolish visions for you, they did not expose your iniquity so as to avert your captivity. They had visions for you of doubtful value, and expelled you* (v. 14). By foretelling pleasing things, they proved an obstacle to repentance, and did not allow them to desist from their extreme lawlessness. (792) *All the passersby clapped their hands at you, they whistled, they wagged their heads at daughter Jerusalem* (v. 15). This is typical of people marveling at a change for the worse. He mentions also what they said, *Was this city a crown of glory, a beautiful ornament, joy of all the earth?* He means that all this has come to pass according to the divine prophecies. He conveys also the words the impious used in their delight at the troubles that had befallen her. *This is the day we looked forward to, we found and have seen it* (v. 16). Blessed David in fact also foretold it, "We have become an object of mockery to our neighbors, of ridicule and taunting by those around us," and again, "You made us an object of mockery among the nations, a wagging of the head among the peoples."[5]

Once again the prophet employs personification and bids the ramparts and the city weep night and day on account of the manifold calamities, mentioning also the extremity of the troubles. *Do women eat the fruit of their womb? A cook did the scarifying* (v. 20), that is, he boiled fruit late in riping; he proceeded to say, in fact, *Many infants at the breast will be slain.*[6] He goes on to mention a further anomaly, *Will they kill priest and prophet in the sanctuary of the Lord?* He brought out the degree of the affliction by the nature both of the persons and of the place. After lamenting the enslavement of the elderly, youths and maidens, he went on, *You invited the settlers from roundabout me as to a feast day. On the day of the Lord's wrath no one was saved or survived*: in fear of the enemies' incursion they took to flight as to a fortified city, but they were all captured there. Everyone normally made their way there at the time of the festivals – hence his comparing the capture to a festival.[7] *I reared them, strengthened them and made them prosper, and the foe disposed of them*: my effort proved futile; I was robbed of all my nurslings.[8] At this point he concluded the second lament.

Chapter Three

He begins the third one this way, *I am a man with my eyes on poverty* (v. 1). In other words, the prophet in particular beyond all others prophesied the time of the calamities; so by *poverty* he refers to the lack of good things. (793) *With a rod of anger he took me up and led me into darkness and not light* (vv. 1-2). He makes his own the sufferings of the city, by *darkness* referring to misfortune. *But he turned on me, he changed his hand all day long* (v. 3): once the source of good things for me, now he applies chastisement (the phrase *changed his hand* suggesting as much). *He made my flesh and my skin grow old, he broke my bones* (v. 4). Discouragement does this, of course. *He walled me up and encircled me* (v. 5), that is, I cannot escape the troubles brought upon me. He suggests also the outside wall which the enemy built in the course of the siege. *He piled troubles on my head, he sat me in darkness like those long dead* (v. 6). In this he touches on the harsh servitude: after putting out the eyes of Zedekiah he consigned him to a mill,[1] as the sequel also indicates. *He loaded the yoke on my neck* (v. 7): he obliged me to serve the cruelest of masters. *Though I shout and cry* (v. 8): he does not accept my prayer when I pray. *He blocked my way with rock, and obscured my paths* (v. 9):[2] I am hampered by troubles I cannot escape.

He has become a bear lying in wait for me like a lion in hiding, he pursued me as I gave way, and alarmed me (vv. 10-11). He brought out the justice of the chastisement, saying, I was the first to give way, and thus he on his part inflicted punishment. The other prophets in olden times, of course, cite these prophecies.[3] *He left me for dead. He bent his bow and set me up as a target for his arrow* (vv. 11-12). Those firing at a target for practice of their skill normally release not two, three or four arrows but a lot; through these images he suggested the rapid succession of the calamities. He mentions also his pain of soul, by *kidneys* referring to his thoughts, and says that he was a source of glee to the enemy, who also kept singing of the calamities inflicted on it. He stripped me of all strength, he is saying, as is suggested by the verse, (796) *He cast out my teeth with a pebble, and fed me ashes* (v. 16), whereas the Syiac, "With a rock he deprived me of the former peace and the manifold good things." *I said, My victory has gone and my hope from the Lord* (v. 18): I despaired of sounder prospects, yet I cause my soul to fail with the memory of the troubles,[4] and I draw the Lord to mercy.

The Lord's mercies are many because we did not fail, because his compassion was not exhausted (v. 22):[5] if he had applied punishment commensurate with the sin, we should not even have escaped slaughter. The prophet next offers supplication on their behalf. *Renew us like early morning* (v. 23). Since he had called calamity *darkness*, he compares the change in it to *morning*. *Your faithfulness is magnified to the morning*: with the change occurring, they will apply themselves to piety in a more genuine manner, for my groans are many and my heart has failed. *My portion is the Lord, said my soul – hence I shall wait for him* (v. 24): I have no other recourse than to wait for your help.

He next brings out the value of hope in God. *The Lord is good to those who wait for him, the soul that seeks him will live. It is good to wait and to hope in the salvation of the Lord* (vv. 25-26). For the consolation of the disheartened he brings out this and other things. *It is good for a man when he lifts up the yoke from his youth. He will sit on his own and keep silence because he lifted up on himself a heavy yoke* (vv. 27-28). Blessed David also said as much, "It is good for me that you humbled me so that I might learn your ordinances."[6] The phrase *He will sit on his own and keep silence* recommends being patient and enduring sorrows. What follows is also in harmony with it, *He will put his mouth on the ground in case there is hope of endurance. He will offer his cheek to the striker, and be sated with insults* (vv. 29-30). This is the evangelical law: the Lord commanded us to offer one cheek after the other to the striker.[7] (797) For the phrase *He will put his mouth on the ground* the Syriac said "to the soil," that is, He will keep silence and nobly bear the abuse and insults, as though having his mouth full of soil. The divinely-inspired David also suggested as much, "With the sinner holding his ground before me, I was humbled, I was mute and I made no mention of good things."[8]

He then stresses that the Lord in his lovingkindness does not have recourse to correction for long; rather, after the correction he applies mercy. *He did not humble me with all his heart nor repulse human beings* (v. 33): his appearance is that of an angry person, but his intention is full of lovingkindness. He has recourse to correction, of course, for the good of human beings, as he went on to say, *For humbling under his feet all the imprisoned on earth* (v. 34), that is, those bound to the earth and without a lofty attitude: they live a life of iniquity and have no respect for the one who observes them. *Who spoke in these terms and it came to pass? The Lord did not give instructions. From the mouth of the Most High bad things and good will not issue forth* (vv. 37-38). The verse criticizes those who do away with providence: they attribute what happens to fate and chance.

Why will any living mortal complain, a man about his sin? (v. 39) In other words, it is indifference, not nature, that is responsible for sin,[9] as a result of which the judge also imposes punishment on the sinners. *Our way has been scrutinized and examined* (v. 40): he saw the lawlessness committed by us. *Let us turn to the Lord*: let punishment be for us an occasion of repentance. *Let us lift up our hearts and lift up our eyes to the Most High, who dwells in heaven* (v. 41): ridding our thoughts of idle concerns, let us beg God for mercy. *We sinned and acted with impiety, and you were not appeased* (v. 42): the punishment you imposed was just. *You wrapped yourself in anger, you persecuted us, you killed and did not spare. You enveloped yourself in a dense cloud to stop our prayer getting through to you* (vv. 43-44). God said this also through another prophet, "Because your sins came between you and me."[10] He compared this to the cloud which hindered the approach of the prayer.

He laments and bewails particularly on seeing the adversaries offering mockery and insults to the people; (800)

he says they hunted, slaughtered and threw him into a pit, pelted him with stones and submerged him in water. In all this he indicated the awful extent of the troubles. The divinely-inspired David on the part of these same people also said, "Save me, O God, because waters have invaded my soul. I was cast into the muddy depths, and there is no firm footing. I went to the depths of the sea, a tempest submerged me," and again, "Do not let the flood of water drown me, or the deep swallow me, or the well close its mouth on me."[11] Likewise here.

I invoked your name, O Lord, from the bottom of the pit. You heard my voice, do not close your ears to my plea and my cry (vv. 55-56). He brings out also how he won over the loving God. *You came near on the day I called on you, and you said to me, Do not fear* (v. 57). Even this brief word is sufficient for consolation. He then recounts that he rendered justice to them and to the adversaries, consigning the latter to slavery and regaling themselves with freedom. With a request for the destruction of the impious he concluded the third lament.[12]

Chapter Four

How gold has become dull, how the good silver is changed, the sacred stones are scattered at the head of all exits (v. 1). He compares the piety of the forebears to these materials, and laments the change occurring in their offspring. What follows confirms this. *Zion's children, precious, exalted, more valuable than gold, how they are reckoned as earthenware pots, works of the potter's hand* (v. 2). The Lord had foretold this also through the divine Isaiah, "They will be useless like a pot smashed into pieces in which water cannot be drawn or fire taken from the furnace."[1] *Even dragons bare the breast, suckle their young; daughters of my people were beyond help, like an ostrich in the desert* (v. 3). The most savage beasts, he is saying, care for their offspring, whereas the extremity of Zion's suffering caused the inhabitants even to forget nature itself: when most were slaughtered and the rest taken off into slavery, some few remained like a solitary ostrich wandering through the desert.

He indicates the troubles produced by the famine. (801) *A suckling's tongue stuck to its throat through thirst; infants begged for bread, and there was no one to break it for them* (v. 4). He brings out also their former luxury. *Those who ate delicacies perished in the streets* (v. 5), that is, thrown out into the market place. *Those reared in purple were clad in dung.* He says their sin was responsible for this, and compares it to that of Sodom. He mentions also the pride of the Nazarites before the calamities and their wretched condition in time of calamity; he says death in war is preferable to the shafts of starvation. He inserts in the lamentation also the worst affliction of all. *Hands of compassionate women cooked their own children; they became food for them in the crushing of the daughter of my people* (v. 10).[2]

The Lord in his anger justly inflicted this on Zion. *Kings of the earth and all the inhabitants of the world did not believe that foe and oppressor would enter through the gates of Jerusalem* (v. 12). After all, as good grounds for so believing they had the fate of Sennacherib, whose army he wasted in a short space of the night.[3] But it was surrendered to the enemy on account both of the deception of the false prophets and the killing by the priests. *Her young men crept through the exits* (v. 14). By *exits* he refers to the highways and what were called streets. *They were stained with blood in their powerlessness, they were cast out along with their garments.* While starvation forced them to be cast out, the besieging enemy prevented their being buried, and the dogs ate them when cast out.[4] He mentions also what was shouted out by the enemy. *Keep away from the unclean* (v. 15). It was us they referred to as unclean. Then to bring out whom he calls unclean, he repeats the saying, *Keep away from the unclean, keep away, do not approach them because they provoked* – God, that is. *They were left alone and were unsteady*: they were deprived of divine assistance on account of their lawlessness. *Say to the nations, Let them have no further dwelling in the sight of the Lord*: he renounced us completely.

Our eyes failed in watching for help when our gaze was on futile things; we looked for a nation, but it could not save (v. 17): trusting in the assistance of the Egyptians, (804) we were deceived in our expectation. He next brings out the enemies' cruelty: they neither spared the elderly nor even showed any respect for priesthood.[5] *We hunted down our little ones lest they go on to the streets* (v. 18). The Syriac gave the rendering "they hunted," which is logical: the enemy hunted down the young along with the old. We suffered this, he is saying, *because our time had come, our days were up*. The verse brings out that in using plumb line and measuring line the God of all exercises both longsuffering and punishment:[6] when he exercises longsuffering but observes our scorn for it, he applies punishment to put an end to our sin. He then explained that the speed of the enemy surpassed even the velocity of eagles.

The spirit of the face of our anointed Lord was taken in our corruption, to whom we said, In his shadow we shall live among the nations (v. 20). Let the Jews tell us whom the inspired word refers to by *anointed*: which of those called *anointed* by them – king, prophet, priest – was named *Lord*? They would, however, be unable to show it, despite having recourse to extensive doubletalk. It is clear, therefore, that the prophet foretold our Savior and Lord, taken by them on account of the corruption of their impiety. The biblical authors say they will live *in the shadow*.[7] They came to faith through the sacred apostles and through their divine oracles which were preached to the nations. Now, let us try to find his meaning with the all-holy Spirit enlightening us. He says, *The spirit of the face of our anointed Lord*. The prophet, of course, inserted this prophecy among the laments to teach the Jews of that time that, despite their expectations not having been realized by then, they would obtain mercy and enjoy the recall, even though they were due to surrender the Savior of the world to the cross.

Rejoice and be glad, daughter of Idumea, who dwells in the land of Uz; the cup of the Lord will come to you, you will drink, be intoxicated and vomit (v. 21). The inspired word predicted for them the extent of the troubles, the phrase *you will be intoxicated and vomit* suggesting it. The divinely-inspired David says of them, "Remember, Lord, the children of Edom on the day of Jerusalem, who said, Raze it, raze it, down (805) to its foundations."[8] Though brothers and neighbors, they refused to live in peace, instead maintaining the ancestral hatred. *Your iniquity has come to an end, daughter Zion; he will not go to the extent of deporting you any longer. He called you to account for your iniquity, daughter Edom, he made revelations of your impiety* (v. 22). He forecast prosperity for Zion, but the opposite for Idumea: he said retribution would befall it. The statement *he will not go the extent of deporting you any longer* is true: those reduced to slavery were not completely destroyed, and came under the power of the Persians.[9]

For his part, then, the prophet gave this conclusion to the laments.[10] We for our part sing the praises of the one who gave a mouth to a human being and instilled knowledge into a human being, for the reason that we have both made clear the meaning of the prophet to the extent it was possible for us to achieve it, and added this commentary as well to the other prophetic books, thus leaving not even a single piece of prophecy without comment, thanks to his grace. Now, I beseech the readers in turn to accept what was well and properly expressed, while forgiving any deficiency; being human, after all, and falling short of perfection, we contributed our own enthusiasm to the task of providing some benefit to those fond of God and of hard work.[11] We exhort them to repay the labor of commentary with the support of prayer so that, relying on it, we may complete what is left of our life, serving in word, deed and thought our God and Savior and Lord, to whom with the Father and the all-holy Spirit belong glory and magnificence, now and forever, for ages of ages. Amen.

Notes

Notes to the Commentary on the Book of Jeremiah

Introduction

[1] We do find J. Quasten, *Patrology* II, Westminster MD 1953, 121-23, speaking in a local and physical sense of "the school of Antioch founded by Lucian of Samosata" in opposition to the "school of Caesarea," Origen's refuge after his exile from Egypt. But we prefer to use the term only of a fellowship of like-minded scholars joined by birth, geography and scholarly principles, even if some members did exercise a magisterial role in regard to others.
[2] F. M. Young, *From Nicaea to Chalcedon. A Guide to the Literature and its Background*, 267, who also concedes (268) the extent of Theodoret's pastoral responsibilities (on the evidence of *Ep.* 113).
[3] Y. Azéma, *Théodoret de Cyr. Correspondance II*, SC 98, 202, *Ep.* 82, written to Eusebius of Ancyra.
[4] For a somewhat more lengthy summary of Theodoret's life and works, see J.-N. Guinot, "Theodoret von Kyrrhos," *TRE* 33.250-54.
[5] Hom.2 *In Oziam* (SC 277.88).
[6] Cf Pref. to Psalms Commentary (PG 80, 860). Before even those works Theodoret produced (under pressure again) a Commentary on the Song of Songs, in the preface to which he laments the many concerns, "urban and rural, military and political, ecclesiastical and civil," that impeded him as a commentator. See the introduction to my translation, *Theodoret of Cyrus. Commentary on the Song of Songs.*
[7] PG 80. 860.
[8] *Theodoreti Cyrensis Quaestiones in Reges et Paralipomena*, 299. This disclaimer is made in identical terms at the close of the Questions on 2 Kgs. The two series of Questions seem to have been composed in failing health a decade later than Jeremiah (around 453, suggests Guinot).
[9] For details of dating of all these commentaries, see my *Theodoret of Cyrus. Commentary on the Psalms* I, 2-4.
[10] PG 81, 9-14.
[11] Cf CPG 6205, citing the doubts of M. Faulhaber, *Die Propheten-Catenen nach Römischen Handschriften*, 113sq. J. Paramelle also in a survey article on "Christianisme Byzantin" in *Annuaire de l'Ecole Pratique des Hautes Etudes* 88 (1979-80) 379-86 makes a passing reference to "l'inauthenticité du Commentaire de Jérémie" (380), but without elaboration.
[12] *Commentaire sur Isaïe* I, SC 276, 13, n.2. Guinot nevertheless feels we are confident in claiming "l'on est désormais en possession de tous les com-

mentaires de Théodoret sur les prophètes" (15), not being prepared to dismiss the claim to authenticity of the Migne text of Jeremiah, even if it may have to be conceded to be "composite et lacunaire."

[13] Unfortunately, it is not all modern commentators, nor the most eminent, who take the versions into account at all. While William McKane, *Jeremiah*, is aware of the Lucianic recension, he does not consult it regularly (as he might through Ziegler's edition of the LXX Jeremiah); noting the appearance there of verses often declared missing from ch. 29, he observes, "It is probable that (the Lucianic recension) is a correction modeled on MT (the insertion of v.16-20)."

[14] This is the authoritative conclusion of N. Fernández Marcos, *The Septuagint in Context. Introduction to the Greek Versions of the Bible*, xi, who nonetheless does not accept the idea of a number of versions like the targums proposed by P. Kahle, *The Cairo Genizah*, 2nd ed., 256-57.

[15] N. Fernández Marcos, "The Lucianic text in the Books of Kingdoms," in *De Septuaginta*, ed. A. Pietersma, C. Cox; Missisauga: Benden Publications, 1984, 102.

[16] *Praef. in Paral.* (PL 28.1324-25).

[17] *Ep.* 106.2 (PL 22.838).

[18] Cf D. S. Wallace-Hadrill, *Christian Antioch*, 30; B. Drewery, "Antiochien," 106; S. P. Brock, "Bibelübersetzungen I,2," TRE 6, 166-67. Lucian is not a name we find on the lips of Theodoret or Chrysostom, not surprisingly considering his flawed reputation.

[19] Cf D. Barthélemy, *Les Devanciers d'Aquila*, 126-27; E.-L. Guillaumin, "Problèmes posés aux éditeurs de Jean Chrysostome par le richesse de son inspiration biblique," ΣΥΜΠΟΣΙΟΝ. *Studies on St John Chrysostom*, ΑΝΑΛΕΚΤΑ ΒΛΑΤΑΔΩΝ, Thessaloniki: Patriarchal Institute for Patristic Studies, 1973, 62-63; Guinot, *L'Exégèse de Théodoret de Cyr*, 171-72.

[20] So K. G. O'Connell, "Texts and versions," *NJBC* 1092, who places the origins of this revision in Palestine, matching Palestinian Hebrew manuscripts from Qumran. S. Jellicoe, *The Septuagint and Modern Study*, 160-61, denies the provenance of the revision directly from the Hebrew.

[21] Cf Fernández Marcos, *Scribes and Translators. Septuagint and Old Latin in the Books of Kings*, VTS 54; Leiden/New York: Brill, 1994, 28: "One of the reasons for the uncertainty concerning the Lucianic recension of the Octateuch was the lack of critical editions of the Antiochene Fathers."

[22] There is an authentic homily on Jer 10.23 by Chrysostom (PG 56.153-62). I have noted also the existence of a putative commentary on Jeremiah by Chrysostom dismissed by Henry Savile in the seventeenth century as "sheer fanciful trifles;" see my article, "'Norms, definitions and unalterable doctrines': Chrysostom on Jeremiah," *ITQ* 65 (2000) 336.

[23] These distinctive readings in Theodoret's biblical text are noted in the translation below. As well, for convenience the column numbers of the PG 80 text are included.

[24] M. P. Weitzman, *The Syriac Version of the Old Testament*, 253, holds that the Peshitta version of the Prophets already existed and had attained authoritative status by around 170.

[25] *Jeremiah 1-25*, 612,616.
[26] *Bibliotheca* 203 (PG 103, 676).
[27] Cf my "On looking again at *synkatabasis*."
[28] PG 80, 860.
[29] *Biblical Exegesis and the Formation of Christian Culture*, 182,296. Cf C. Schäublin, *Untersuchungen zu Methode und Herkunft der Antiochenischen Exegese*, 170, who likewise sees an accent on *alêtheia* typical of Antiochene hermeneutics. Schäublin attributes the accent to the influence of pagan grammarians in the course of the Antiochenes' education.
[30] Cf J. N. D. Kelly, *Early Christian Doctrines*, 373-74.
[31] We should heed the qualification made by J. N. D. Kelly, *Golden Mouth. The Story of John Chrysostom, Ascetic, Preacher, Bishop*, Ithaca NY: Cornell University Press, 1995, 94: "Neither John, nor any Christian teacher for centuries to come, was properly equipped to carry out exegesis as we have come to understand it."
[32] *Theodoreti Cyrensis Quaestiones in Reges et Paralipomena*, 299.

Chapter One

[1] This prophet, like Isaiah, is not listed by Theodoret in the preface to his Psalms Commentary amongst the biblical authors he had initially commented on; in fact, at the conclusion of this Commentary we shall see him claiming that with it he completes work on all the prophets – which may account for an even more concise treatment than is customary with him. For the difference in the opening to the text from the form in the manuscript discovered in Constantinople, see Introduction.
Theodoret speaks here of Jeremiah's work as *prophêteia*, inspired composition, as he and other Fathers do of all Old Testament works, even if this work is (also) prophecy in our more limited sense of the word. He will speak of Bar as also part of the whole work, *prophêteia* (in commentary on Bar 3.32).
[2] An Antiochene can have difficulty balancing the respective roles of divine grace and human effort in spiritual matters, as we shall see in the course of this and other of Theodoret's commentaries. In his Isaiah Commentary, completed not long before, he makes the same double acknowledgement, as he does in closing the Jeremiah Commentary.
[3] Conciseness, *syntomia*, is the feature Theodoret principally aspires to – and achieves – as a commentator, perhaps with the *makrologia* of homilists like John Chrysostom in mind. We shall see him resolutely abjuring in his work the role of a preacher.
[4] To help people grasp the sense or drift (*dianoia*) of Jeremiah's work, Theodoret begins by stating the book's theme (*hypothesis*), beginning with a foreword or synopsis (*protheôria*). Frances Young, in *Biblical Exegesis and the Formation of Christian Culture*, remarks, "The scholars of the Church, notably the Antiochenes, would ask about the *hypothesis* of a particular

prophetic book or Pauline Epistle, or the *skopos* (intent) of a particular Psalm, but... Athanasius in confuting the Arians would look for the mind (*dianoia*) or aim (*skopos*) of scripture as a whole."

[5] At this point our text notes the beginning of volume (*tomos*) one, which contains the first four chapters of Jeremiah. The division, which is one of content or volume and not structure (vol.2 here, for instance, finishing within ch.8 of Jer), is not registered in the Sirmond text of the Isaiah Commentary, acknowledged to be from the catenae; so perhaps its inclusion here strengthens the case for direct transmission of the text.

[6] An alternative form of Jehoiachin. Theodoret thus clarifies the confusing table of succession in Judah in these tumultuous years, filling out the picture given in Jer 1.1-3. He had done the same in introducing the book of Daniel, being particular about backgrounding his text.

[7] True to his word, Theodoret has concisely summarised in advance the topics to be covered by Jeremiah. Predictably, he confined his introduction to matters of history and content, not entering critical matters such as authenticity and order of the oracles that interest modern commentators.

[8] For details of the precise local form of the LXX in use by Theodoret, see Introduction. The text of the verse in Heb. and Grk is ambiguous on Jeremiah's priestly status, probably referring only to Hilkiah as being of a priestly family. But some modern commentators side with Theodoret.

[9] The text suggests Theodoret is not interested in quoting v.3 verbatim, dealing as it does with succession details. Is it that he does not want to get embroiled further in historical matters? or do this and similar examples of paraphrase imply that he intends to move briskly through the text? or does this feature betray the provenance of our text, i.e., from the catenae?

[10] Exod 3.14.

[11] Exod 3.11-12.

[12] Matt 28.20. Already a difference in interpretation is notable from the hermeneutical stance in the Isaiah Commentary, influenced so much by Alexandrian commentary: the commentator is focussing on the historical situation of the prophet and his listeners, extending his hermeneutical perspective both retrospectively and prospectively, whereas Eusebius and Cyril encouraged Theodoret to a less historical, more eschatological interpretation, with no retrospective view.

[13] Theodoret was a native Syriac speaker, Pierre Canivet assures us, but it appears he knows no Hebrew; he can access the original text only through the Peshitta Bible (*Syros*), which seems to have been compiled by this time (see Introduction). So he is aware here of the differing accounts of the fruit on the twig; but his lack of Hebrew does not allow him to pick up the word play in the original between *shaqed*, almond tree, and *shoqed*, I am watching. Antiochene precision, however, obliges him to pursue the differing significance of Hebrew original and Greek version, respectively, as he sees it, his explanation being assisted by his awareness that the Peshitta rendered the word as "hastening."

[14] Pss 44.23; 78.65.

[15] Ezek 11.7. Theodoret omits comment on v.14 of his text, though citing

it in the course of other commentaries; conciseness requires a brisk pace here, explicit citation given only where necessary, and paraphrase frequently sufficing.
[16] An individual reading.
[17] Matt 16.18.

Chapter Two

[1] Ps 78.36-37, Theodoret's form of the LXX reading (by a copyist's error?) *êgapêsan,* loved, for *êpatêsan,* deceived.
[2] Deut 32.9. Theodoret has already noted what strikes modern commentators as well, the similarity of Jeremiah's call and message to that of Moses – that retrospective viewpoint.
[3] Exod 4.22.
[4] Hos 9.10, the similarity of accent on this relationship in Hosea also being noted by modern commentators.
[5] Isa 37.10.
[6] Theodoret has been paraphrasing vv.6-7 of the LXX text, which speaks of the Lord bringing the people to Carmel, the Hebrew phrase being rendered in modern versions as "a plentiful land" (NRSV) or "a garden land" (NAB), *carmel* suggesting an orchard, a generic meaning probably lost on Theodoret (and the LXX). He also shows no interest in the literary genre of the lawsuit, *rib*, developed here, which fascinates modern literary critics of prophetical discourse.
[7] More sociologically minded commentators today would suggest Jeremiah is referring rather to the official or cultic prophets as distinct from a prophet personally called by the Lord like Jeremiah himself.
We note Theodoret's discipline in not moralizing on the dereliction of duty by these various office-holders as a preacher might.
[8] An Antiochene does not let the significance of different forms (middle and active) escape him: theological meaning lies in morphological distinction. (Moderation also appeals to this commentator.)
[9] In giving a precis of vv.10-11, Theodoret is with modern commentators in suggesting the term Kittim denotes the west generally, a meaning not emerging from a version like the NRSV's "the coasts of Cyprus," and he likewise grasps the full force of Kedar.
[10] Deut 32.1, cited to throw light on v.12 of this chapter, paraphrased in a form that suggests (as it does when vice versa he cites it on the Deut text in the *Quaestiones*) that it is a local reading, and to head off any possible misunderstanding of anthropomorphisms in the biblical text; figures such as metonymy and synecdoche are also not lost on the commentator. The commentary is proceeding economically, but with sufficient attention to points needing explication or admonition.
[11] As emerges in his other works, Theodoret is at pains to bring out the full force of imagery in the biblical text.
[12] The final clause is according to the LXX.

[13] John 19.15. Seeing the New Testament correspondence of this situation, Theodoret recites the traditional explanation of contemporary Jewish misfortunes, viz, the crucifixion of Jesus. It is not a gratuitous observation: Theodoret sees the New Testament encouraging a typological interpretation of this passage.
[14] Deut 32.32. Theodoret, looking back to the Song of Moses and forward to the Johannine Supper discourse, takes what Frances Young would call a typically Antiochene view of "narrative coherence." (Though he had previously commented on Isaiah, Theodoret makes no reference here to the celebrated parable of the vineyard in Isa 5.)
[15] John 15.1.
[16] Theodoret's text in this form is commenting on the LXX, which reads *en polyandrio* for the Heb. "in the valley," i.e., the Valley of Hinnom, where children were sacrificed, a place referred to explicitly in 7.31 and evidently known to Theodoret. The Bavarian codex at this point in the text is less elliptical, spelling out the different readings and going into greater detail of the heinous practices – but in its lack of conciseness it has a less authentic ring, as is true of its later glosses.
[17] Jer 31.19 LXX.
[18] These LXX verses continue to diverge from the Heb. See Introduction for the relation of the LXX and our Masoretic Heb. text.
[19] Cf Deut 32.30.
[20] LXX. The vv.25-26 were briefly paraphrased.
[21] A similar bland paraphrase of the colorful verse in Heb. and LXX, "A sword consumed your prophets like a destructive lion," on which the Bavarian codex elaborates even further (though without developing the image).
[22] Ps 106.37-38.
[23] Theodoret showed similar morphological precision to make a point on v.9.

Chapter Three

[1] Ezek 16.6 LXX.
[2] The verb *ekphuro* that Theodoret finds in the LXX is a hapax legomenon; he is encouraged to arrive at its meaning by reference to its uncompounded form in Ezek and by the Syriac translation in the Peshitta (though, as McKane observes, the Peshitta was dependent on the LXX, which was available to the Syriac translator). The Heb. would not help him, could he access it, as the meaning of *shegal* in this context ("ravished") is also unparalleled. His native Syriac is an asset to him as a commentator; others, like Chrysostom, could only turn to alternative Grk versions or to similar forms in the LXX.
[3] Perhaps not without purpose Theodoret passed over v.1, where the LXX speaks of the "many shepherds" Judah has lain with – surely a puzzling phrase. By reference to a passage like 16.19-20, he comes up with a plausible

explanation, all unaware that the LXX (and Peshitta) has misread the Heb. *re'eh*, friend, lover, as *ro'eh*, shepherd.

[4] Ps 31.2. The LXX, unlike the Heb., includes the word "house" in v.4, and Theodoret is exercised to rationalize its occurrence with a scriptural parallel (not being in a position to question its place in the text).

[5] This clause seems to belong to the local form of the LXX, though known also to Aquila and Theodotion (but not to our Heb. text). Modern commentators treat vv.6-18 as an insertion, deriving from a different period of the prophet's ministry or beyond; but Theodoret would not be likely to debate such redactional issues.

[6] Exod 20.3.

[7] Cf Ezra 3.2.

[8] Cf John 21.16. If an Antiochene must find a scriptural basis for recognising typology operating in a text, Theodoret is stretching things to come up with this biblical parallel. He insists Jeremiah goes on to confirm his application of the text.

[9] Theodoret finds the mention of incinerating in his local text, and provides an appropriate commentary on it.

[10] Rom 6.21 – no moralizing, simply leaving reinforcement to "the divine apostle" (whom Theodoret rarely presumed to call Paul in his Commentary on the letters).

Chapter Four

[1] Matt 5.33-34. The Greek of vv.1-2 is at variance with our Heb. text.

[2] Rom 2.28-29. Theodoret is free to recognise typology operating if Paul has already seen it in this text. (Theodoret's local text of the verse speaks of "uncircumcision," while other forms of the LXX interpret it to read "hardness of heart.")

[3] This comment by Theodoret seems to be meant to avoid any possible misunderstanding of "breath," *pneuma*, as somehow relating to the Holy Spirit.

[4] Theodoret is always concerned to ensure scriptural images are not lost on his readers, even if the text of the verse is reduced to paraphrase in the process.

[5] Cf 1 Sam 3.20, a phrase suggesting from north to south. Today the site of Dan is identified with Tell el-Qadi.

[6] Jer 52.9 (where LXX and Theodoret call this other town Deblatha, here Reblatha); 2 Kgs 25.20-21. The reason for the shift in Theodoret's thinking from Dan to Riblah is not clear. What is clearer, from his other commentaries, is his interest in geography (and other natural sciences).

[7] Cf 2 Sam 8.9, a reference to Hamath (called Epiphaneia in the version of Aquila). He will trace the same connections in comment on 49.23.

[8] Cf Jer 52.4; 2 Kgs 25.1.

[9] Cf notes 6 and 10 on ch. 2 for the sense given by the LXX to Heb. *carmel* (though Theodoret has some reservations about its likelihood in this con-

text) and for his sensitivity to the text's figurative language.
[10] A clause in the local form of the LXX.
[11] The reader needs reminding, at least occasionally, not to misinterpret anthropomorphisms in the text , whatever the value of its figurative language generally.
[12] A typically concise comment: the comparison hardly needs explication, and Theodoret is not about wringing the withers of his readers, let alone moralizing, as a preacher might. It is noteworthy that the brevity of comment and paraphrase does not lend itself to scriptural documentation.
[13] It is in fact a Pauline maxim (Rom 12.15); perhaps Theodoret thinks it is a dominical saying found in the Gospels.
[14] Cf note 5 on ch. 1 for the division of Theodoret's work into volumes, or *tomoi*, which are simply divisions imposed by capacity rather than suggested by structure. One such volume now closes – hence the doxology; there is certainly no lengthy moral peroration such as we might get from Chrysostom. The divisions and accompanying perorations suggest direct manuscript tradition.

Chapter Five

[1] Cf 4.2.
[2] Theodoret's local text does not include the opening "Lord."
[3] Cf Jer 40; 2 Kgs 25.
[4] Dan 7.6 Grk. We have seen Theodoret independently, if tentatively, offering his own opinion in interpreting obscure references. As he stated in the preface to his Commentary on Paul, he is aware of his predecessors in the field, but confident he has a contribution to make – especially in the natural sciences, like zoology.
[5] LXX.
[6] Where the ancient versions generally take the rare Heb. words in v.10 to mean walls, modern versions speak in terms of vines.
[7] Unlike the nomination by ancient and modern commentators of Babylonians and Scythians for this title, Theodoret chooses the Assyrians, tracing their antiquity and forebear back to Gen 10.8-11 – an historical datum he finds more relevant (like some geographical and zoological items previously) than blood-curdling details in this section of the text.
[8] The absence of this powerful image, which Theodoret's local text preserves, modern commentators regret in other forms of the LXX. His explication of it for his readers corresponds remarkably (if less effectively) with that of a modern, William McKane: "The arrows fired by enemy deal out death and so their container is described as an open grave." Otherwise, Theodoret does not dwell on the pathos of the verses, briefly paraphrasing the account of future horrors; he finds theological significance elsewhere, as usual.
[9] All the ancient versions give a meaning "law" where "boundary" is intended, McKane observes, adding, "The functioning of the sand as a

boundary for the sea is as old as the created order itself." Theodoret, aware perhaps of a different sense in LXX and Peshitta, anticipated his modern counterpart (as in his Commentary on Paul he likewise had much to offer the moderns, if only they had read him).

[10] Since the text elaborates on the image of the bird snare, Theodoret feels no need to explicate it himself.

Chapter Six

[1] These adjectives appear in the Heb. but not in LXX generally; Theodoret's local form of the text must contain them.

[2] Again the text (vv. 11-13) is verbose in its basic message, so Theodoret reduces it to a precis.

[3] John 14.6. The commentary thus far has been generally very concise, even for Theodoret, with verses reduced to paraphrase where not thought significant, and scriptural documentation rare. Elements of this verse, by contrast, strike Theodoret as Christological, as well as ringing Old Testament echoes; and the commentary becomes relatively expansive as the commentator sees another level of meaning.

[4] Deut 18.15.

[5] As observed in note 1 to ch. 1, *prophêtes* and *prophêtikos* refer generally to Old Testament inspired authors (as distinct from New Testament authors, *apostolikoi*), and not simply specifically to the Latter Prophets. We need to be sensitive to this more general meaning to grasp the full sense of Theodoret's commentary on these verses.

[6] Ezek 3.17.

[7] Grk.

[8] Acts 13.46-47, citing Isa 49.6 (with some dittography).

[9] The description in those vv.22-23 is in fact gripping; but it is not what interests Theodoret. The ensuing despair of the populace is also passed over rapidly.

[10] Of the puzzling elements in the text of the verse, Theodoret chooses for comment one term which his local form of the LXX alone offers.

[11] Ancient and modern commentators admit the difficulty of the text of vv.29-30 and the thinking behind the employment of the figure. Theodoret, however, is by no means inclined to pass it over, finding it grist to his theological mill, and he takes the trouble to explicate all its elements for his readers.

[12] A clear statement of a basic dogmatic and moral principle that absolves Theodoret of accusations of pelagianism (on which Kelly finds the need to defend him and others of his school). In the wake of the Fall, human nature is not impaired; people's failings – and especially the Jews' situation, to which he often applies this principle – are due not to such a flaw but to their own acts of free will, *proairesis*, or (elsewhere) their mindset, *gnome*. Cf note 2 to ch. 8.

Chapter Seven

[1] Modern commentators debate the reasons for the omission in the LXX of an opening verse to this chapter in which the prophet is bidden stand at the gate of the Temple and make an announcement to those entering: did the LXX abridge the Heb., or has our Heb. incorporated a later addition? Theodoret seems to know of this verse, though not citing it verbatim. He also gives but a precis of other verses, as is his wont, not even bothering to recite the mini-Decalogue in v.9.

[2] Hos 3.1.

[3] This terminology of God showing considerateness (*synkatabaino*) for human limitations (*astheneia*) we associate particularly with Chrysostom in connection with the language of the Scriptures and in events of sacred history, including the Incarnation. It is rare to find them in Theodoret's vocabulary.

[4] Cf Deut 12.13-15.

[5] Cf 2 Kgs 21.

[6] Cf Ezek 8.

[7] Again Theodoret does not elaborate on these descriptive verses with their gruesome details. He does not chance his arm on the etymology of Topheth at this occurrence, whereas when he met it at Isa 30.33, he referred to Syriac, and on finding no satisfaction in the meaning "food," he proceeded to a resource he had not elsewhere used, *Translation of Hebrew Terms*, which gave him the meaning "closure" – both of which meanings he cites here (modern scholars preferring to see a root meaning hearth or fireplace). Once again one gets the impression he has no time to waste; a brief summary of previous research suffices.

Chapter Eight

[1] Theodoret expresses what his practice to this point has suggested, that he finds some passages somewhat verbose and less relevant to his theme (for all their color) – hence his leaving them to precis or paraphrase – whereas the people's act of choice is grist to his mill, as the following note confirms.

[2] As observed in note 12 to ch. 6, an Antiochene commentator cannot let pass reinforcement of the belief that nature is not inherently evil – only acts of free will.

[3] We have noted that Theodoret likes to respond to figures from nature; so he is exercised by these two comparisons, from the behavior of horses and of winged creatures, which puzzle commentators. With the former he has the double recourse to Syriac and to Greek texts (not Heb., of course); he reads v.7 in such a way as to confirm his option for the Greek approach, finally admitting the doubts of all commentators about the names of the winged creatures referred to there.

[4] As in Deut 32.9, a text Theodoret quoted at the beginning of commentary on ch. 2. The sense of "pen" for *schoinos* does not seem to occur to him. Nor is he as commentator interested in sociological matters like the existence of groups in the community of Judah such as sages and scribes; priests, false (cultic) prophets and kings come in for mention from a moral point of view.

[5] The precis of verses from 10b to 18 is particularly abbreviated, partly because the LXX omits vv. 10b-11 (Theodoret having access to the passage, perhaps from the Peshitta), and partly because again the expression is verbose.

[6] Rom 15.4. Jeremiah might be in full flight; but the second volume has come to an end, and so Theodoret has to conclude with a (typically concise) peroration.

[7] Is Theodoret just chancing his arm again here? Gilead, as McKane says, was "apparently renowned for its *materia medica* and its doctors," and 46.11 and Gen 37.25 speak of its curative balm (cf note 3 to ch. 22). The message underlying the metaphor, however, he has probably grasped.

Chapter Nine

[1] There is no clear break in thought at this stage, and Theodoret sees only continuity with the preceding verses (ancient texts, of course, not numbering chapters and verses). It is probably more helpful to follow the numbering of our Migne text, which corresponds to that of the NRSV Bible, Theodoret here citing a phrase from v.2.

[2] The relevance of the mention of interest, *tokos*, in the LXX puzzles modern commentators as well, and this time Theodoret makes no attempt to explain it.

[3] Ps 66.10.

[4] Chrysostom himself could not have better expressed the principle of scriptural *synkatabasis*, a term that we observed in note 3 on ch. 7 Theodoret does not generally use. He has let this particular anthropomorphism pass without comment to this point, but thinks the reader could do with the reminder.

[5] Theodoret the naturalist feels he can improve on the biblical text with information on the habits of birds and serpents. In fact, however, the LXX text in referring to serpents (v. 11) is confusing similar Heb. words, the creature being rather a jackal or wolf – but natural science would not help him there.

[6] Theodoret, who likes to explicate a metaphor in the text, is not alone in justifying the figure of death entering through the windows; modern commentators come up with a range of possible explanations. So he feels he can admit not simply a moral explication but also a psychological one, the senses being described as the windows of the soul.

[7] Theodoret does not resolve the ambiguity of these verses as to the nations' being circumcised that puzzles all commentators; he simply supports

each contradictory verse, and weighs in on the basic moral thrust of the passage. He also makes one of his complimentary statements of the value of the Old Testament.

Chapter Ten

[1] Modern commentators find vv.1-16 of our present Heb. text "a passage which has been built up by piecemeal contributions" over time (McKane); the LXX generally does not know vv.6-8,10,and it places 9 after 4. Theodoret's text is fuller than this – complete even (though he is still inclined to precis where prolixity is unnecessary), and he concurs with Benjamin Wambacq in seeing v.2 as the core of the passage. As to the port in question in v.9, *Tharsis*, which is generally represented as Tarshish and located in Spain, Theodoret as usual sees a reference to Africa, as does the Targum here; at its occurrence in Ezek 27.12 he remarks, "The Syriac and Hebrew call Carthage *Tharsis*" – the geographer speaking, as we have seen before, and with some encouragement.

[2] Ps 104.32.

[3] Theodoret is quick to insert a rare (for this Commentary) piece of Christological polemic against Arian subordinationists. What he is unaware of, though a Syriac speaker, is that this v.11 is an "Aramaic gloss" which McKane dates to the fifth century, predating the verses missing from the LXX – though Theodoret in the first half of that century is reading them. As emerges also from his Commentary on Paul, modern commentators could do with reading their ancient counterparts, like Theodoret – even on textual matters.

[4] Pss 33.9; 135.6.

[5] The verses are obscure and the text uncertain, as modern commentators admit; but Theodoret presses on, thinking repetition may lead to clarity.

[6] The Heb. *tannim* here the LXX at 9.11 misread to mean serpents instead of jackals; this time it opts for sparrows, which Theodoret the naturalist finds unlikely, and proposes a larger, desert bird.

[7] At first flush, it seems odd that Theodoret should suddenly leave the historical context of these verses to use them in support of a general moral principle, albeit important and one that he has harped on before in this Commentary. But we know from Chrysostom's Antioch homily on v.23 that it was one of many scriptural tags bandied about and misquoted at the time to support a denial of moral accountability; see my "'Norms, definitions and unalterable doctrines:' Chrysostom on Jeremiah." In Theodoret's defence, we recognise that the general principle is applicable to the historical context (one of Chrysostom's "norms" for responsible hermeneutics).

Chapter Eleven

[1] Deut 27.26. Theodoret would agree with some modern commentators that Jeremiah was in sympathy with the Deuteronomic movement. He would

also agree that vv.1-8 represent variations on a theme – and conciseness is not about playing variations – and that vv.3-4 are the nucleus of this theme; so he reduces the rest to a precis.

[2] Ps 95.2.

[3] Ps 40.6 in the local form of the LXX.

[4] Ps 51.16-17.

[5] John 15.2. Though we have seen Theodoret reducing to a precis sections of the text he finds verbose, he does not shirk difficult passages if he finds them ad rem. He is confronted here with one such, where the Heb. *hamulla* is already rare and obscure (probably "din") but has been read by the LXX as *himmola*, "circumcision" – "which makes nonsense," McKane observes. But Theodoret wrestles with it nonetheless.

[6] John 6.51. The Christological echoes of vv.18-19, akin to Isa 53, are familiar to Theodoret, if only from Passiontide liturgies. He does not, however, discount their immediate application to Jeremiah's situation before proceeding to see them fulfilled more completely in the case of Christ's passion, invoking further scriptural support.

Chapter Twelve

[1] Again Theodore shows the advantage of his acquaintance with Syriac to clarify the sense.

[2] This verse is a veritable *crux interpretum*, to judge from the myriad commentators (including – uniquely – Theodoret via J. Ziegler) assembled by McKane, who does not even consider that the verse is directed at the people, not Jeremiah – despite this being obvious to Theodoret (and to this modern reader), who, aware of the difficulty of the Greek, looks to the Syriac for clarity, and then offers a paraphrase of both to the readers in an admirable spirit of detachment: "I have cited both senses, leaving the choice of the better one to the readers" – a justified piece of flattery? Perhaps it is his way of implying the superiority of the Syriac without impugning the status of The Seventy responsible for the LXX, in whose divine inspiration he is a believer (cf his preface to his Psalms Commentary).

[3] This time it is Theodoret who has not considered the fairly obvious possibility that v.6 is directed at the prophet rather than the people. To document his interpretation, he has referred to one of those unusual biblical characters who seem to take his fancy (as emerges also in his Psalms Commentary), like the Rabshakeh of 2 Kings 18&19.

[4] John 19.15.

[5] Cf 7.11.

[6] As he (like other Fathers) does at intervals, Theodoret takes occasion of passages describing the Jews' continuing misfortunes to spell out the theological justification for it, namely, the crucifixion. At least he does not labor the point in the manner of a moralizing preacher.

[7] Modern commentators on vv.14-17, like other pericopes in this book, are much exercised to identify within a composite unit a "Jeremianic core"

based on appropriate historical references; other suggest a reordering of verses. Such criticism of the text is not an issue for Theodoret; he accepts its integrity *a priori*, seeing the commentator's role merely as discovery of the prophet's thought.

Chapter Thirteen

[1] Theodoret has no problem with what Jeremiah recounts in these eleven verses, by contrast with the difficulties modern commentators find: for him it is simply a prophecy in action and a literary device, *eikôn*. He has no doubt it is the Euphrates that is referred to (not some local watercourse of similar name); he raises no quibble about the seven hundred miles involved in a journey to Babylon or the absence of onlookers; he is not concerned about the way a loincloth gets sweaty and dirty or the prohibition against washing it; he does not raise McKane's point that "if it is a dramatic parable or allegory, this is a form of communication nor normally associated with the prophet Jeremiah." Theodoret is clear as to what the text says (and much of this can be reduced to a precis) and more importantly what it means – hence his choice of verses to cite verbatim. He is not primarily concerned to get the narrative to stand up historically; Frances Young warns us against presuming "Antiochene literalism meant something like modern historicism" – they were interested solely in "narrative coherence" (or at least textual coherence of whatever sort).

[2] Theodoret, ever interested in the (moral) meaning to be derived from the text (without proceeding to moralize to his readers in the manner of a preacher to his congregation), bides his time before determining the precise force of this *eikôn*, which depends on whether the text is speaking of a wineskin and scattering (so the LXX) or a wine jar and smashing (Heb.).

[3] Gal 6.10.

[4] As the chapter closes with some obscure phrases, especially in the LXX, Theodoret's conciseness comes into play. He does not unpick the proverbial statement of the difficulty of reversing habit, only rephrasing it in terms of the moral principle we have heard from him on the role of free will. He does not repeat the image in v.27 that had already occurred in v.22.

[5] Only the end of his third volume elicits from Theodoret any remark that could be construed as parenesis. He is scrupulous about letting the inspired text – adequately (if concisely) commented on – speak for itself. As to "the remedies of repentance" available in his church to those who were guilty of those human falls, he elsewhere contests Novatian rigorism that would deny forgiveness for such falls after baptism, but he does not speak of a separate sacrament of reconciliation.

Chapter Fourteen

[1] Once again Theodoret is not concerned to represent the litany of examples of the drought's effect, settling for a mention of the gasping asses ("like a

snake" an individual remark not in the LXX) perhaps because as a naturalist he finds it an accurate brushstroke.

[2] Theodoret, without saying as much, agrees with his modern counterpart McKane's judgment on the LXX version , "the sense which this yields is poor" by comparison with the Syriac, which only the former cites.

[3] Form critics like Sigmund Mowinckel recognise in vv.1-10 the elements of a communal lament found also in many psalms. Theodoret, on the other hand, is not interested in form criticism; it is the (moral) content that concerns him, not structural or formal aspects. Nor do sociological matters take his fancy, such as the implication from these verses that Jeremiah is acting as a cultic prophet. He would most of all be surprised at McKane's conclusion that these verses "are not attributable to the prophet Jeremiah. They are connected with later, perhaps exilic, reflections on the failure of Jeremiah, acknowledged to be a true prophet, to prevail with Yahweh as an intercessor."

[4] A mistaken recall of Matt 5.34-35.

Chapter Fifteen

[1] Exod 32.10.

[2] Does Theodoret have in mind Elijah's drought-breaking miracle in 1 Kgs 18.41-45? Editor Schulze thinks he has in mind some such intercession on Samuel's part as that mentioned in 1 Sam 7.5-6, and that a copyist has omitted Elijah's name from the second clause.

[3] Theodoret's response to the poetry is more sensitive to its pathos than modern commentators who think there is simply reference to an attack by day rather than by night.

[4] Again Theodoret leaves the reader to choose between Syriac and Greek versions of this pathetic complaint by Jeremiah, with which he does not proceed to empathize; detachment in a commentator is productive of explication, not empathy. The prophet can wring his own withers.

[5] In his efforts to find his way through this difficult part of the text, Theodoret evidently refers to other forms of the LXX available to him. Such other *antigrapha* he consulted in his Commentary on the Psalms, though there he also had Origen's Hexapla available for reference to the versions associated with Aquila, Symmachus and Theodotion – not to mention his predecessors in the field (not acknowledged here).

Chapter Sixteen

[1] For Theodoret Jeremiah in these vv.1-9 is making but one point, and that a well-worn one, and hence the content can be reduced to a precis. The distance between his focus as a commentator and many moderns' is illustrated by McKane's summary of critical opinion: "It is doubtful whether the right way of approaching 16.1-9 is to distinguish between a Jeremianic core and a Deuteronomistic elaboration of that core (Rudolph, Thiel, Nicholson),

or to suppose that these verses are entirely Jeremianic (Weiser, Weippert) and give us direct access to a stance of the historical prophet Jeremiah." Theodoret's response would probably be: does it matter, to me and my readers? does it help grasp the *dianoia* of the text?

[2] Theodoret is ready to concede elsewhere in his works as well the advantage the Jewish people enjoyed in having the Old Testament by comparison with the gentiles, who had "only" the New Testament. It is the Jews of his time who deserve the tribulations they experience.

[3] Our text of Theodoret is suspect here. The "former proverb" occurs at 2.11.

Chapter Seventeen

[1] Theodoret's text differs from other forms of the LXX, that have no trace of vv.1-4.

[2] Unlike modern commentators who play down the reference to conscience and look to religious practice in smearing altars with blood on the Day of Atonement, Theodoret indulges in a rare excursus of a moral nature on the incorruptibility of conscience.

[3] The Heb. word is a hapax legomenon, and Theodoret would at least note that the versions differ in their renderings; but, he says, the message is the same.

[4] One might wonder why Theodoret sees a warning about an Egyptian liaison here unless one were to note a similarly-phrased warning in Isa 31.1-3, which was perhaps on his mind after his earlier work on that prophet.

[5] Cf Dan 5.18-21. Theodoret is naturally interested in the behavior of the partridge; but being bent on relating the verse to Nebuchadnezzar (perhaps in the wake of the referral of vv.5-8 to Egypt), he ignores the partridge's habit of stealing eggs to concentrate on the decoy sounds of the hunters.

[6] Again Theodoret's text of v.12 retains elements of the Heb. lost in other forms of the LXX.

[7] Even for Theodoret in his conciseness, this precis of nine long verses is drastic. We may presume that he feels Jewish sabbath observance is not a burning issue for his readers; and his brevity reflects (not his but) his modern counterparts' scepticism about it being an issue in the time of Jeremiah, either.

Chapter Eighteen

[1] The LXX has come up with a version that parts company with the Heb., reference to "breasts" and "wind" stemming from misreading of Heb. forms; but Theodoret as usual focuses on the moral point underlying the figures and clarifies it well.

[2] Once again Theodoret wants his readers to be in no doubt about the image depicted.

[3] His fourth volume has come to an end with only a few remarks left to

make, and so concludes with the briefest of perorations.
[4] Or, as McKane puts it, "Jeremiah's opponents are saying that the pillars of the establishment stand firm and that each is secure in his own specialty. Against Jeremiah they range a powerful coalition of intellectual and spiritual leadership." Has McKane been reading Theodoret?

Chapter Nineteen

[1] Reducing a whole chapter to little better than a precis may seem drastic; but its content has been addressed before – the people's worship of idols, the symbolic action with the earthenware jar, and Topheth – so Theodoret clearly feels nothing is lost by brevity of treatment. Unlike the loincloth incident in ch. 13, the narrative does not represent both prophecy in action and an *eikôn*, a literary device.

Chapter Twenty

[1] The inclusion in Theodoret's text of "roaming," *kuklothen*, which the Heb. would suggest, is a significant difference from other forms of the LXX in McKane's view – just one more indicator of the value of the Antiochene form of the LXX for establishing the biblical text.
[2] Acts 17.16.
[3] The similarity of these verses to Job's cry in ch. 3 of that book, noted by modern commentators, escapes comment by Theodoret, who in this Commentary is not providing many gratuitous scriptural parallels. But he does offer existential reflections in case readers find Jeremiah's behavior under stress inexplicable; and McKane observes in the same vein, "The one who brought the good news now falls under the curse, for the day of birth can no longer be regarded as an occasion of rejoicing."

Chapter Twenty-One

[1] We have noted that Theodoret is not inclined to apply to the biblical texts the kinds of critical scrutiny that his modern counterparts might adopt. Redactional criticism of the kind he applies here is forced upon him here by historical references in the text itself, eliciting from him the admission that the oracles do not occur in the book in historical order (cf note 1 to ch. 25 & 26, and his comment on Isa 51.9). Though showing his characteristic flexibility in this, he is still reluctant to give it the importance it has for modern commentators.
[2] Depending on vocalisation the Heb. word can have either of these two meanings, occurring in the versions of Theodotion and Symmachus respectively, and also the meaning Tyre, which the LXX and Aquila seem

to be taking – a meaning Theodoret with reference to the Syriac does not entertain here, unlike Ezek 26.2 (though some modern commentators also have difficulty with the phrase as a description of Jerusalem). Jerome admits the possibility of all three readings.

Chapter Twenty-Two

[1] Cf Heb 6.13.

[2] Isa 13.3. We know from this that Theodoret had previously completed his Commentary on Isaiah (as in its preface he admits he has yet to treat of Jeremiah).

[3] Theodoret the geographer is interested in teasing out Jeremiah's figures involving places. He can relate the mention of Lebanon with the cedars later in the verse, which he sees referring to conceited people (rather than buildings). Gilead, which in 8.22 he had unaccountably called "a city of priests," he now thinks of as two places, one in Lebanon and the other in Israel, perhaps thinking of two cities in that general area of Gilead such as Jabesh-Gilead to the north and Ramoth-Gilead to the east; the more mountainous character of the former may account for his associating it with impiety.

[4] Cf 2 Kgs 23.31-35; 2 Chr 36.1-4. The "some" Theodoret cites in support of reading Shallum as Jehoahaz would include several Antiochene mss of the LXX, according to J. Ziegler. But where Theodoret sees vv.13-17 also directed to this king (presenting his evidence below), modern commentators prefer to see them plus vv.18-19 as a philippic against Jehoiakim.

[5] Other forms of the LXX convey the sense of this passage less adequately than Theodoret's local text.

[6] Matt 7.21.

[7] Theodoret is referring here to the plain statement in 2 Kgs 24.6 and 2 Chr 36.8 (LXX) that Jehoiakim died in Jerusalem and was buried in the family grave; Jeremiah (here and at 36.30) contests only the manner of interment. As to this manner, Theodoret's text first says he is not (properly) buried, then he says he is treated like dead birds, *oiônoi;* the LXX says he is given the burial of an ass, *onos,* as does our Heb. – which intrigues commentators on it. Jerome sees birds entering the picture to tear the corpse to pieces as happens with dead asses. The "dunghill" of Theodoret's text may arise from a confusion of similar Heb. forms *hemur,* ass, with *homer* – or vice versa.

[8] As a geographer Theodoret knows the two mountain ranges mentioned in this v.20; the LXX has misread the Heb. for a third, Abarim, to mean "to the seashore," and his Syriac version does no better.

[9] Other forms of the LXX do not register this clause. The word in the Heb. which Theodoret's text renders "mouth" is a hapax legomenon, possibly "idol" (McKane) or "pot" (Jerome, NRSV); Theodoret does not feel secure enough to attempt to unpack the image.

[10] Eph 1.21. Though Theodoret is mainly concerned that his readers grasp

Jeremiah's moral message, he knows they would also want factual statements in the text to stand up if they are to take the prophecy seriously ("narrative coherence" again); and as well he wants to show that Jews could not claim Jesus was their king in the sense that David was. So, recalling but conveniently ignoring Gabriel's promising Jesus "the *thronos* of his ancestor David" (Luke 1.32) and the entry of both Zerubbabel and David in Luke's genealogy of Jesus (3.27,31), he substitutes an elegant variation in denying Jesus the Davidic *thôkoi*. The moderate Theodoret (with apologies for the assonance; Gustave Bardy calls him "modéré") does not normally use a mallet to kill a gnat.

Chapter Twenty-Three

[1] Other forms of the LXX do not have the verb "be in disagreement," an important inclusion for Theodoret, who uses it to dispose further of Zerubbabel as a fulfillment of prophecy in competition to Jesus.
[2] Theodoret in his approach to these verses, as part of his polemic against Jews who (like many modern commentators) want to see Zerubbabel referred to, is not helped by the LXX rendering *anatolê*, generally meaning "east," "dawn," for the *blastêma*, "shoot" of Symmachus, and by the attachment of the phrase about the prophets to v.6 instead of the opening of v.9 as in the Heb. The most he is prepared to concede to Zerubbabel – reluctantly (there being no scriptural support) – is the role of a type of Jesus; cf his comments on the similar 33.15-16. His term for the Jews, "stupid," is etymologically linked to thunder, as Eng. "lunatic" is to the moon – strong stuff for a man of moderation.
[3] Other forms of the LXX version of v.10 make no such charge, leading some commentators to question our Heb. text. But the Syriac agrees with it and with Theodoret's text, to which it would be good for the moderns to refer.
[4] The meaning of the passage depends on the form of the Heb. word which Theodoret's text takes as something like "pledge, loan" and which others (cf NRSV) take as "burden," and on whether Jeremiah is thus being taunted (as Theodoret feels).
[5] In his customary brief peroration closing his fifth volume, Theodoret hints at Jeremiah's detractors in upholding the vivifying effect of both OT and NT (*prophêtikoi* and *apostolikoi*) writings, through both of which God speaks. Contemporary detractors of the OT may also have been in his sights, even if it was Jewish promotion of Zerubbabel's claims over Jesus' that occupied him in these two chapters.

Chapter Twenty-Four

[1] Modern commentators tend to see this chapter with its endorsement of

Judaism in exile as a mere "compilation in which other parts of the Hebrew Bible are used... a historical riddle which cannot be completely solved" (McKane), not the work of the prophet. Theodoret, of course, entertains no such deconstructive criticism, merely suggesting here that we should leave suspended the question of how the vision of the figs should be taken; and as usual he concentrates on the import of the vision.

Chapter Twenty-Five

[1] As we have observed (cf note 1 to ch. 21), under pressure from internal evidence Theodoret is prepared to admit that the order of oracles in the text is not consistently sequential; but he sees the author to be in control of the material.

[2] The fact that other forms of the LXX do not incorporate this annotation about Nebuchadnezzar is used by modern commentators to postulate a prejudice in the Seventy against Babylon or a learned gloss creeping in to synchronize Judean and Babylonian chronologies in a late edition of the Heb. text. Again one has to wish that reference might be made to the text available to Antiochene commentators in the fourth and fifth centuries before such uneducated guesses are arrived at.

[3] At this point the Heb. and LXX part company in ordering the text. The LXX sees a cue to present here the oracles against the nations (Heb.46-51) and sets the opening oracle (Heb.25.15-38) at the end of that block as 32.15-38 – perhaps the original order. Theodoret's editor Schulze thought fit to adhere to the order of our Heb. (and modern versions).

[4] Ps 75.8.

[5] Theodoret the geographer is not content to let the nations pass without explicit mention, even though, as he acknowledges, his previous commentaries on all the other prophets have likewise touched on them. Location of them is not clear in every case to modern geographers.

[6] Cf Gen 25.2; 1 Chr 1.32. McKane takes the omission of Zimri from the LXX as a guarantee it was not in the Heb. text the Seventy translated; but Theodoret tells us he found it one such Heb. text (accessed through the Syriac, as usual) – as well as in his own local form of the LXX, does he mean?

[7] The final clause of v.26 "is not indicated by Sept. and is certainly secondary," McKane observes – but again it is in Theodoret's text; and he hazards another personal interpretation of it (if not speaking of cryptograms or atbash, as do his modern counterparts: cf note 13 to ch. 51) as well as justifying its inclusion, his focus being primarily theological rather than paleographical.

[8] Theodoret repeats his morphological observation (middle voice of the verb *krinô* rather than active) to make a subtle theological point (as before), but prudently avoids the more demanding challenges of these verses – how relate "on high," "holy habitation," "his place," why the reference to the

treading of grapes. If he has no light to shed on obscure textual matters, better to say nothing.

Chapter Twenty-Six

[1] As at the opening of chs 21 & 25, Theodoret is implying oracles are not arranged in chronological order. Modern commentators suggest ch. 26 is related to Jeremiah's Temple discourse in ch. 7.
[2] Ezek 2.5 in Theodoret's form of the LXX. Divine ignorance or mutability is inadmissible in his theology.
[3] Mic 3.12 (the house being the Lord's). Theodoret does not advert to the fact that this is the only explicit quotation in the Bible of one prophet by another.
[4] At the rate Theodoret is moving through the text he merely paraphrases it; but it would seem his text (but not the LXX generally) attributes vv.19-23 to the leaders and people making accusations against priests and false prophets.
[5] Theodoret does not acknowledge mention of this Ahikam in Josaiah's time in 2 Kgs 22.12,14.

Chapter Twenty-Seven

[1] If his text, which corresponds to one Heb. reading (the whole verse missing from other forms of the LXX), is to be taken at face value, then this chapter would precede ch. 27, even though it goes on to speak – more appropriately – of Zedekiah (the opening rogue time-reference coming from 26.1). Too complicated for Theodoret, who has been flexible enough to allow for some rearrangement of oracles – but this is too much.
[2] Theodoret does not give us his text of v.3, so we do not know if it agrees with the "send them (the bars)" of Heb. and other forms of LXX (*pace* Jones), or is a conjecture like modern versions that are similarly expressed.
[3] The anthropomorphic phrase may be misconstrued by his readers, Theodoret feels, and encourage a depreciation of divine transcendence; so it is explained as a concession to their human limitations – an example of *synkatabasis*, in Chrysostom's terminology.
[4] "The dark prophecy of v.7... is absent from the LXX," says Jones – wrong again (because not consulting its variant, and specifically Antiochene, forms). Theodoret, in the particular conciseness typical of this his final prophetic commentary, is picking the eyes out of the text. How Zedekiah now enters the picture after the earlier (rogue) time-reference to Jehoiakim he cannot stop to unravel. (Unfortunately, this extreme conciseness deprives us of greater light on the Antiochene LXX text, there being no other extant commentary from that school on this work.)
[5] The Heb. text of v.19 and obviously Theodoret's refer to the bronze stands and vessels made for Solomon, as 1 Kgs 7.27-47 records. Other forms of

the LXX omit the verse, an omission which Jones says some commentators attribute to the "abridging tendency of LXX at work" but which he prefers to take as "an earlier form of the tradition" – unaware, of course, of its presence in the Antiochene text, an integral part of the puzzle. Decisions about original text cannot be taken without retrieving all available data.

Chapter Twenty-Eight

[1] While continuing to pick the eyes out of the chapter, Theodoret carefully analyses the dynamic between Hananiah, respectable but still false prophet, and Jeremiah, wishing he were right but unable to endorse him. The pathos of the situation is not lost on him.
[2] One would think this meaning would emerge; but Theodoret is not for letting images go unappreciated.
[3] An unusually moral elaboration on the text.

Chapter Twenty-Nine

[1] That is, Jehoiachin (son of Jehoiakim), taken captive to Babylon in the first deportation in 597. Again Theodoret admits the narrative is not in sequence.
[2] 1 Tim 2.1-2 – a rare piece of scriptural documentation by the hastening commentator, but the paradoxical affirmation of a foreign power requires some comment.
[3] The Heb. term here, as compared with the one used of bad figs in ch. 24, is a hapax legomenon. It may be through his native Syriac that Theodoret comes to this statement of its meaning (cf note 8 below); it is a typically heuristic stance he adopts as a naturalist to the neologism, testifying to the authenticity of our text. Jones, probably on the basis of his copy of Rahlfs, declares vv.16-20 "missing from the LXX," and on these (faulty) grounds opines that "LXX represents an earlier form of the text and the expansion in MT is the result of *literary* activity."
[4] A popular imprecation Theodoret often recalls, as in the Isaiah Commentary.
[5] Pss 79.4; 44.14.
[6] The NRSV's "persisently" leaves a lot to be desired in conveying what Heb. and Theodoret's text literally say; he could not be so unresponsive.
[7] Other forms of the LXX omit mention of the dispatch of letters found in our Heb. and Theodoret's text. Jones again naively presumes, "It is clear that MT has embellished the earlier text," whereas Theodoret goes on to insist on letter after letter.
[8] Theodoret's text has simply transliterated the Heb. for "stocks;" but with his ignorance of the language he has to check with the Syriac to find a meaning.

[9] Only at the close of (his sixth) volume does Theodoret, as we have observed, permit himself any parenesis.

Chapter Thirty

[1] Jones declares the final phrase "missing from the LXX" and therefore a gloss, if a helpful one. Theodoret expands on the image, and proceeds to mention a different one he remembers from 2.37. He has no choice but to admit that Jeremiah's ministry was at times not simply one of preaching but also of committing oracles to writing, whereas on Isa 51.9 he was at pains to stress that the order of the oracles was determined by later redactors.
[2] Vv.11-12, which occur again at 46.27-28, are here missing from other forms of the LXX. Theodoret comments on them at both places. He is finding this material, a moral discourse from the Lord, more to his purpose than the narrative of former chs.
[3] A modern commentator would do well to note that the mention of the Temple, *naos*, in the Antiochene text (and, strangely, adopted in Rahlfs' text) is paralleled by *laos*, people, in other forms of the LXX (as though by a copyist's error) – making a significant difference in the nature of the prophecy. Our Heb. text speaks of palace or citadel, *'armon*.
[4] The LXX reading is awkward: Theodoret gets a quite different alternative from the Syriac, but is not in a position to proceed further to the Heb. to settle the question. And unlike the more leisurely Isaiah Commentary, he does not go to the trouble of showing the reader that both versions have a worthwhile meaning. Pressure of time brings the incidental advantage of a reduction in rationalizing.
[5] Theodoret probably has Sir 2.10 in mind.

Chapter Thirty-One

[1] Theodoret's text of v.2, which he calls simply the Greek version, departs markedly from other forms of the LXX and our Heb. For light on it he turns to the Hebrew via the Syriac, and typically (though unconvincingly) declares there to be similarity in meaning, which he is not clear about, failing to admit any reference to a new Exodus that modern commentators find. He is too much in haste to refer to the Hexapla for the alternative versions and "the Septuagint" (that form of the LXX mentioned only once at the very beginning, on 1.12), as he so often did in the Isaiah Commentary to resolve obscurities. He seems to think his text of v.3, which corresponds to other forms of the LXX, is supported by the Syriac (the Peshitta version of the prophets being available at this time, we recall, though influenced by the LXX).
[2] This is a fair paraphrase of the verse, though its sentiments on the gratuity of divine mercy are not generally to the liking of an Antiochene.

[3] Among Jacob's sons, that is; cf Gen 46.8-27.
[4] Theodoret the topographer is following the location in Gen 35.19, thought now to be a gloss (but where today's guides will show you the tomb – and possibly did in his day), contradicted by Gen 35.16 and 1 Sam 10.2 that place the grave at Ephrath on the northern border of Benjamin.
[5] Cf Matt 2.16-18.
[6] Jer 5.3.
[7] Hos 10.11; 4.16.
[8] Ps 119.67,71.
[9] By contrast with the Isaiah Commentary, influenced so strongly as it was by Alexandrian hermeneutics, recourse to an eschatological interpretation of Jeremian verses is very rare, Theodoret generally content to stay with the historical sense. An exception is made here, for one reason perhaps because the final clause in our Heb. (rendered by the NRSV as "a woman encompasses a man") has been classed by R. P. Carroll as "perhaps the most incomprehensible saying in the whole book." Theodoret, as we have seen, prefers not simply to throw up his hands, even if the historical sense is opaque.
[10] In commentary on Ezek 18.2, completed well before this (and the Isaiah Commentary), Theodoret had recourse to the version of Symmachus as well to clarify the meaning of the rare verb here rendered "were set on edge," whereas there his text read "became blood-red."
[11] We could be somewhat disappointed by Theodoret's response to this prophecy of the new covenant, a passage that has been called by John Bright "one of the profoundest and most moving passages in the whole Bible," and on the other hand we are impressed by his not immediately giving it an eschatological sense that NT passages might encourage. He sees it first confirming the previous proverb, and only then makes a comparison of the two covenants before proceeding to its Christological and indeed polemical (but not eucharistic) content.
[12] Exod 3.14.
[13] There are some individual features of Theodoret's text of this verse – the inclusion again of Judah, the phrase "the breasts of their hearts."
[14] Again Theodoret admits redactional activity affecting the composition of biblical books, the prophets in particular. Cf note 1 to ch. 30, and Theodoret's comment on the date in Ezek 30.20.
[15] The bishop can always find a baptismal reference in a text.
[16] Isa 10.22; Rom 9.6. Does Paul really support Jeremiah and Isaiah – and Theodoret?
[17] Again Jones fails to take account of the Antiochene text (at least) in observing, "LXX places v.35 after v.37 and thereby destroys its point. MT is to be preferred." The "point" is not lost on Theodoret.
[18] 18.9-10. The directions are obscure in a passage modern commentators would see as an addition from the period of Nehemiah's rebuilding of the city. Theodoret with his interest in topography stays with it, even seeking enlightenment on names from the Syriac.

Chapter Thirty-Two

[1] Again Theodoret is signaling the lack of sequence in chapters, and the gap between the placement of oracles and their "actual delivery," *energeia*.
[2] Mere narrative is not of significance, and a precis suffices – but not without depriving us of a knowledge of the Antiochene text of Jeremiah. The custom of giving right of purchase to the relative, prescribed in Lev 25.25-31, is acted out in the book of Ruth.
[3] Ezek 8.16.
[4] Theodoret had examined these rites fully in comment on Isa 30.33, as also the derivation of Topheth/Tapheth/Thapheth; he digests the information in comment on 7.31 (see note 7 there) and here. His text makes a reference to "towers in Geb" in place of the sacrifices to Moloch in LXX and Heb., though the latter is paraphrased here.
[5] Even when reducing large sections of this prose narrative and sermon to brief precis, Theodoret can still pause for topographical precision. But from the viewpoint of "narrative coherence" he is also concerned to show that God's puzzling instructions (to man behind bars) about buying a property did make sense.

Chapter Thirty-Three

[1] The prose sermon again is thought reducible to precis. Theodoret pauses to comment on the hapax legomenon, *synoulosis*.
[2] Jones (along with other commentators) comments: "Startlingly, LXX does not have vv.14-26, the longest single passage which LXX lacks. There is no obvious reason why LXX should have deliberately omitted it. The conclusion must be that it is a relatively late addition to MT. The content supports this." Not only does Theodoret's text give the lie to this baseless conclusion, but he sees vv.15-16 repeating elements of 23.5-6 (a reason for omission by other forms of the LXX?), where he had vigorously contested Jewish claims of Zerubbabel's fitting this role except as a type and denies him the title Jozadak.
[3] Gen 49.10, a favorite locus of Theodoret's. He is insistent, even more than on 23.5-6 (where he did proceed to the person of Jesus), on examining the prophecy's applicability to the history of Judah, canceling Zerubbabel's eligibility but seeing a realisation in the exercise of priestly power after the Exile. This attachment to the historical sense of prophecy is noteworthy, and typical of Theodoret, by comparison with the Isaiah Commentary.
[4] Theodoret has finally conceded that only in NT terms can the prophecy fully make sense. Unlike modern commentators who see the "two tribes" as those, not of David and Levi, but of Israel and Judah, he is happy to confirm that the orders of Christian clergy in the performance of their clerical ministry are fulfilling the Lord's intentions mediated by Jeremiah.

Chapter Thirty-Four

[1] Again Theodoret notes lack of sequence in the material.
[2] Deut 15.12.
[3] Cf Gen 15.9-10.

Chapter Thirty-Five

[1] Though he cuts to the bones of the story, the Rechabites' fidelity wrings this unaccustomed exclamation from Theodoret.
[2] Anxious to see the Rechabites' virtue not lost, Theodoret maintains that the tradition has lived on – though the Bible does not seem to know of it (could the nineteenth century Independent Order of Rechabites have had a precedent in early Antioch?). In finding a (false) reference to Rechab in the LXX version of Judg 1:19, Theodoret in his Quaestiones on the Octateuch (Q.6 on Judg) compliments him and his descendants for their religious spirit.
These chapters are being reduced to a readable precis; it is not simply a question of the survival of individual verses as found in a catena. Theodoret has never considered mere narrative worth delaying on; theological significance is what is important.

Chapter Thirty-Six

[1] As he has implied before, Theodoret sees Jeremiah's ministry as one of oral delivery of oracles later re-arranged in imperfect sequence by redactors. Chapter 36 thus recounts Baruch's written recording of them at this late stage. Where our Heb. speaks of this being done in a scroll (of papyrus) and the LXX generally of paper leaves, the Antiochene text speaks of a chapter (*kephalis*) of a book, which to Theodoret means *eilêmata*, volumes.
[2] The prophet's being inspired, *energoumenos* (*empneomenos* below), is taken for granted by Theodoret, and not often mentioned. Chrysostom will use *katêchoumenos*, less often *entheos*, for this charism (see my "Chrysostom's terminology of the inspired Word"). .
[3] The inclusion of "the Lord," which makes the good sense Theodoret proceeds to explicate, occurs only in his text. As well, his text refutes Jones's claim that the LXX on good grounds does not say "all" his servants were involved, exceptions about to be listed.
[4] Christological comment, we noted, has been rare in this Commentary (by comparison with Isaiah, e.g., or even the Psalms). This comparison and the expression of the hypostatic union both leave something to be desired, frequent though the latter is in this Antiochene.
[5] Theodoret has to tie up the loose ends, disposing of the brief reign of Jehoiachin (cf 2 Kgs 24.8-12) and that intriguing phrase about Baruch's inclusion of other items, lest "coherence" of the prophetic narrative be impaired. Thus – after a precis of the dramatic narrative of ch. 36 (treated

somewhat differently by Chrysostom in his first homily on the obscurity of the OT) – the seventh volume is brought to a close.

Chapter Thirty-Seven

[1] Modern commentators see the work of redactors introducing this chapter with a condensed account of Zedekiah's accession in 2 Kgs 24.17-20. Theodoret – or his text – shows the influence of this source, which mentions the king's age and length of reign, not occurring here in Heb. or LXX. He also gives the king a role in convincing the Egyptians to supply temporary assistance.
[2] The final phrase is an unusual moral comment of Theodoret's.
[3] Neither our Heb. nor other forms of the LXX give the buying of bread as the reason for the prophet's journey, nor make the comment that the public prison was passed over on account of its being full.

Chapter Thirty-Eight

[1] Though modern commentators tend to see this account as a doublet of the imprisonment arrangements in the previous chapter, Theodoret unusually goes into particular detail in paraphrasing the incident. The device of rags under armpits (presumably to avoid rope burn) is not found in other forms of LXX, nor naming of the pit insisted on here; and for the Heb. term for the obscure meeting place in the Temple which the LXX attempts simply to transliterate, he even goes to the trouble of invoking the Syriac. Theological significance is surely yet to come.
[2] This is more to the theological point for any reader of the chapters: why would God give a guarantee of safekeeping and of destruction, respectively, on those conditions? The text does not supply the answer; but Theodoret is not prepared to take a hint from the Kings account to settle for a moralizing solution, Zedekiah's impiety – rather, he comes up with his own partly political, partly religious analysis.
[3] A phrase that commentators relate to Obad 7, but not Theodoret here or in that place. He has, however, well brought out the dilemma and tragic error of Zedekiah, this being at the focus of attention in commenting on this chapter.

Chapter Thirty-Nine

[1] The fact that vv.4-13 do not appear in the other forms of the LXX leads modern commentators to debate whether the shorter text or the longer Heb., which is presumed to have taken these verses from 2 Kgs 25, represents the original. Theodoret's text, however, includes these verses (unbe-

known to the moderns), though as usual he is not much taken with mere narrative, contenting himself with a precis and remarking more typically on topographical details and on Zedekiah's ingratitude to his benefactor as he had done in the previous chapter. (We shall see the passage recurring in ch. 52, where Theodoret does not advert to his previous account; and, as editor Schulze notes, he recounts the events in commenting on Ezek 12.4-5.)

[2] Significance lies, Theodoret believes, not in bare narrative but in revealing incidents, in this case involving two foreigners, not Jews – a perception not labored in the text.

[3] Cf 1.18.

[4] The final clause is "missing from the LXX," opines Jones.

[5] Pss 146.5; 144.15.

Chapter Forty

[1] Modern commentators debate the authenticity of material in these chapters in which Jeremiah is not personally involved. For his part Theodoret is not interested in commenting on machinations involving Johanan and Ishmael, nor does he share Jones's view that Gedeliah is a central character as being an "alter ego" of Jeremiah.

Chapter Forty-One

[1] The story may not be worth dwelling on; but if there is light to be shed on topography, let there be light.

[2] No moralist, Theodoret is nevertheless concerned to find some theological significance in these bloody narratives.

Chapter Forty-Two

[1] This material is grist to Theodoret's theological mill, and he cites the text verbatim. He also ventures a comment on the detail of time provided, which incidentally differs from the response of a modern commentator, G. Couturier, "The answer came to Jeremiah only 10 days later; the delay certainly aggravated the situation, for the fear of the Babylonians could only have increased. Also this delay proves well enough that true prophetical inspiration does not depend on human insight."

[2] One is reminded that the prose form of the text has not given Theodoret scope to comment on figurative language, such as found in earlier oracles. This is a rare exception; another appeals to him in the following chapter, the shepherd delousing his cloak as a figure of Nebuchadnezzar despoiling Egypt.

Chapter Forty-Three

[1] Cf Exod 1.11 LXX (On being the Heb. form of the Egyptian name for Heliopolis). Theodoret does not go into the question – here or at Ezek 29.19 – as to whether Nebuchadnezzar did in fact invade Egypt, a fact known to us from a fragmentary tablet, but probably unknown to him

Chapter Forty-Four

[1] The text of this verse resembles our Heb. but differs from other forms of the LXX.
[2] Schulze suggests the better reading is "the more impious." Perhaps the Babylonians came to mind in connection with the queen of heaven mentioned in these verses, an originally Mesopotamian goddess.
[3] 7.17-18.
[4] Theodoret is not giving his readers much credit for general knowledge. Or is it that he himself is short on knowledge of this Hophra, the pharaoh (otherwise known as Apries) who gave assistance to Zedekiah against Babylon and was killed by a pretender? (One manuscript of the Commentary does in fact supply further historical information.)

Chapter Forty-Five

[1] The final phrase "absent from the LXX," says Jones, "almost certainly a gloss."
[2] Cf 1 Cor 10.13. It is an appropriate moment for Theodoret to close his (eighth) volume, the conclusion of the prose narratives.

Chapter Forty-Six

[1] As was observed in note 3 of ch. 25, this chapter, introducing oracles against Egypt and other nations, is numbered 26 in the LXX, and follows an oracle about the people of Judah. Theodoret's editor Schulze thought fit to follow the order of chapters in our Heb. and modern versions.
[2] Cf 2 Kgs 23.29. Theodoret's text seems to contain no mention of the precise site of Neco's defeat, Carchemish.
[3] Cf Gen 43.11. Theodoret the naturalist pauses to add this detail.
[4] This comment encapsulates Theodoret's style of commentary. He knows what the author's mind is, but his LXX text – probably by confusing similar Heb. forms – has come up with a puzzling reference to a yew tree; the Syriac, to which he turns for enlightenment, reproduces the Heb. and seems to make no such reference. But, as a naturalist and with his habitual insistence that all versions are saying the same thing, he enters into the author's supposed use of imagery to rationalize the versions and bring out

the meaning – not unlike a magician producing a rabbit out of a hat.
[5] Again the mention of Greeks is puzzling – and again arising from confusion of similar Heb. forms by the LXX; but Theodoret can rationalize his way out of it, having nowhere else to turn (his Hexapla not available for recourse to Symmachus and company?).
[6] When it comes to Hebrew terms (like this nickname) retained in the text by the LXX, Theodoret, ignorant of that language (*pace* Guinot and Rondeau), can only fall back on his native Syriac (a dialect of Aramaic).
[7] Isa 19.13.
[8] Cf Matt 7.26.
[9] Theodoret, as is his wont, has been helpfully explicating the images in the text; but this comment seems otiose.
[10] Cf 43.8 (which, interestingly, is 50.8 in LXX ordering of chapters, whereas we are in LXX ch. 26 at this point).
[11] "Verse 26 is missing in the LXX," declares Jones.

Chapter Forty-Seven

[1] "The original title [i.e., v.1] was only 'Against the Philistines,' as in the LXX," maintains Couturier, not having seen Theodoret's paraphrase of his Antiochene text; and Jones concurs.
[2] Cf the comment by Theodoret on Isa 23.1. He would like to tidy up all the obscure references in this passage if he could.
[3] Jer 7.29, a verse paraphrased to this effect.
[4] Theodoret may be recalling the reference to these giant people in Jos 11.21-22.

Chapter Forty-Eight

[1] Isa 46.1. Modern commentators admit difficulty in identifying the place names in this chapter. Theodoret, topographer that he is, had done his best in the Isaiah Commentary (cf chs 15 & 16 there, verses from which recur below).
[2] Theodoret has been dutifully commenting, albeit briefly, on these verses referring to Moab, which might be thought less relevant to the prophet's message. So, perhaps in desperation, he lets slip – uncharacteristically – a moral one-liner by way of application to his readers.
[3] Even if Jeremiah's thought is proving a little tedious, he can at least earn a compliment for his imagery.
[4] Cf 1 Kgs 12.25-30; Amos 3.14; 4.4; 5.5.
[5] Topographer though he is, Theodoret sees no value for his readers in listing and locating a dozen obscure cities of Moab mentioned in vv.21-24.
[6] When this obscure verse appeared as Isa 16.7 as part of an identical oracle against Moab, Theodoret had Symmachus to fall back on for some light.

Here, unmindful of the parallel, and evidently without that alternative version to hand, he has recourse to the Syriac, faring no better, and coming up with a different paraphrase. Like many a modern commentator, he is struggling with the material.

[7] Jazer gains a mention in Num 21.32, but not in the context of weeping; Theodoret, here and at Isa 16.8, is vague about the occurrence.

[8] Cf Ezek 17.3-6.

[9] Again Theodoret does not acknowledge that vv.43-44 replicate Isa 24.17-18.

[10] This time it is the song in Num 21.27-30 from which the author borrows, unbeknown to Theodoret. Vv.45-47 do not occur in other forms of the LXX – "missing from the LXX," in Jones's view.

Chapter Forty-Nine

[1] The LXX text (not our Heb.) refers to these giant people, on whom Theodoret had commented on 47.5.

[2] Jones comments: "In v.6 the salvation of Ammon is envisaged, like that of Moab (48.47) but, as there, the passage is lacking in LXX."

[3] Presumably Theodoret is gleaning this information on Eliphaz (king?) of Teman from Job.4.1. He does not advert to the similarity of vv.7-16 to the text of Obadiah.

[4] Theodoret may be distinguishing the Bozrah in Idumea (Edom) from the city of Moab mentioned in the list in 48.24 that he passed over.

[5] Ps 78.49. Theodoret is strangely not content with the sense of "messenger" for *angelos* in this verse. In his Commentary on Paul's letters he showed a particular interest in angels, e.g., in comment on Col 2.18.

[6] The Exod 12 account does not mention an angel, but its midrash in 1 Cor 10.10 and Heb 11.28 refers to "the destroyer," an avenging angel.

[7] Cf 2 Sam 24.15-17.

[8] Theodoret often remarks on a particular prophecy that it proved true, *apseudes*; narrative – or in this case prophetic – coherence is at stake.

[9] Theodoret distinguished these two possible locations in comment on 4.15 (see also notes 6 and 7 there). The two cities, symbolizing former Aramean power, appear as a couple also in 2 Kgs 19.13; their similar occurrence in Isa 36.19; 37.13 goes without mention by Theodoret, that Commentary being of the kind it is.

[10] The final clause of this verse, found several times above, is "missing from the LXX," in Jones's terms.

[11] Cf Gen 25.13. Theodoret's variant of a title going back to the third century BC is interesting.

[12] Where our Heb. speaks of "kingdoms of Hazor" and "people of the east," the LXX reads different forms and comes up with "queen of the court" and "sons of Kedemah" (as also in v.33).

[13] A slip of the tongue for the Persian Gulf?

[14] Another comment along the lines of narrative coherence, though which city is now a pious site of the Lord's throne is not clear.
[15] It is rare in this Commentary for Theodoret to introduce a spiritual interpretation. Perhaps the close of another volume encouraged him to do so by way of peroration.

Chapter Fifty

[1] Theodoret has got himself into a spot of bother here by confusing the principal god of the Babylonian pantheon, Marduk/Merodach (with whom the god Bel from Nippur had become identified), with the king Merodach-baladan who appears in Isa 39.1, and to whom in his final comments on Isa 37 he had credited with the transfer of power from Nineveh to Babylon that had in fact occurred under Nabopalassar, father of Nebuchadnezzar. But he can find an appropriate meaning, despite the confusion – like all rationalizers.
[2] If Medes or Persians are intended, as Theodoret believes, perhaps he might have suggested that east was the more precise direction.
[3] Ps 95.7.
[4] Cf Dan 8. A modern commentator like Jones also finds the image a little unlikely; Theodoret suggests he look further for enlightenment, finding it in the Syriac and scriptural parallels.
[5] In fact, of course, as occurred earlier at 46.16, the LXX comes up with "Greek sword" for "destroying sword" by confusion of similar Heb. forms; and so this discursus on Greeks is wide of the mark – but not without a rationale by the commentator.
[6] We have noted that Theodoret consistently omits the reign of Sargon II, 721-705, from the list of Assyrian kings of the period (as he likewise does not occur in the Bible).
[7] Theodoret had discussed these terms and various translations of them in commentary on Isa 13.21-22, where he also enunciated the principle (which Chrysostom had styled *synkatabasis*) of Scripture's adoption of human forms of expression. He is not ready, like modern commentators, to note the similarity of these verses to material found elsewhere in the prophets and suggest they are a pastiche of these other loci.
[8] The present course of the Euphrates and the desolation of the site are quoted as a further index of the reliability of prophecy.
[9] Ps 137.9.

Chapter Fifty-One

[1] Dan 2.32,38. Commentary on this book was one of Theodoret's first exegetical works.
[2] Isa 14.13.
[3] Though Theodoret does not hint at it, the passage replicates 10.12-16.

[4] As before when enlightenment was required on an obscure verse, Theodoret has his Syriac version to refer to, but no "Greek version" other than his local form of the LXX; the form in the Hexapla is obviously not to hand, nor The Three also contained there.
[5] The final phrase is "absent in LXX," in Jones's terms. An unusual image calls for some explication, and Theodoret as usual supplies it.
[6] Individual verses, repetitive though they be, are coming in for comment, even if brief, where theological content may be thought to be thin. But we recall that the chapter is numbered only 28 in the Greek, and so is early in the work as a whole. Later chs in the version (placed earlier in our Heb.), especially of a narrative character, we noticed receiving less individual comment.
[7] The question is, however, not that there are two ways of referring to the one city, but how did the difference arise. Today's scholars explain it as a case of atbash, a code or cryptogram in which the last letter of the Heb. alphabet replaces the first, the second last the second, and so on, the word in question here being *Babel*. Naturally, Theodoret, unaware of this, would think in terms of two unrelated names, one replacing the other in the course of time; and he recalls it happening also in 25.26.
[8] Dan 14 LXX.
[9] For Jones, vv.44b-49a are "lacking in LXX" owing to haplography.
[10] This comment of Theodoret's represents a clause (49b) in his text that reads differently from Heb. and other forms of LXX.
[11] Powerful portrayal of retribution like this, even if thought derivative by modern commentators with an eye to earlier oracles, requires no elaboration, let alone moralizing. And so we appreciate Theodoret's bare commentary, faithful to his initial promise of conciseness and his scrupulous avoidance of the role of a preacher.

Chapter Fifty-Two

[1] LXX ch. 28, naturally, does not close with the redactor's words in the Heb., "Thus far are the words of Jeremiah" – but does Theodore know of some such closure at some point before ch. 52 opens?
[2] Theodoret had given a precis of this same account occurring as ch. 39 (see note 1 there), and for all his conciseness does the same here – incl. the v.15 that speaks of the committal of the land to the poor ("absent in LXX," says Jones). He even clarifies for his readers some of the items of the spoils – a rather extreme instance of Antiochene *akribeia*.
[3] Numbering of the captives in vv.28-30 Theodoret is aware of, despite modern commentators declaring the verses missing from the LXX
[4] Thus, even at the close of this sorry story, Theodoret has only the briefest of moral conclusions to offer his readers; he could never be classed another Jeremiah. He does not even breathe a sigh of relief for having finally brought to a close his work on all the prophets: (Baruch and) Lamentations await, when closure may properly be drawn. As he suggested at the begin-

ning, this Jeremiah Commentary has simply been an afterthought – though in its directness it may reveal the true Theodoret more authentically than the more leisurely and derivative Isaiah Commentary.

Notes to the Commentary on the Book of Baruch

Chapter One

[1] The Commentary on Baruch, of course, a book not in the Heb. Bible, occurs in most mss of LXX and of Theodoret between Jer and Lam (though in the Vulgate after Lam). Theodoret is aware that the material in Bar is not by Jeremiah himself, but in commentary on Bar 3.32 he speaks of it as part of the one work, *prophêteia* – hence its occurring before the work's conclusion at the end of Lam. The so-called Letter of Jeremiah, occurring at the end of Bar (LXX) or as its sixth ch. (Vulg), is not in Theodoret's text, at least in the major mss (his mention of a "letter" – see note 4 below – is probably not in reference to that).

[2] Modern commentators highlight the errors in historical details made by the author, such as Belshazzar's being described as the son of Nebuchadnezzar instead of the later Nabonidus, an error occurring also in Dan. Theodoret seems anxious to avoid other errors, such as the decision in v.8 to send back to Jerusalem the sacred vessels (Ezra mentioning this occurs under Cyrus) and the suggestion in v.14 that the Temple is still standing. He also notes the Hebrew term *manna* occurring in v.10, known also from NT usage, e.g., John 6.31,49.

[3] Cf 1 Tim 2.1-2. Theodoret can be quoted elsewhere for this statement of coherence between OT and NT teaching, as in commentary on Ps 33.6, "Old Testament inspired composition, *prophêteia*, anticipates the Gospel teaching."

[4] If it strikes us a strange that the letter (Theodoret's term for *biblion* in LXX v.14) should be "read out to God," we may see the expression arising from his anxiety to avoid the anachronistic expression in v.14 "in the house of the Lord." (But cf note 2 on ch. 2).

[5] Throughout his commentary on the prophets, Bishop Theodoret has been insistent that the clergy were involved in infidelity – just as in his Psalms Commentary he observed that the clergy of his day have no monopoly on spiritual goods.

[6] Rom 1.30.

[7] Cf Lev 26.3-39; Deut 28.

Chapter Two

[1] Theodoret is simply conducting a brief paraphrase of the verses, pausing only to unravel an obscure or figurative expression, as is his wont.
[2] After seeming in ch. 1 to avoid expressions that spoke of the Temple as still standing, here Theodoret cites and clarifies such an expression without correction.
[3] Anthropomorphisms in particular call for the clarification referred to in note 1 – and for an admonition.
[4] The LXX text speaks vaguely in v.26 of the Temple being "in the condition it is today." Theodoret is less non-committal.
[5] Deut 32.24-26.

Chapter Three

[1] Theodoret's is the obvious interpretation of the statement, an interpretation the NRSV finds so little to its liking (shades of Luther in debate with Johann Eck on 2 Mac 12.42-46) that its renders the phrase "the *people* of Israel," adding the puzzling footnote "Grk 'dead'" as though its editors were working from a Heb. text (which we do not possess, though it is presumed once to have existed) rendered inaccurately by the LXX. Theodoret sees its implications and baldly states them; the fact that he moves on without further comment is all of a piece with his being ready to credit OT authors with NT eschatology, as emerges often in his Psalms Commentary.
[2] Cf Jer 31.30.
[3] Baruch it is, and Sirach, who identify wisdom with the Law; and Theodoret has no qualms about making this identification for the author. He has no quarrel with OT Judaism.
[4] While acknowledging (as he often does) the OT Jews' prerogatives, Theodoret is encouraged here – perhaps by reading of this passage in Christian liturgy – to see a reference to the Incarnation.
[5] The former phrase occurs immediately above in 3.12, the latter not in Bar but early in the book, *prophêteia*, of Jer at 2.13. Theodoret, we noted, follows tradition in seeing Bar as closely associated with the prophecies of Jeremiah and included in "the book."
[6] Twice in this chapter Theodoret has found this rare word *exeuriskô*, and twice he has cautioned his readers not to take the anthropomorphism literalistically.
[7] Prov 8.22 has aroused much debate among commentators for its apparent hypostatization of Wisdom and the duality in the Godhead it could be thought to be suggesting, especially if the verb in the Heb. is taken to mean "acquired" rather than "created." The LXX, however, takes the latter sense, which is unacceptable to Theodoret for the subordinationism it implies; so he does not develop any trinitarian meaning or Christological sense of wisdom in vv.35-37 in the way the NT liked to do.

Chapter Four

[1] While Theodoret was happy to see Baruch identifying wisdom with the Law in the previous chapter, this is too much; and – against the intention of the text – he prefers now to see the old covenant expiring, the OT people failing to take up the offer, and Jesus introducing a new covenant, which the Gentiles have accepted.
[2] Theodoret is moving along at a brisk pace, but can still pause to offer an independent interpretation. In the following section the speakers are not clear, owing to ambiguities in the text.
[3] Ps 126.6.
[4] Again Theodoret thinks it important to find in the text confirmation of the prophecy; and he adduces a fact highlighted by Jeremiah (so he remarked previously in an identically disparaging phrase; cf 50.39).

Chapter Five

[1] Theodoret is aware that Exod 28.36-37; 39.30-31 made this prescription for Aaron's priestly attire, and so recognises that, as Aloysius Fitzgerald remarks, "Lady Jerusalem, the city of the worship of the true God, has become a priest." But only because of Jesus' passion there, Theodoret adds.
[2] An Antiochene, of course, has to establish that no details in the text are contradictory.
[3] Ps 114.4.
[4] Cf Ps 89.15.
[5] As noted above, Theodoret's text knows nothing of a Letter of Jeremiah, whether as ch. 6 of Bar or elsewhere, at least in the better mss.

Notes to the Commentary on the Book of Lamentations

Chapter One

[1] Most manuscripts of the LXX put Baruch before Lamentations (the Hebrew Bible not containing Baruch, and placing Lam in The Writings as one of the five Scrolls), Codex Sinaiticus the exception. This order occurs in mss of Theodoret's works as well, despite his admission that the material in Bar is not by Jeremiah himself, though part of "the book." So it is only at the end of Lam that he brings to a close his work on both Jeremiah and all the prophets (as the conclusion indicates).

[2] As a pastor, Theodoret sees a moral and not simply an affective dimension to the work; like his own purpose as detailed in the conclusion, Jeremiah was composing – this time directly in writing (a slight hint at a difference in authorship?) – for the good of his contemporaries and later generations.

[3] Hebrew and Greek texts run to five laments; Schulze finds a fifth only in some Latin codices. Theodoret obviously finds his four appropriate. He gives no indication that his text contains the introductory description of Jeremiah sitting among the ruins of Jerusalem as found in other forms of the LXX (not in the Heb.). His knowledge of Hebrew being what it is, it is predictable that he makes no mention of the acrostic pattern in each lament that does not pass into the Grk.

[4] Not surprisingly, Theodoret is not much moved by the plight of the defeated Jews; he moves briskly through the material, not really resonating with the pathos of their situation, being content with paraphrase. No wonder he came up with a different reason above for Jeremiah's composition other than mere sympathy and affection. He can barely suppress his usual diagnosis of Jewish misfortune, They had it coming; and he dwells on statements of their responsibility for it all.

[5] Deut 28.43; 32.25.

[6] Deut 23.3. Though not disposed to be moved by the lament, Theodoret is as usual interested in supplying details of Jewish liturgy in OT times.

[7] While 2 Kgs 25.3 mentions famine during Nebuchadnezzar's siege of Jerusalem under Zedekiah, this ghoulish detail is probably derived from Lam 4.10.

[8] Both these strange phrases (Theodoret by his reference to the Syriac making a futile attempt to gain some light on his rare Grk term from agriculture suggesting rough treatment) probably correspond to "he humbled me" in other forms of the LXX.

[9] Cf Isa 63.2; Jer 48.33.
[10] Cf Lev 18.19. Brisk though the pace is, Theodoret as is his wont cannot pass over images like the wine vat, the wringing hands and the menstruating woman without ensuring his readers have got full value from them.

Chapter Two

[1] Ps 99.5.
[2] Ps 89.40,41.
[3] Cf Zech 2.1-2 (5-6 Heb.), a vision Theodoret seems to take negatively, perhaps in the light of the following verses. Iain Provan, who like many a modern uses the term LXX univocally and declares that it reads here "The Lord turned to destroy," wonders how a measuring line could be used in the context of destruction; but Theodoret has no difficulty coming up with the sense of "measure and find wanting," finding confirmation in that negative connotation of Zechariah's vision.
[4] Theodoret does not think comment is necessary (or possible) on the term "glory" here, which arises from LXX reading a similar form for "liver." His brief paraphrasing of these verses suggests the lament is hardly wringing his withers.
[5] Pss 79.4; 43.14.
[6] Theodoret seems to recognise that the LXX has come up with both a translation of a rare Heb. word and a paraphrase of it.
[7] His readers may not resonate with the feelings of the plaintiffs, but they must not miss the point of a comparison.
[8] Again Provan is unaware of the Antiochene text in commenting, "LXX's alternative here, 'I have strengthened and multiplied all my enemies,' makes little sense." Theodoret, thanks to his text, understands the author's meaning perfectly.

Chapter Three

[1] Cf 2 Kg 25, a rare piece of scriptural documentation as Theodoret fairly flies through the verses of what is going to be a long lament.
[2] For mention of the rock, "LXX has no equivalent," Provan believes.
[3] Mention of the Lord as bear and lion calls to Theodoret's mind Hos 13.8 and Amos 5.19, on which he had commented earlier in his career.
[4] Things are in desperate straits for the plaintiff; but apart from explicating images like archers at target practice, Theodoret skims over the recital of abandonment.
[5] "Vv.22-24 are not present in the LXX," claims Provan.
[6] Ps 119.71.
[7] Matt 5.39.
[8] Ps 39.1-2.
[9] A classic statement of the Antiochene position on human nature and

sinfulness, consistent with the correlative position about the respective roles of divine grace and human effort in salvation (underlying Theodoret's unease about Paul's accent on the former). While pelagians took heart from the accent on the latter, the Antiochenes were in no doubt of the Fall and at the same time insisted that human nature was not impaired – a balance the West did not always achieve. Sin is attributable instead to *rhathymia*, indifference, sloth – and so punishment is due.

[10] Isa 59.2.

[11] Ps 69.1-2,15.

[12] Theodoret has patiently been commenting, if very briefly, on the verses of this long lament; but he finally runs out of patience and telescopes the last part.

Chapter Four

[1] Isa 30.14.

[2] This harrowing detail, which is probably the basis for Theodoret's comment on 1.11, passes without elaboration here. He seems unaffected by the people's plight. Cf note 4 on ch. 1.

[3] Cf 2 Kgs 19.35.

[4] As was observed in that note 4 on ch. 1, Theodoret is capable of adding a further macabre detail to an already ghoulish text.

[5] Reference to these groups is found not "next" but in v.16 in Heb. and at least other forms of the LXX. Theodoret, however, has a difficulty with v.18, the Syriac version of which makes better sense if related to v.16.

[6] Apprently a reference to 2.8; see note 3 there.

[7] Theodoret may have texts like Pss 23.4; 44.19; 107.10; Isa 9.2; Jer 13.16 in mind. In his haste to dispose of the Lamentations, he has hardly had time to dwell on the misfortunes of the sixth century people (which he sees Jeremiah reflecting) without proceeding to give the work an eschatological dimension; but mention of *pneuma* and *christos* prove too much to ignore it here.

[8] Ps 137.7.

[9] As often in commentary on Jeremiah, Theodoret as an Antiochene is keen to uphold that prophetic "coherence." He does not, however, remark on Edom's eventual fate.

10 As was remarked at the opening, Theodoret's text does not contain the fifth lament found in Heb. and (at least some) other forms of the LXX. Modern commentators, who find in the fifth lament some peculiar features, might have taken this lacuna into account in judging its authenticity.

[11] Thus Theodoret concludes his massive (and happily extant) corpus of commentary on all the prophets, not without a note of self-satisfaction. It resembles the conclusion to the Isaiah Commentary (and the Song of Songs), completed not long before by the late 440s, in its Antiochene acknowledgement of indebtedness both to divine grace and to his own

effort/enthusiasm, its concession of possible deficiencies, and its request of prayers from the reader (who likewise is expected to rely on both God and human effort). Its appearing here represents a difference from the Isaiah Commentary, where the conclusion is found in the 'Constantinople' ms but not in the Sirmond and thus PG edition, suggesting (as the text has all along) that the Jeremiah Commentary in the latter editions comes to us in direct manuscript tradition (fortunately, as the 'Constantinople' ms is now beyond access).

General Index

Index of Biblical Citations

Made in the USA
Monee, IL
11 September 2026

62770620R00152